Adriana Cavarero

Critical legal scholars have made us aware that law is made up not only of rules but also of language. But who speaks the language of law? And can one lawfully speak in one's voice? For the Italian philosopher Adriana Cavarero, to answer these questions we must not separate who is speaking from the very act of speaking; moreover, we must recuperate the material singularity and relationality of the mouth that speaks. Drawing on Cavarero's work, this book focuses on the potentiality of the voice for resisting law's sovereign structures. For Cavarero, it is the voice that expresses one's living and unrepeatable singularity in a way that cannot be subsumed by the universalities and standards of law. The voice is essentially a material and singular passage of air and vibration that necessarily reveals one's uniqueness in relationality. Speaking discloses this uniqueness, and so one's vulnerability. It therefore leads to possibilities of resistance that, here, bring a fresh approach to longstanding legal theoretical concerns with singularity, ethics and justice.

Elisabetta R. Bertolino has completed a doctorate in law and legal theory at Birkbeck Law School in London, UK, where she has also taught seminars in jurisprudence and criminal law. Currently, she teaches legal subjects at the University of Palermo, Italy. She has been interested in the theme of the voice and the work of Adriana Cavarero for several years, and conducted an interview with the Italian philosopher which was published in *differences: A Journal of Feminist Cultural Studies* in 2008.

Nomikoi: Critical Legal Thinkers

Series editors: Peter Goodrich
Cardozo School of Law, New York, USA
David Seymour
School of Law, City University, UK

Nomikoi: Critical Legal Thinkers presents analyses of key critical theorists whose thinking on law has contributed significantly to the development of the new interdisciplinary legal studies. Addressing those who have most influenced legal thought and thought about law, the aim of the series is to bring legal scholarship, the social sciences and the humanities into closer dialogue.

Other titles in the series:

Rancière and Law, edited by Monica Lopez Lerma and Julen Etxabe

Hannah Arendt: Legal Theory and the Eichmann Trial, Peter Burdon

Žižek and Law, edited by Laurent de Sutter

Roberto Esposito: Law, Community and the Political, Peter Langford

Bruno Latour: The Normativity of Networks, Kyle McGee

Deleuze & Guattari: Emergent Law, Jamie Murray

Althusser and Law, edited by Laurent de Sutter

Henri Lefebvre: Spatial Politics, Everyday Life and the Right to the City, Chris Butler

Carl Schmitt: Law as Politics, Ideology and Strategic Myth, Michael Salter

Jacques Derrida: Law as Absolute Hospitality, Jacques de Ville

Niklas Luhmann: Law, Justice, Society, Andreas Philippopoulos-Mihalopoulos

Giorgio Agamben: Power, Law and the Uses of Criticism, Thanos Zartaloudis

Evgeny Pashukanis: A Critical Reappraisal, Michael Head

Judith Butler: Ethics, Law, Politics, Elena Loizidou

Adriana Cavarero

Resistance and the Voice of Law

Elisabetta R. Bertolino

Routledge
Taylor & Francis Group
LONDON AND NEW YORK

First published 2018 by Routledge

2 Park Square, Milton Park, Abingdon, Oxfordshire OX14 4RN
52 Vanderbilt Avenue, New York, NY 10017

Routledge is an imprint of the Taylor & Francis Group, an informa business

First issued in paperback 2019

British Library Cataloguing in Publication Data
A catalogue record for this book is available from the British Library

Library of Congress Cataloging in Publication Data
Names: Bertolino, Elisabetta, author.
Title: Adriana Cavarero: resistance and the voice of law/Elisabetta Bertolino.
Description: New York, NY: Routledge, 2018. |
Series: Nomikoi: critical legal thinkers | Includes bibliographical references and index.
Identifiers: LCCN 2017037133 | ISBN 9780815366317 (hbk)
Subjects: LCSH: Cavarero, Adriana. | Law–Philosophy.
Classification: LCC K230.C395 B47 2018 | DDC 340/.1–dc23
LC record available at https://lccn.loc.gov/2017037133

ISBN: 978-0-8153-6631-7 (hbk)
ISBN: 978-0-367-26433-8 (pbk)

Typeset in Galliard
by Sunrise Setting Ltd, Brixham, UK

Contents

Overview

Critical legal scholars have underlined that law is made up not only of rules but also of language and the language of law expresses the violence of a sovereign and abstract subject, disconnected from her body and the community. Such a legal violence reflects both the general voice of an essentialized sexual difference divide – privileging the mind over the body and associating the body with the feminine – and the limits of a liberal philosophical and political framework. It is thus pertinent to ask some questions in relation to this. Who speaks in law? Can one speak in one's voice with respect to law?

For Adriana Cavarero, to answer those questions we must not separate *who* is speaking from the very act of speaking and we must recuperate the material singularity and relationality of the mouth that speaks within language and signs. For Cavarero, the voice that comes from one's mouth is capable of recuperating the very meaning of signification. One's voice expresses a living and unrepeatable singularity that cannot be subsumed under universalities and standards. Drawing on Cavarero's theory, the book focuses on the singular and unique voice (as opposed to law's general voice) and its potentiality for resisting law and its structures.

Within the critical legal tradition – following Jacques Derrida – there has been a political demand to return to the lived experience of *who speaks* by using signs and texts. This book intends to take the voice as its point of departure, supplementing the critical legal discourse with an understanding of the singularity that emerges from a material and corporeal self through one's voice. A focus on one's voice changes the approach to the voice. I am using the term "one's voice" as it implies less possessiveness than, for instance, "one's own voice." One's voice contains multiple implications in terms of subjectivity, sexual difference, ontology and justice, thus reversing the Derridean understanding of the voice as metaphysics and as a system constructed as voice.

Furthermore, any subject of resistance within law can be said to be limited since it is caged within the narrow boundaries of the liberal framework that appears to conceive the subject as autonomous, independent and, in a way, righteous and vertical. Yet I consider such an approach as partial, embedded in particular ideological assumptions. The subject of resistance offered by John Rawls and Martha Nussbaum marks the limits of this approach. On the contrary, in this book, I focus on a resistance that begins with one's voice, as opposed to a linguistic and political frame already conceived for us.

In the case of female genital cutting (FGC),[1] law attempts, for instance, to resist the practice of cutting and wounding the vagina through the linguistic production of non-consenting subjects and by constructing mutilated bodies that lack integrity within an illusion of a discourse on autonomy, freedom and informed consent; whereas in the case of women in the sex industry law re-appropriates a moralizing objectified notion of woman that reflects an essentialist understanding of sexual difference, in which the female self is constructed as object, or less than a subject.

In critical distance from such a frame of thought, I understand scholars such as Jacques Derrida, Judith Butler and Adriana Cavarero to have contended that the corporeal and sexed subject is always already cut, impeded by the linguistic structure, and any attempt to stitch the subject into a whole results in incoherence, and loss of autonomy and independence; they have thus argued for the necessity to look for moments of rupture and aporia. Yet, in my opinion, it is only with Cavarero's corporeal and unique voice that suspension from such a linguistic and political imposition becomes possible.

I have divided the book into three main parts. The first part – which comprises the introduction and Chapter I – deals with the theoretical focus on one's voice. The positions of John Rawls, Martha Nussbaum, Jacques Derrida, Judith Butler and Adriana Cavarero are mentioned or explored in relation to resistance and the voice.

The second part of the book consists of Chapters II and III, which concern two case studies – female genital mutilation and commercial sex. These are intended to be illustrative of the argument for focusing on one's voice, supporting such a focus while showcasing it and bringing one's voice alive. Female genital cutting and commercial sex are seen as situations in which the cuts that are performed on the legal subject are ingrained in the self and the body. Female genital cutting and commercial sex show how a focus on one's voice radicalizes resistance.

The third part comprises Chapter IV and the concluding remarks. Chapter IV brings up the question of ethics and justice in relation to one's voice, exploring in particular the relation between the possibility of forgiveness, one's voice and the law. Speaking in one's voice discloses one's uniqueness and the awareness of vulnerability and, therefore, leads to potentially ethical possibilities of resisting violence and resentment. Chapter IV offers the possibility of a level of justice that escapes the institutional approach of law and politics but that can run parallel to those levels. In the chapter, I talk of unpredictable actions such as forgiveness,

1 We shall use the term female genital cutting (FGC) rather than female genital mutilation (FGM) because it is more neutral and avoids negative valence on the ritual.

where forgiveness is disconnected from standards and institutional requirements. Forgiveness is rather connected to one's voice, a singular and personal approach from within, not imposed on one. Finally, in the concluding remarks I offer some reflections on why a focus on the voice may bring newness and fresh perspectives to resistance.

Acknowledgments

This book is the result of years of interest in Adriana Cavarero's thought and the voice and includes Cavarero's approach to the voice as well as my own speculation and developments. Cavarero's work and especially her 2005 book on the voice – *For More Than One Voice: Toward a Philosophy of Vocal Expression* – has had a deep bearing on the structure and operation of this book, permeating my body and life. At times, I would experience my own suspension from the linguistic experience, making the completion of this study seem an impossible task.

I would like to thank many people for helping me along the way with this project. Firstly, I want to thank Adriana Cavarero for her inspiration, as well as for allowing me to interview her in Verona in 2005. Secondly, I am grateful to Elena Loizidou, whose guidance has been invaluable. However, I am indebted to Elena in a more profound way. Her passion for Judith Butler has launched my adventure with Adriana Cavarero's thought, while my search for radical forms of resistance has been inspired by her interest in anarchic disobedience. Thanks to Elena, Cavarero's focus on one's unique voice appeared challenging to me and became my point of reference.

Thirdly, I am grateful to the School of Law at Birkbeck for offering a vibrant and excellent environment for my research at the beginning of this project, as well as for supporting me in various ways. I would like to thank Adam Gearey, Michelle Everson, Patrick Hanafin, Linda Mulcahy, Elena Loizidou, Costas Douzinas, Maria Aristodemou, Stewart Motha, Patricia Tuitt, Peter Fitzpatrick, Sara Paiola, Sara Ramshaw, Matt Stone, Pablo Ghetti, Emanuel Barreto, Illan Wall, Victoria Riddle, Ben Golder, Jose Bellido, Piyel Haldar, Daniel Monk, Oscar Guardiola-Rivera, Bill Bowring, Brenna Bandhar, Sundhya Pahuja and many others who offered comments and support in seminars and other informal settings at the time. Thanks also to the University of Brighton, Tim Huzar and Louise Purbrick, the series editors of Nomikoi, Peter Goodrich and David Seymour, Colin Perrin, the two anonymous reviewers, and Hilary Arundale, Catherine Tingle and Colin Read.

Finally, intellectual conditions are not the only ones that make a book possible. One has to take into account the wider world that forms a backdrop for the life of the mind. Thanks, then, to all those around me who contributed to building a shared community worth being in.

Introduction

> *The World is there, it is visible, but it is up to us to look or not. The visible world is not a world that interrupts, interferes, or surprises everywhere with its sounds; it is, rather, a stable, immobile, objective world that lies in front of us. This guarantees the reality of being and thus the status of truth as presence.*[1]

In *Critical Jurisprudence*, Costas Douzinas and Adam Gearey note that jurisprudence is today impoverished both cognitively and morally, reduced to the *legitimation of the existent* and to *technocratic legalism*.[2] In contrast, their critical jurisprudence signals the return to a general philosophy of law and to a law without an absolute commandment. For both Douzinas and Gearey, a conception of legal education as solely technical knowledge that needs to be remembered and repeated by law students amounts to a sort of *death of the soul and of the intellect* and to a *diminution of the scope of law*.[3] In *Critical Jurisprudence*, Douzinas and Gearey suggest approaching legal education via a general jurisprudence concerned with the law of the law rather than through a restricted notion of jurisprudence.[4]

This book espouses such an approach to law, that is, a notion of law as general philosophy, law as law of the law that returns to ethics by focusing on the voice; it rests on the work of critical legal scholars such as Peter Goodrich and Costas Douzinas in its search for ways of speaking other than the general and normative language of law.[5] Drawing in particular on the theory of Adriana Cavarero and her notion of vocal ontology, this book centers on the notion of speaking in one's

1 Adriana Cavarero, *For More Than One Voice. Toward a Philosophy of Vocal Expression*, trans. Paul Kottman (Stanford: Stanford University Press, 2005), 37.

2 Costas Douzinas and Adam Gearey, *Critical Jurisprudence: The Political Philosophy of Justice* (Oxford: Hart Publishing, 2005), 3–10.

3 Douzinas and Gearey, *Critical Jurisprudence*, 3–10.

4 Douzinas and Gearey, *Critical Jurisprudence*, 17.

5 Peter Goodrich, *Languages of Law: From Logics of Memory to Nomadic Masks* (London: Weidenfeld and Nicholson, 1990); Costas Douzinas, Matthew Stone and Illan Wall, eds, *New Critical Legal Thinking. Law and the Political* (New York: Routledge, 2012); Costas Douzinas, Peter Goodrich and Yifat Hachamovitch, *Politics, Postmodernity and Critical Legal Studies: The Legality of the Contingent* (New York: Routledge, 1994).

voice and calls for an ethics of law inspired by one's voice. I prefer using the term "one's voice" rather than "one's own voice" because in "one's voice" the emphasis is less on ownership as the voice is not owned but is constitutive of *who one is* and always exposed to others.

Thus the voice that is focused on is intended here not as a general and abstract voice but rather as a singular, unique and corporeal voice that is always revealed in relationality, when speaking with others. The sound of such a unique voice is able to interrupt, surprise and interfere with the status of truth as presence.

For Cavarero, the voice communicates the uniqueness and corporeality of each one of us and resonates in the flesh of one's throat.[6] In one's voice there is the experience of a singular being in relationality. In contrast, the voice of law is the voice of the general, silent and visible Logos that organizes the disembodied substance of the signified of law and shapes itself as the voice of a *what,* where experience is repressed and the reality of being is guaranteed.

While critical legal scholars informed by Derrida's philosophy, such as Goodrich and Douzinas, attend to the interpretation and infinite deferral of signs in order to recapture what has escaped the text of law,[7] Cavarero focuses instead on the voice as that which reveals *who someone is* and the materiality of one's unique body, thus interrupting and suspending the normative symbolic order of law.

In my opinion, the implications of her focus on the voice are multiple and of great significance, not only for "the subject of law," but also for questions of sexual difference, ontology and the ethics of law's justice that are inherent in law but that transcend the legal field to include language in general. I argue that the voice represents the excess and the superfluous, what is cut out and left out by law and language, and therefore a focus on the voice implies a diverse selfhood. While the subject of law renounces the singularity of experience, the voice reveals precisely the experience of oneself as unique and corporeal in the plurality of voices.

A first point to consider is the fact that the focus on the voice has a significant impact on the binary logic of the hierarchical divisions that characterize an essentialist view of sexual difference within and beyond law. According to such logic, the body becomes associated with the feminine and emerges as secondary to the dominance of the mind that is seen in terms of the quality of maleness. The essentialized sexual division is reflected in the subject of law, who is constructed as general and neutral but is in reality a cut subject with only masculine traits. The voice as one's voice goes beyond such hierarchical divisions. It looks for the singular and accepts vulnerability beyond sexual difference. For Cavarero the voice or body is not an abstract. It is always one's voice and one's body, already sexed. Sexual difference has been given meaning either from a masculine or feminine perspective. Cavarero changes the understanding of sexual

6 Cavarero, *For More Than One Voice*, 30.

7 Jacques Derrida, *Of Grammatology*, trans. Gayatri Chakravorty Spivak (London: Johns Hopkins University Press, 1997); Jacques Derrida, *Speech and Phenomena: And Other Essays on Husserl's Theory of Signs*, trans. David B. Allison (Evanston: Northwestern University Press, 1973).

difference, seen now in relation to such categories as singularity, corporeality and uniqueness. I will focus on a critique of the essentialized sexual difference perspective within law through the voice in this book's case studies on female genital cutting and objectification in commercial sex.

Thinking through the voice also produces an ontological discourse that dismantles the ontology of metaphysics of presence, intended as the essence, which has traditionally been supposed to capture and represent reality in Western philosophy. Contrary to such a metaphysical thinking, the ontology of the voice is an empty ontology; it is simply a passing of air, a vocal sound, an exposure of one's singularity, a connection to other voices, contingency and changeability.

Finally, the focus on the voice shifts attention to ethical aspects such as overcoming law and justice conceived in terms of retribution – this will be explored in more detail in Chapter IV. Retribution signifies a subject that is righteous and disconnected from her voice, her vulnerability and the community of other voices. In my opinion it denotes a subject separated from her-self that speaks the language of norms; norms that fail to realize the value of a subject's experience, relationship and reciprocity. I think that attending to the voice instead reveals a way of suspending the *commandments* of law, listening instead to the possibilities for justice that come from within oneself and one's voice in relation to others. The unpredictability of a forgiveness spoken in one's voice and coming from within – in the sense of letting go and continuing one's life without necessarily acquiring retribution or embracing a subjectivity of resentment – constitutes one of those relational possibilities of a justice from within and with others.

Regarding this latter ethical aspect of the voice and justice, I will connect Cavarero's approach with that of Arendt. Cavarero's thought on uniqueness is rooted in Hannah Arendt's *who-ness*, which is the theorization of an ontological selfhood beyond identities and beyond *what*. There are other potential links between the two scholars' thought. For Arendt, it is speaking that makes a person political.[8] A focus on speech allows for a radical rethinking of politics in terms of action.[9] Both Cavarero's voice and Arendtian action go beyond the act of signifying something; they reveal precisely *who someone is* and allow for *natality* and newness in a political horizon of plurality.[10] The voice as action beyond the predictable normativity of justice calls for a different response to violence and for new forms of theorizing subjectivity and justice, springing from uniqueness and vulnerability.

In particular, the idea of vulnerability intersects with ethical conduct. Both Cavarero and Arendt touch on the idea of *being born*.[11] Arendt stresses the

8 Hannah Arendt, *The Human Condition* (Chicago: The University of Chicago Press, 1958).

9 Arendt, *The Human Condition*.

10 With her notion of "natality" Arendt points to the fact that each human being begins life with birth, that is, with newness. Natality also indicates that each of us takes initiatives and is prompted into action. Thus, natality in Arendt becomes a political category of freedom from the already spoken and expected, because natality is rooted in material birth and unexpected newness.

11 Arendt, *The Human Condition;* Adriana Cavarero, *Horrorism: Naming Contemporary Violence*, trans. William McCuaig (New York: Columbia University Press, 2009).

vulnerability of natality in terms of action that produces unpredictable ways of doing and being,[12] whereas Cavarero emphasizes the defenseless vulnerability of the newly born and the fact that one begins one's existence in such an utterly vulnerable condition.[13] Even though Arendt does not talk directly of vulnerability, I assume that vulnerability is necessarily implicit in her idea of acting as unique beings in the frailty of the human condition. Of necessity, the vulnerability of being born, for both philosophers, requires active involvement and ethical responsibility.[14] For both scholars, ethical responsibility is understood not as a universal imperative but as the ability of a singular and material selfhood to respond to another with response-ability. And birth seems to suggest a break and a suspension of the normative and sovereign imposition of representation. Those are all aspects that I will deal with in Chapter IV.

The voice might be seen by some legal scholars as having nothing to do with law, its rule and its substance, as it is disconnected from the legal and symbolic text and its ethical developments. The voice is also on a different level from law and the social reality of how law functions. To talk about the voice and law, then, one has to pass through the voice of the critical legal studies movement and tradition. As a matter of fact, I contextualize the focus of the book on the voice within the critical legal tradition and thus on a more "general" approach to jurisprudence and on law's ethical aspects.[15]

It might then be necessary to trace briefly the turn of events related to the critical legal tradition, given its complexity and contradictions.

In the late 1970s, critical legal studies was a movement in the United States committed to destabilizing traditional conceptions of the law and to unfolding and challenging existing legal institutions; soon afterwards, a critical legal studies movement also emerged in Britain.[16] The critical legal tradition criticizes many aspects of law and the legal system. A central attack of critical legal studies can be located against legal liberalism.[17] The struggle against legal liberalism has been characterized as a struggle against the liberal state and its institutions that become visible through the neutral and formal approach of law, or its depoliticizing process. In particular,

12 Arendt, *The Human Condition*, 177.

13 Cavarero, *Horrorism*.

14 Arendt, *The Human Condition;* Cavarero, *Horrorism*.

15 The term "general" is intended here as general philosophy of law, as opposed to the technical and narrow knowledge of law.

16 Michael Freeman, *Lloyd's Introduction to Jurisprudence*. Eighth Edition (London: Sweet & Maxwell, 2008), 1209–1224.

17 Lloyd cites Kelman's three fundamental contradictions in liberalism. A first contradiction is that liberalism commits to mechanical rules as the appropriate form of resolving disputes; a second contradiction lies in the fact that liberalism commits to a notion of desire as being arbitrary and subjective, whereas reason is objective and universal; and the third contradiction alludes to the liberal commitment to a self-determining individual will and determinist discourse. See Mark Kelman, *A Guide to Critical Legal Studies* (Cambridge: Harvard University Press, 1987); Freeman, *Lloyd's Introduction to Jurisprudence*, 1210.

critical legal studies puts the emphasis on reality and experience. In an article that appeared in the American *Review of Law and Social Change*, Peter Gabel and Paul Harris show that a critical legal approach is not a utopian philosophical approach disconnected from reality but it can be applied concretely in the case law. [18]

For Gabel and Harris, the critical legal approach can be used against the state that attempts to legitimize a social order by manipulating symbols and ideas. Gabel and Harris suggest that a critical legal strategy needs to go even beyond legal rights and to focus instead upon a wider political strategy of consciousness, breaking away from treating law apolitically as agent of the state and of liberal ideology.[19]

In practical legal terms, this means it is necessary to avoid the distance between lawyer and client and ceasing to treat the client's case as if it were abstract. The issue is political and the client needs to be seen as a human being with human needs. In other words, it is necessary to assert the material and unique meanings put forward by the client and overcome the abstract and formal sense of legal language and thus "demystify" the legal system.[20] However, in this context, when talking of critical legal studies I will refer mainly to the British critical legal studies movement that consists of a plurality of approaches to law. Costas Douzinas explains that like most movements this tradition has produced several themes of thought, such as deconstruction and postmodernism, post-colonialism, critical race, queer theory, the ethics of otherness and the ontology of singularity.[21]

An article in *Law and Critique* by Tim Murphy explores some of the intellectual influences which have outlined the development of critical legal studies in Britain.[22] Although British scholars know more about America's legal system than any other in the world, Murphy stresses that the theoretical interest of critical legal studies has come essentially from Europe and European theories.[23] Murphy refers to an emerging second generation of critical scholars who, while dealing with theory in more

18 Peter Gabel and Paul Harris, "Building Power and Breaking Images: Critical Legal Theory and the Practice of Law," *Review of Law and Social Change*, XI (1982/1983): 369–411.

19 Gabel and Harris, "Building Power and Breaking Images."

20 In their article, Gabel and Harris offer several examples of case law, where a critical and political approach has been applied in case trials. In a case of a rape, the victim Inez Garcia shot and killed the assailant. In the first trial, the victim succeeded as she was not convicted of first-degree but only of second-degree murder. To achieve this, Garcia had to show through a psychiatric testimony that she was not conscious of what she was doing. Thus, for the purpose of her defense, Garcia had to embrace a subject that was not herself and speak the voice of law. In the retrial, Garcia was instead represented by a radical feminist attorney, Jordan. Jordan confronted the myths about rape and the male rules, and was able to capture the singular experience of Garcia when facing the attack. As a consequence, the rape was unfolded as a violent assault rather than a sexual act resulting from female flirtation. The second trial demonstrates that it is possible to adopt a political approach in trials, escaping reification in practicing existing law.

21 Costas Douzinas, "A Note from the Editor," *Law and Critique*, 20 (2009): 1–2.

22 Tim Murphy, "Brit Crits: Subversion and Submission, Past, Present and Future," *Law and Critique*, 10 (1999): 237–278.

23 Murphy, "Brit Crits."

sophisticated ways, seem to have succumbed to certain institutional dynamics.[24] For example, some critical feminist and race theorists promoted their own programs for social justice, focusing on eliminating disadvantages rather than on critiquing liberalism. Those theorists preferred to proceed through diagnosis and solutions rather than long-term goals.[25] By the mid-1970s, Marx was the main reference point for the critical legal scholars, followed by Freud, Lacan, Foucault and Derrida. Feminism in particular pushed toward Freud and Lacan.

In relation to this, Michael Freeman describes a sort of feminist "off-shoot of the Critical Legal Studies Movement" that focused on analyzing how law contributed both to the perpetuation of patriarchy and the undermining and elimination of patriarchal domination.[26] As reported by Freeman, various feminist schools of thought affirmed themselves within critical legal studies, namely the liberal, radical, cultural and poststructuralist schools.[27] In particular, some feminist critical legal scholars joined postmodern and poststructuralist critical legal thinkers and looked for ways to legitimize women's concrete experience as against the abstract truth of the legal text by challenging the structures of legal thought as well as those of liberal law.

For example, in the United States Catharine MacKinnon employed the concept of dominance to discuss critically the subordination of women to men and attacked male supremacy; while Robin West underlined the failure in the understanding of the subject and the necessity of seeing it as connected to others.[28] In Britain, Maria Drakopoulou's work engages with critical explorations of the feminist politics of legal change; Patrick Hanafin draws on Italian feminism to disrupt law's male symbolic order; Elena Loizidou makes use of the thought of Judith Butler to deconstruct the legal subject and Maria Aristodemou shows that, similarly to literary texts, legal texts are fictitious.[29]

24 Murphy, "Brit Crits."

25 See: Banu Ramachandran, "Re-Reading Difference. Feminist Critiques of the Law School Classroom and the Problem with Speaking from Experience," *Columbia Law Review*, 98(7) (1998): 1757–1794; Jeffrey J. Pyle, "Equality and the Rule of Law. Critical Race Theory's Attack on the Promises of Liberalism," *Boston College Law Review*, 40(3) (1999): 787–827.

26 As Freeman underlines, feminist critical legal studies was deeply influenced by Anne Scale's article "Towards a Feminist Jurisprudence" and Catharine MacKinnon's article "Feminism, Marxism, Method, and the State: Toward a Feminist Jurisprudence." See: Freeman, *Lloyd's Introduction to Jurisprudence*, 1285–1407.

27 Freeman, *Lloyd's Introduction to Jurisprudence.*

28 Catharine MacKinnon, "Feminism, Marxism, Method, and the State: Toward a Feminist Jurisprudence," *Signs: Journal of Women in Culture and Society,* 8(4) (1983): 635–658; Robin West, "Jurisprudence and Gender," *University of Chicago Law Review,* 55 (1988): 1–72.

29 The scholars mentioned above are only indicative of several critical legal theorists who currently engage with feminist theory and the law in the UK. Maria Drakopoulou, "Introduction: Reading Law, Reading Woman," in *Feminist Encounters with Legal Philosophy*, ed. Drakopoulou, M. (Oxon: Routledge, 2014), 1–8; Patrick Hanafin, "A Voice Beyond the Law: Reading Plato, Reading Cavarero," in *Feminist Encounters with Legal Philosophy*, ed. Drakopoulou, M. (Oxon: Routledge, 2014), 9–19; Elena Loizidou, *Judith Butler: Ethics, Law, Politics* (Oxon: Routledge, 2007); Maria Aristodemou, *Law and Literature: Journeys from Her to Eternity* (Oxford: Oxford University Press, 2000).

This work on the voice complements such a feminist critique of the law and supports the possibility of developing a more concrete approach while situating itself in the tradition of those critical legal scholars who mainly take Derrida as their point of reference. The study belongs to the postmodern and deconstructive critical legal tradition, its focus being in particular on the elements of corporeal concreteness and relationality that spring from the voice.

In *Postmodern Jurisprudence*, Costas Douzinas explains how critical scholars generally brought together two types of theory: jurisprudence and postmodern deconstruction.[30] The postmodern deconstructive approach to critical legal theory involves reading texts of law. The texts of law present themselves as being coherent and expressing sovereignty and patriarchy. On the contrary, postmodern jurisprudence opposes the faith in a real and complete legal system, distrusts the reality and objectivity of law and shows that things can be told differently:

> *It appears that the most typical move of jurisprudence, the presentation of law as a unified and coherent body, is rooted in the metaphysics of truth rather than the politics and ethics of justice. The truth of justice is justice as truth [. . .] The task of postmodern jurisprudence is to deconstruct such a logocentric tendency in the texts of law.*[31]

By attending to the voice, this book supplements the critique of legal textual language and justice as it has been articulated by Douzinas in *Postmodern Jurisprudence*. Similarly to Douzinas, Peter Goodrich in *Languages of Law* denounces law on the grounds of its being a language that requires no justifications and that contains a fixed legal identity, a language that regulates our speech and that operates through repetition:[32]

> *Language thus carries the legal tradition, a tradition that is embedded in our very speech and of which our speech, our phrases, are the unwitting witnesses. Law in that sense is our grammar, the rule of our speech. It is the trace or imprint of the past in what we live and how we live, repossessed through iteration or diction [. . .] In Derrida's term, it would be the unwritten writing that precedes and structures speech, the "arche-writing," the trace, which acts as the imprint of an absolute past, a legal past, one beyond memory, one which could never be reactivated or awakened to presence.*[33]

Hence, Goodrich poses a crucial question: *who speaks?* In order to answer this question, Goodrich approaches case law and judgments as pure text and sign, so

30 Costas Douzinas and Ronnie Warrington with Shaun McVeigh, *Postmodern Jurisprudence: The Law of Text in the Texts of Law* (London: Routledge, 1991), 3–51.

31 Douzinas and Warrington with McVeigh, *Postmodern Jurisprudence,* 27.

32 Goodrich, *Languages of Law.*

33 Goodrich, *Languages of Law*, 120.

as to expose the circularity of judgments and case law, the excess, the flaws and silences of law. By drawing on Derrida's notion of the trace, Goodrich sees in the analysis of the written sign an anti-metaphysical strategy: since writing works against the system of presence of metaphysics, it thus allows the emergence of what stands as peripheral and marginal, what is excluded by the law. Within this framework, signs have meaning only in a specific context and their meaning changes in different contexts.

Derrida called the attitude of law "logocentric" because there is in law a presence of concepts that are supposed to exist in themselves.[34] In opposition to this, Derrida showed that objects always refer to other concepts, that there is circularity, which in turn can reveal multiple inconsistencies. For Derrida, as for postmodern deconstructive critical legal scholars such as Goodrich and Douzinas, meaning is a process of continuous differentiation, it is never fully present and never natural and the search for the truth is simply a mistake.

Yet, unlike Douzinas and Goodrich, the Italian philosopher Adriana Cavarero offers an anti-Derridean perspective without discarding Derrida's brilliant work of deconstruction – this will be shown in more detail in Chapter I.[35] Cavarero focuses on the voice rather than the sign as a means of resistance. For Cavarero, it is necessary to avoid thinking of the text as if it speaks on its own. To answer the question *who speaks?* we must not separate the *who* who is speaking from the very act of speaking and it is necessary to recuperate the reality of the mouth that speaks within language and signs. Cavarero, therefore, suggests one's unique voice as a means to fight metaphysics.[36] For Cavarero, the voice is capable of recuperating the very meaning of signification. One's voice expresses a living and unrepeatable singularity that cannot be subsumed under the universality of metaphysics.[37]

The voice in Cavarero is understood in terms of one's voice. And it is through a specific voice that one is able to articulate language. The stress on the singularity of the voice implies the uniqueness of each voice and a radical materiality of a body. In Cavarero, it is precisely a focus on the mouth that speaks in relationality and with others that can reveal what is excluded in the understanding of representation and the sovereign subject. There is an emphasis on the relational dimension of the material voice but also on the singular and vulnerable condition of speaking in one's voice.

Drawing on John Langshaw Austin, some scholars, using a deconstructive approach, have focused on the act of speaking in language rather than on the written sign of language, unfolding the excess of language.[38] For instance,

34 Derrida, *Of Grammatology*; Derrida, *Speech and Phenomena*.

35 Cavarero, *For More Than One Voice*.

36 Cavarero, *For More Than One Voice*, 213–241.

37 Cavarero, *For More Than One Voice*.

38 John Langshaw Austin, *How to Do Things with Words* (Cambridge: Harvard University Press, 1975).

Shoshana Felman has made use of the elements of the voice and speaking but in terms of bodily acts.[39] In Felman, the act of speaking, rather than the written sign, resists the sovereign subject. The speech act exceeds what it intends or knows and scandalizes language boundaries. By doing this, the body becomes part of the speech act, failing to comply with the promise made by consciousness.

A similar theory is put forward by Marianne Constable.[40] Constable proposes an alternative to understanding law as a system of rules, underlining the excess of legal language. She shows how law includes and consists of performative, passionate utterances and social acts. Therefore, neither law nor justice can be reduced to what lawyers and judges say. She concludes by saying that law and justice depend on the claims and responses that we make to one another in the name of the law.

Work influenced by Austin's speech act theory has also been carried out by Judith Butler.[41] For Butler, the body is not a fact of nature but is produced by discourses and thus by language and the law as well. Butler argues that the body can be performatively re-inscribed and this constitutes the subject's agency within the law or the possibility of subverting the law against itself to radical political ends. Identity, gender and sexual difference thus has a social existence and is something one does, is a sequence of acts, is doing more than being.[42] I will talk of Butler's approach to resistance in Chapter I.

The approach to resistance that I will consider in this book is the one offered by Adriana Cavarero through one's voice. One's voice in Cavarero comes from one's mouth and represents the corporeal condition necessary for one's production of language and signification. Such a material condition for Cavarero is also social or relational, because it happens when speaking with other voices. Yet, in Cavarero, one's voice is a rupture with the very logic of signification and an unpredictable element of the saying that goes beyond the linguistic agent-subject. Cavarero also emphasizes the element of uniqueness and thus the radical corporeality of the voice, revealed when one speaks.

One's voice in Cavarero is not the general voice but springs from a singular and material mouth. Although one can speculate about one's mouth and voice through language, one can also focus on one's voice and become aware of such a corporeal possibility of uniqueness, inherent in language and speaking and always revealed when one speaks to others.

Attending to the voice as corporeal and singular is not the same as attending to the meaning of the sign that remains within the text of law. The voice, more than the written sign, seems to be able to suspend the law and show the excess,

39 Shoshana Felman, *The Scandal of the Speaking Body. Don Juan with J.L. Austin or the Seduction in Two Languages*, trans. Catherine Porter (Stanford: Stanford University Press, 2003).

40 Marianne Constable, *Our World Is Our Bond. How Legal Speech Acts* (Stanford: Stanford University Press, 2014).

41 Judith Butler, *Bodies That Matter: On the Discursive Limits of Sex* (New York: Routledge, 1993); Judith Butler, *Gender Trouble: Feminism and the Subversion of Identity* (New York: Routledge, 1990).

42 Butler, *Bodies That Matter*.

because the voice springs from the singular and corporeal body as opposed to the general sign of representation. If the voice is a rupture with representation, then it becomes important to ask a few questions, such as: what type of resistance can a focus on the voice signify? Would this happen within law and its institutions? Or would this imply a permanent moment of suspension outside the law?

When we think of the voice in relation to ethics and justice, the corporeal and vulnerable voice implies unpredictable ethical actions of newness and natality that escape the retributive logic of the justice of law. Is then the focus on the voice leading to a different ontology? Has this any implication for subjectivity and for sexual difference? To answer these questions, I will have to explore some theoretical and methodological approaches that resist law with reference to justice and the voice.

In the first part of the book, which comprises Chapter I, I engage with different scholars who have looked for the possibilities of thinking about resistance of the current legal framework and subjectivity position. Scholars such as John Rawls, Martha Nussbaum, Judith Butler and Adriana Cavarero will be taken into consideration. The theories proposed by those scholars are interpreted in terms of a hypothesis of resistance against the normative authority of law. I will explore what Rawls, Nussbaum, Butler and Cavarero suggest in terms of allowing voice and justice to people.

These scholars either reframe justice within the institutional parameters of law to allow more equality, as in the case of Rawls and Nussbaum, or appear to be radically critical of all the normative and fictitious frameworks of law, as in the case of Judith Butler (even though she does not deny the necessity of the framework itself – this will be explained in Chapter I). I will be looking instead for a radical position, one that is capable of suspending the normative frame, even if just temporarily, and that allows connection to oneself and one's voice beyond the legal institutions and principles; a position that presupposes a different ontology.

This study is closest to the work of Adriana Cavarero. More specifically, it draws mainly on Cavarero and her Arendtian roots and aims to develop, in an ethical sense, the perspective on the voice. Cavarero theorizes a space of resistance that begins from a non-essentialized account of oneself, from one's uniqueness and *who-ness.* This is a space which is never the same, always changeable and always corporeal. By engaging with such an excess and an excluded dimension of subjectivity, Cavarero remains critical of the possibility of resistance within the frame and the institutions of law and engages with this frame and its subjectivity. Walter Benjamin does something similar in his theorization of the general strike.[43] I will connect Cavarero's resistance to that of the critical legal tradition and Walter Benjamin in Chapter I, while discussing the methodological engagement and disengagement of one's voice with regard to law and its institutions.

43 Walter Benjamin, "Critique of Violence," in *Reflections: Essays, Aphorisms, Autobiographical Writings*, ed. Demetz, P., trans. Edmund Jephcott (New York: Harcourt Brace Jovanovich, 1978), 277–300.

In the second part of the book, I will compare and juxtapose the ontological approach of this study with gendered situations in case studies. These case studies are intended to give more voice to the argument of one's voice and have the purpose of supporting, bolstering and showcasing the theme of the voice. Female genital cutting (FGC) and commercial sex can be seen as situations where the cracks and the wounds operated on the subject are ingrained on the self and body; they mark radically the sexual difference division within subjectivity. The case studies embrace the underlining critique of an essentialized sexual difference.

In Chapter II, I analyze the legal approach to FGC. I argue that law, via the principles of consent and the integrity of the body, denies the possibility of speech and the exercise of autonomy and choice. Law deems women who insist on FGC as consent-less and their body is constructed as mutilated in contrast to the intact legal body. The theories of Rawls and Butler are also taken into consideration as well as the position of Renata Salecl on body art and FGC. I advocate for the necessity to approach the cut via ambivalence and one's voice.

In Chapter III, I consider the case of sex work and objectification. After taking a look at the objectification of sex workers by law itself, I explore the perspectives of Nussbaum and Butler on objectification. I will argue that the ontology of one's voice, by revealing one's uniqueness and by coming from one's body, challenges the essentialized sexual difference division that is responsible for the objectification of women in commercial sex and the idea that women are less than subjects.

Finally, in the last part of the book, which includes Chapter IV, I bring up the question of ethics and justice in relation to the voice. Justice in law is grounded on emotions of retribution and resentment, expression of a general legal subjectivity divested of the voice and cut out from one's corporeal body and one's vulnerability. Thus, in this chapter, I explore the ethical implications of one's voice.

If we go back to the critical legal studies movement, Douzinas talks about justice by reminding us of the tragedy of Antigone.[44] We could use this tragedy to understand the conflict between one's voice and the general voice of the justice of law. Antigone's voice lives in the action of a singular being, whereas the law made by Creon rests in public proclamations. Creon's edict establishes publicly that the traitor Polynices needs to be left unburied; he proclaims his cut and divided vision of the law and justice. But Antigone chooses to follow her own voice, the divine law, and buries her brother against Creon's will.

Antigone shows her inner voice, her awareness of the vulnerability of life and death, and acts with ethical responsibility. She is a singular person with a unique voice and is capable of reversing the ontological principles of law into her ontology of singularity and vulnerability. Her action is pure expenditure, a gift with no return, absolute love as opposed to Creon's utilitarian approach to life through

44 Costas Douzinas and Ronnie Warrington, "Antigone's Law. A Genealogy of Jurisprudence," in *Politics, Postmodernity and Critical Legal Studies*, eds Douzinas, C., Goodrich, P. and Hachamovitch, Y. (London: Routledge, 1994), 187–225.

law. She challenges the legal and institutionalized symbolic order. Antigone's action signifies a different type of legality that suspends Creon's law.[45]

However, rather than Antigone it is the character of Medea that will be explored in Chapter IV. Medea is employed to show that following the righteous law of revenge and punishment reflects a subject that is cut and separated from itself; that does not show an awareness of itself; that is not aware of its vulnerability and that of others; that is not able to respond following the voice of its own uniqueness. This last part of the book suggests that justice beyond revenge – connected to an awareness of one's voice and unpredictable actions such as Arendt's forgiveness – could represent a path of justice for feminism that moves beyond the justice of law. Forgiveness makes one strong without being sovereign. Yet forgiveness is intended here as a possibility that springs from speaking in one's voice and from within; an unpredictable action that one embraces to break with the cycle of violence and get on with one's own life; something that can never be generalized or institutionalized.

In relation to this, an important element I deal with in the first part of the book consists of the methodology employed in resistance. Resistance can be achieved by means of accommodation within law and institutions, as in Rawls and Nussbaum, or by engagement with ethical responsibility, as in Butler as well as in Douzinas, or by suspension from the normative frame, as in Benjamin. Cavarero's voice suggests the possibility of a space of resistance as suspension from the institutional framework and as ethical responsibility. However, we are aware that suspension from the symbolic order is possible only temporarily; therefore I propose resistance through an ontological approach that runs parallel to the ontology of law and deals with the ethics of law. In such a way, we engage with law but we remain nevertheless beyond law.

To sum up, this study complements in some ways the field of the critical legal studies movement and its later adoption of a feminist perspective by continuing the themes of deconstruction through the ontology of singularity and the focus on the voice. The study makes use of the voice as a means of showing that excess, the margins and the peripheries of law are severed and left out. By focusing on the voice it is possible to resist the law as being general and disconnected from one's experience, and thus subjectivity as being cut and divided from our uniqueness. The voice signifies *who someone is* rather than the *what* of identity and subjectivity. Consequently, this study of the voice represents a critique not only of the limited perspective of law, but also of the philosophical and political perspective of liberalism as well as the traditional way of understanding representation and its referent subject.

In addition, the case studies on FGC and commercial sex focus on women and are specific to women, because rethinking the voice in terms of one's voice is essentially a feminist rethinking of representation and the subject. In the case

45 Douzinas and Warrington, "Antigone's Law."

studies, I investigate the possibility of a rupture with the monopoly of the cut (masculine) subject and explore how consent, agency and sexual relations can be referred back to a woman, as singular, corporeal and unique, from the perspective of one's voice. Through one's voice, when a woman speaks she cannot comply with an understanding of a subject as sovereign, autonomous and self-referential, cut and thought of as masculine. On the contrary, she only refers to her own awareness in relationality.

Yet one's voice is not only specific to women. Though not tackled in this book, people in different life conditions could benefit. In the new matrix of history in which homosexuality gets affirmed in our culture, and migration is the new community issue, one's voice could challenge any cut and divided construction of subjectivity, bringing back more awareness of vulnerability from within in relationality, and helping imagine an alternative community.

Chapter I of this book focuses in more detail on the critical legal tradition within which Cavarero's voice is situated in this study. In the chapter, I explore the thought of John Rawls, Martha Nussbaum and Judith Butler and connect the idea of one's voice to the issues in the book.

Part I

The voice and its possibilities of resistance

Chapter 1

Can one speak in one's voice? One's voice and the critique and resistance of the law: a review of the literature

> *The ontological horizon that is disclosed by the voice – or what we want to call a vocal ontology of uniqueness – stands in contrast to the various ontologies of the fictitious entities that the philosophical tradition, over the course of its historical development, designates with names like "man," "subject," "individual." For what the universal categories share is the neglect of the "uniqueness" of those human beings.*[1]

For Adriana Cavarero, the voice is essentially unique, springing from a specific and corporeal mouth. It implies a corporeal selfhood, in that there is the passing and breathing of air in one's throat and a singular body in action.[2] I will be using the term "one's voice" to distinguish it from the voice as general and abstract. The voice I am referring to is the voice emitted by a singular and corporeal selfhood. I prefer the term "one's voice" because it slightly downplays the sense of possessiveness of the voice, whereas in the term "one's own voice" the emphasis is more explicitly on ownership. The voice is not possessed by one but it is rather constitutive of *who one is* and one's uniqueness. One's voice is revealed in the exposure, when one speaks, and thus it expresses a situation of relationality and plurality.

The voice carries possibilities for thinking about sexual difference, ontology, politics, subjectivity and ethics. From a traditional and essentialized sexual difference perspective, the subject reflects the masculine traits of being, whereas the feminine subject is marginalized and objectified by being associated with the body. A focus on the voice, however, implies paying attention to those traits of our subjectivity that are stereotypically associated with the feminine. The gendered traits become unraveled and one's voice shows that those traits are part of the uniqueness of anyone. Thus the voice allows us to go beyond gender and sexual difference distinctions by touching the radical uniqueness and materiality of each of us.

1 Adriana Cavarero, *For More Than One Voice. Toward a Philosophy of Vocal Expression*, trans. Paul Kottman (Stanford: Stanford University Press, 2005), 173.

2 Cavarero, *For More Than One Voice.*

Adriana Cavarero's thought comes from a position of sexual difference. She was originally part of a group of Italian scholars called *Diotima* who chose to cut themselves off from the language of men, took a separatist stance and worked to construct their own language, valorizing the originality and strength of women as a group.[3] Cavarero began to deconstruct the text of Western philosophy, to work both with and against language. Her focus on the voice as corporeal and singular represents her original position on sexual difference.

In ontological terms, the voice carries a relational and anti-metaphysical ontology because it occurs in communication with another and belongs to a unique being made of flesh and bones. The uniqueness of selfhood always resonates in the voice: one's uniqueness is always revealed when one speaks, because one's voice is always different from another's.

The ontology of one's voice provides an anti-metaphysical strategy, capable of re-vocalizing Logos, politics and the law. One's voice interrupts the symbolic and normative order of thinking.[4] The ontology of the voice also contains radical political aspects because it is capable of giving one the possibility of speaking with a unique voice, together with other voices, as opposed to the sovereign, general and devocalized voice of current politics. One's voice offers a different way of speaking in law, too, going beyond the voice in terms of consent. Consent in law refers to a rational individual, thought of in terms of a divided subjectivity. I will say more in relation to consent in Chapter II.

In terms of subjectivity, from the Cavarerian perspective on voice the current legal subject is cut off and divided from her uniqueness, corporeality and relationality. The voice, understood as one's voice, exemplifies precisely the excess, what is cut out from our subjectivity and a moment beyond the general naming. One's voice and thus singularity, corporeality and relationality, are those unique aspects of the self that are excluded by the normative symbolic order and its related subjectivity. Those aspects become superfluous and are not taken into consideration by the symbolic framework. In legal discourse, the voice in terms of singularity is not spoken.

Law as a discourse of the symbolic order speaks the voice of the general and universal legal subject and is unable to include singularity and uniqueness. Law also reflects the liberal perspective of an autonomous and independent subject who enjoys rights; whereas speaking in one's voice implies awareness of vulnerability, connection, relationality and leaning toward others. Our voice has a profound relationship with our selfhood and the way we imagine our subjectivity.

Finally, ethically, the voice – being an expression of singularity and corporeality – connects to vulnerability. A focus on the voice leads to awareness of one's vulnerability and that of others. Such awareness leads to the possibility of ethical

3 Graziella Parati and Rebecca J. West, eds, *Italian Feminist Theory and Practice. Equality and Sexual Difference* (London: Associated University Press, 2002), 57.

4 Cavarero, *For More Than One Voice*, 173–182.

conduct beyond the justice of law. The justice of law, in fact, requires punishment in the case of inflicted wounds because the law insists on restoring balance, on what is right, after an injury, focusing on a specific type of righteous and independent subjectivity. Hence I explore the possibility of speaking through an ontology that resists the cuts and divisions operated upon the subject and the reproduction of violence. Such an ontology reminds us that although one may be constructed in law and other symbolic discourses as sovereign and righteous, there is an aspect of one's existence that does not belong to such a formation of subjectivity.

Cavarero's insights on the voice call for a reflection on a series of questions, allowing us to rethink resistance. Can such a space of resistance be applied to the law? Would this space be a moment of suspension or an engagement with law and institutions? Can the focus on the voice provide an ontology that overcomes the cut and separations of the legal subject? What type of ontology would this be? Would this approach have significance for the division of essentialized sexual difference? Can a critique and resistance that starts from the voice be applied to empirical and gendered contexts such as female genital cutting (FGC) and sex work? Is there an implication in terms of ethical responsibility? What would this mean for law and justice?

The focus on the voice and on those juridical questions attempt to continue the critique of law as developed by the critical legal studies movement and its feminist thinking. The focus on the voice relates also to feminist scholars within critical legal studies, in that it has a similar intention of deconstructing the masculine and abstract subject of law. The recent book edited by Maria Drakopoulou, *Feminist Encounters with Legal Philosophy*, illustrates, for instance, how the interpretation of established legal texts has been the most significant form of feminist critical legal practice.[5] Working with texts has allowed the exposure of the patriarchal and phallocentric nature of law and women's exclusion from the legal symbolic order. In *Feminist Encounters with Legal Philosophy*, legal texts are interrogated in order to identify their male and patriarchal thinking. In "Samuel Pufendorf, Feminism and the Question of Women and Law" Maria Drakopoulou scrutinizes the critical insights offered by feminist political and legal theory, whereas Patrick Hanafin, in "A Voice Beyond the Law: Reading Plato, Reading Cavarero," employs Italian feminist philosophy and Cavarero's theory to read law in a different way.[6] In the UK, other critical legal scholars have engaged with feminist critique, operating a sort of deconstruction of the law. In *Judith Butler: Ethics, Law, Politics* Elena

5 Maria Drakopoulou, ed., *Feminist Encounters with Legal Philosophy*, (Oxon: Routledge, 2014).

6 Maria Drakopoulou, "Samuel Pufendorf, Feminism and the Question of Women and Law," in *Feminist Encounters with Legal Philosophy*, ed. Drakopoulou, M. (Oxon: Routledge, 2014), 66–99; Patrick Hanafin, "A Voice Beyond the Law: Reading Plato, Reading Cavarero," in *Feminist Encounters with Legal Philosophy*, ed. Drakopoulou, M. (Oxon: Routledge, 2014); Maria Aristodemou, *Law and Literature: Journeys from Her to Eternity* (Oxford: Oxford University Press, 2000); Elena Loizidou, *Judith Butler: Ethics, Law, Politics* (Oxon: Routledge, 2007).

Loizidou points out, for instance, how the feminist work of Judith Butler on the livable and viable life can question the legal subject itself, whereas in her book *Law and Literature: Journeys from Her to Eternity*, Maria Aristodemou has highlighted the similarities between literary and legal texts as a means to better understand the origin of law and literature. By touching the origins of both texts, she shows the tension between law and literature and underlines how jurisprudence can overcome law's formal structure and become more a cross-disciplinary investigation. In her view literature represents an ancient mode of connecting with what is alive. There is therefore in her work the search for what it means to be a legal subject in terms of a living human being, man or woman.[7]

With the influx of postmodernism and deconstruction, British critical legal studies has moved away from Marxism, rethought the terms of critique and connected more deeply to the continental tradition.[8] The main philosophical tendencies are informed by the works of Freud, Foucault, Lacan, Levinas and in particular Derrida and deconstruction.[9] There is an attempt to criticize the legal discourses and their texts by focusing on what has been repressed and excluded, and thus to have a more diverse voice. The Derridean deconstructive approach has meant, for some critical legal scholars, the analysis of the law as a pure text and as a sign.[10]

Peter Goodrich and Costas Douzinas are among the critical legal scholars who have approached law as text and language. For instance, in his work *Languages of Law* Goodrich gives the example of the annunciation, which is described as the process whereby the Holy Spirit is announced as present, the divinity in the womb of the virgin mother of Christ.[11] Then Goodrich goes on to compare the legal tradition to *a secular version of Christian morality*.[12] Law uses speech to announce something similar to the Holy Spirit. As a consequence, law becomes absolute Law and life gets denied.

Goodrich's critique of the metaphysics of the legal is also inextricably linked to a feminist critique of the patriarchal truth of the law. For instance, in his book *The Law of Love* Goodrich counterposes normative law with amorous law.

7 These feminist critical legal scholars are only indicative of the feminist tradition within the critical legal studies movement. Several other scholars within the critical legal studies movement have become involved in a deconstruction of law from a feminist perspective, putting women at the forefront of their writings.

8 Tim Murphy, "Brit Crits: Subversion and Submission, Past, Present and Future," *Law and Critique*, 10 (1999): 237–278.

9 Murphy, "Brit Crits."

10 Murphy, "Brit Crits."

11 Peter Goodrich, *Languages of Law: From Logics to Nomadic Masks* (London: Weidenfield and Nicholson, 1990), 249. Adriana Cavarero, "Dedicated to Derrida," in *For More Than One Voice: Toward a Philosophy of Vocal Expression*, trans. Paul Kottman (Stanford: Stanford University Press, 2005), 213–241.

12 Goodrich, *Languages of Law*, 249; Cavarero, "Dedicated to Derrida."

Contrary to rules, rights and obligations, in amorous law there are neither absolute rights nor individual autonomy capable of excluding a lover and it is possible to suspend judgments in favour of erotic conversations.[13] In another essay, "Gender and Contracts," Goodrich also reflects on two different conceptions of relationship, namely the legal proprietary and restrictive contract and an agreement that is instead expressive of love. This latter attaches to a relationship occurring at a particular time and in a particular place.[14]

In his metaphysical critique of the patriarchal text of law, Goodrich follows the Derridean perspective, where speech appears to carry the presence of metaphysics whereas the text seems more distant from it.[15] In a grammatological sense, the legal text reiterates a sign of the sign that is already dead and thus more suitable to be studied by deconstruction. Studying legal texts can lead to an understanding of this denial of life. Through repetition, the text's attachment to the metaphysics of presence can be uncovered.[16] Goodrich says:

> *In interpretative terms, the text sees nothing, it hears nothing, it says nothing. It runs scared, scared of its desire, scared of the possibility of speech, scared of life [. . .] My suggestion is that a semiotics of law can show us some of the forms of dying; it can read the signs and interpret the law so as to laugh at it, so as to seduce, to play by invocation of other worlds and more rigorous and living languages.*[17]

Goodrich poses some questions: who speaks? Who is speaking? He analyzes the repetitions, the texts, signs and symbols of law to discover in the text of law who is speaking. He aims through the repetition of the sign to find references to the excess, to what is excluded by law.[18] For Goodrich, the text bears the meaning of the legal tradition and acts as reference to things.

The process of analyzing the law as text becomes necessary in order to unfold the production and repetition of the legal mechanisms of fixation and the attachment to the violence of metaphysics and authenticity. If law is viewed as an established tradition that does not necessitate further justifications and rather constitutes a truth based on identity (a system of law manifesting the metaphysics of presence), approaching law as a text allows an escape from the constant attachment of law to truth and the presence of metaphysics.

13 Peter Goodrich, *The Law of Love. A Brief Historical and Practical Manual* (New York: Palgrave Macmillan, 2006), 203.

14 Peter Goodrich, "Gender and Contracts," in *Feminist Perspectives on the Foundational Subjects of Law*, ed. Bottomley, A. (London: Cavendish, 1996), 17–46.

15 For those concepts see: Jacques Derrida, *Of Grammatology,* trans. Gayatri Chakravorty Spivak (London: Johns Hopkins University Press, 1997); Jacques Derrida, *Speech and Phenomena: And Other Essays on Husserl's Theory of Signs,* trans. David B. Allison (Evanston: Northwestern University Press, 1973).

16 Derrida, *Of Grammatology*; Derrida, *Speech and Phenomena.*

17 Goodrich, *Languages of Law*, 254.

18 Goodrich, *Languages of Law.*

Similarly, in *Postmodern Jurisprudence*, Douzinas argues that the legal text is characterized by unity, totality, authorship and self-referentiality and that historical continuity reflects the desire for presence.[19] In a Derridean way, Douzinas suggests that the meaning of a text is created in a process of endless differentiations that is never present and repetition allows a demystification of the metaphysics of presence, which is believed to be in the text.

> *The text is always an intertext; it is created through a continuous affirmation and denial of other texts. Rather than being a totality of meaning, the text is a system of signs which are to be repeated. Saussure's classical analysis is based on the claim that meaning, the signified, is a function of the differences between signifiers. But, as Derrida points out, every phonic or graphic signifier differs from endless others.*[20]

Marianne Constable, Shoshana Felman and Judith Butler attempt to deconstruct law from the point of the speaking subject, taking account of the context of communication and considering law in terms of speech acts that exceed all legal intentions.[21] These scholars focus on the performative power of language. Performativity is the capacity simply to do or to act. Marianne Constable investigates, for instance, law's relation to language. She claims that law exists rhetorically and that its claims occur through words. Imperfections and incompleteness are key to understanding law and language. Law and justice depend on relations between people through language and in the name of law.

For Shoshana Felman there is no speech act without the body because performative speech acts are forms of doing that draw upon the body. The character of Don Juan becomes central in her argument, because Don Juan reveals the misfires and failed instances of the performative promise via the body. A promise commits the body to an action. Yet the body bears unconscious fantasies and works against the intention of the promise and this constitutes the misfire and failed instance of the promise. The body is the excess of the promise-speech act and is more than it represents, signifying what is unintentional.

Felman lets us understand that any referent subject cannot stand knowingly for itself; rather it is a mix of conscious and unconscious and the body interferes with representation, language and thus law. For Felman, voice and speaking are to be intended as performative rather than claims of truth or the product of a sovereign

19 Costas Douzinas and Ronnie Warrington with Shaun McVeigh, *Postmodern Jurisprudence: The Law of Text in the Texts of Law* (London: Routledge, 1991), 45–46.

20 Douzinas and Warrington with McVeigh, *Postmodern Jurisprudence*, 47.

21 Marianne Constable, *Our World is Our Bond. How Legal Speech Acts* (Stanford: Stanford University Press, 2014); Shoshana Felman, *The Scandal of the Speaking Body. Don Juan with J.L. Austin or the Seduction in Two Languages*, trans. Catherine Porter (Stanford: Stanford University Press, 2003); Judith Butler, *Gender Trouble: Feminism and the Subversion of Identity* (New York: Routledge, 1990).

referent and, in this sense, her speaking body scandalizes metaphysics and every fixed truth. The performative capacity of language has also been embraced by Judith Butler; Section 1.3 will deal with Butler's thought in more detail.

Despite the many differences between the Derridean approach to resistance and those of scholars such as Constable, Felman and Butler, they all work toward the similar goal of eliminating metaphysical assumptions in language, disrupting any idea of a frozen structure and univocal meaning.[22] The work of Constable, Felman and Butler has been widely influential for the critical legal tradition because it has pushed the focus of critical legal thinking toward the analysis of political, social and discursive forces entangled in law.

Adriana Cavarero adds an element of radical materiality to resistance and focuses on the voice. She is interested in one's voice in the act of speaking with others, emphasizing the uniqueness, corporeality and relationality of speaking selfhood. Precisely, her focus on the voice as one's voice, singular and unique, makes of the body and voice something concrete and specific, thus radically material. Cavarero also sees in the voice a space of meaning independent from speech.

In accordance with the approaches proposed by Constable, Felman and Butler, Cavarero emphasizes the spoken language by focusing on the unique voice as a possibility to escape the metaphysics of presence.[23] In the appendix "Dedicated to Derrida" at the end of her book *For More Than One Voice*, Cavarero argues that Derrida identifies in the voice a sort of matrix of metaphysics and maintains the opposition between voice and writing.[24] The focus on writing permits for Derrida the infinite deferral of signs and truth, and, therefore, the possibility of *différance*. For Derrida *différance* opposes and resists the presence of things or metaphysics. Différance indicates that there is nothing but signs, deferrals, there is no origin or fixed point, there is no desire for a present entity that can generate metaphysics.[25] Cavarero explains this when she writes:

> *The sign thus implies the absent presence of the signified – in the sense that the full presence of the signified is not here, because there is only a sign that supplements it and shows it to be absent. Therefore in the last analysis, suggests Derrida, the presence of the signified – or rather the signified as presence – only gets presupposed or constructed vis-à-vis the deferral of the sign to this presence, a deferral that attests to its absence.*[26]

However, for Cavarero, Derrida's thesis on the phonocentrism of metaphysics has blocked any reflection of the anti-metaphysical potential of the voice.[27]

22 On the difference between Speech Act Theories and Derrida, see: Kevin, J. Halion, Speech Act Theory and Deconstruction. McMaster University: Thesis, 1989.

23 Cavarero, *For More Than One Voice*.

24 Cavarero, "Dedicated to Derrida."

25 Cavarero, "Dedicated to Derrida."

26 Cavarero, "Dedicated to Derrida," 217.

27 Cavarero, "Dedicated to Derrida," 213.

According to Cavarero, the voice in Derrida is not a sonorous voice; rather it is the voice of a self- consciousness as self-presence.[28] Cavarero argues that perhaps in connecting the voice to metaphysics Derrida worked upon a solipsistic idea of subjectivity based on the *said* and did not take into account the *saying* and the plurality of voices.[29] Such an approach is rather the Cartesian way of speaking, where there is a silent person speaking alone.[30] For Cavarero, in Descartes speaking is essentially speaking to oneself and self-reflection.[31]

According to Cavarero, then, the Derridean voice is not a voice, but rather a system constructed as voice.[32] The voice as unique allows instead the separation of the embodied person from her name. The one who is speaking inevitably reveals the singular sound of her voice.[33] Cavarero proposes the dismantling of the metaphysics of presence through the voice rather than the sign. *A vocal ontology of uniqueness must therefore first overturn the old metaphysical strategy that subordinates speech to thought.*[34] The question *who speaks,* for Cavarero, means listening to one's voice as opposed to the general and sovereign normative law.

The theme of the voice in this book is contextualized within the critical legal tradition. The voice is intended to continue – in a different way – the critique of the language of law initiated by critical legal scholars such as Goodrich and Douzinas. The political demand of the critical legal tradition – to return to the lived experience through the sign – is continued in this book with a focus on the voice rather than the text; that is, in terms of a selfhood that is understood as corporeal, unique and relational. A focus on the voice indicates precisely that there are elements of ourselves that are excluded and cut off from our subjectivity. As Goodrich argues, the consolidation of truth through the repetition of a historical legal tradition denies life and implies a cut and separation of life from law.[35] The links between voice and subjectivity are at the core of this study.

Thus I could say there is violence in our formation as legal subjects, understood as cut and separation. The theme of the voice is also the theme of the subject, of *who speaks* in law. Adriana Cavarero positions this cut subject within the Cartesian tradition. The subject *in its classic Cartesian clothes has no voice and speaks only to itself through the mute voice of consciousness.*[36] Cavarero continues:

> *Thought has no voice; it neither invokes nor speaks – it cogitates [cogita]. Thinking is structurally immune to the musical and relational interference of*

28 Cavarero, "Dedicated to Derrida," 241.
29 Cavarero, "Dedicated to Derrida," 218.
30 Cavarero, "Dedicated to Derrida."
31 Cavarero, "Dedicated to Derrida," 218–219.
32 Cavarero, "Dedicated to Derrida."
33 Cavarero, "Dedicated to Derrida."
34 Cavarero, *For More Than One Voice*, 174.
35 Goodrich, *Languages of Law.*
36 Cavarero, *For More Than One Voice*, 173.

> *the acoustic sphere of speech. A vocal ontology of uniqueness must therefore first overturn the old metaphysical strategy that subordinates speech to thought.*[37]

> *Reduced to an acoustic signifier, the voice depends on the signified. This dependence is not only obvious, it is decisive, for it captures the voice in a complex system that subordinates the acoustic sphere to the realm of sight. As in the Platonism of Augustine [. . .], sound evokes the idea; the order of the signified appertains to the realm of the eye. This is expressed in Greek by terms such as noema and idea.*[38]

We can say that as subjects we are formulated as cuts and splits; we are posited in general terms and many traits of ourselves are left out and considered as superfluous and excessive. Such violence is also the violence of speech. Being constructed as cut and divided subjects forecloses the promise to speak in one's voice and to have awareness of oneself. The only possibility left is to speak from within the available choices offered by the current ideological frame.

It is important to note that when talking about the voice in this book I will refer to the dimensions underlined above, namely the ontological dimension of one's singularity, corporeality and relationality that the voice foretells. The voice opens up the possibility of experiencing awareness of oneself as opposed to a generalized constituted subject or identity, accountable to linguistic and normative structures. Consequently, and inevitably, in the book I will also address the condition of plurality of the voice and its ethical implications in terms of responsibility toward others. I will deal with this aspect in Chapter IV.

In the sections of this chapter that follow I will engage with some selected literature on resistance. I have chosen to reflect on the theoretical approaches offered by John Rawls, Martha Nussbaum, Judith Butler and Adriana Cavarero. The theories of these thinkers attempt to create a space of resistance within or beyond the legal liberal framework and address questions related to the voice, subjectivity and justice. In Rawls' theory, there is a search for more equality and justice, even though Rawls' subject lies unvoiced and his thinking remains within liberalism. Nussbaum looks for more equal conditions of life, while her thinking still holds on notions of universality, dignity and the human worth of people. However, both Butler and Cavarero go further by showing a concern for materiality and a justice outside the liberal grid and by paying more attention to the voice of the people. Therefore, both scholars take a critical stand against the universal liberal subject and look for other dimensions of justice beyond liberalism.

1.1 Resistance in terms of justice as fairness

In this section I am going to take into special consideration the perspective on resistance offered by John Rawls, reflecting on its main points and limits. Today,

37 Cavarero, *For More Than One Voice*, 173–174.

38 Cavarero, *For More Than One Voice*, 35.

Rawls' theory of the distribution of goods, and his principle of difference, find application in the welfare states of most Western liberal democracies. The approach constructed by Rawls is interesting, because while it remains within the constraints of legal liberalism and individual rights, it attempts at the same time to provide a voice for people and opposes the imposition of the universal legal principles of the time. During Rawls' lifetime, utilitarianism was the dominant tradition.[39] For utilitarianism, what counted was the greatest total of happiness, as society was viewed in terms of a single entity. According to this view, it is reasonable to put the cost on some individuals in order to achieve greater gains and maximize total benefit and utility for society.[40] Under utilitarianism, slavery is, for instance, admissible insofar as it allows an increase in the sum of happiness and this fails to take into account the distinction between people and the rights of minorities.

It has to be noticed that Rawls' theory of justice as fairness begins from the concept of the recognition of the inviolability of each individual, where basic liberties cannot be sacrificed. In *A Theory of Justice*, Rawls discusses the most adequate conception of justice to be used by a democratic society.[41] He proposes the distribution of goods to those who are least well off in society, attempting to provide a sort of equal voice to everyone and resisting the injustices of liberal law and its institutions.[42] Rawls includes among what he perceives to be primary goods: rights, liberties, opportunities, income, self-respect and welfare.[43]

A society is just, for Rawls, if it promotes a commonly held good in legal institutions. In other words, society is seen as a mutually beneficial system, where there is cooperation between its members.[44] The basic structure of society sets the main terms of cooperation and allows justice. The basic structure consists of the way institutions distribute fundamental rights and duties and thus resolve conflicts fairly.[45] People can choose a basic structure from an "original position." The original position implies that people are "individuals" who do not know things about themselves; they are *blindfolded with a veil of ignorance*, so that they are prevented from knowing about time, history or class.[46]

> *I have said that the original position is the appropriate initial status quo which insures that the fundamental agreements reached in it are fair. This fact yields the name "justice as fairness".*[47]

39 Hercules Bantas, *Understanding John Rawls* (Melbourne: Reluctant Geek, 2010), 4.
40 Bantas, *Understanding John Rawls.*
41 Rawls, John, *A Theory of Justice* (Cambridge: Harvard University Press, 1971).
42 Rawls, *A Theory of Justice.*
43 Rawls, *A Theory of Justice*, 178, 155, 440, 386.
44 Frank Lovett, *Rawls's A Theory of Justice: A Reader's Guide* (London: Continuum, 2011).
45 Rawls, *A Theory of Justice*, 12.
46 Rawls, *A Theory of Justice,* 17.
47 Rawls, *A Theory of Justice*, 17.

> *Among the essential features of this situation is that no one knows his place in society, his class position or social status, nor does any one know his fortune in the distribution of natural assets and abilities, his intelligence, strength, and the like. I shall even assume that the parties do not know their conceptions of the good or their special psychological propensities.*[48]

The *original position* appears necessary for individuals to accept justice and ignore themselves, their different welfare needs and their divergent life prospects. If, for instance, one knew oneself to be a black man or a woman, one would bargain for principles that favour black people or women, but if one did not know these facts, one would not have reason to do so. The veil of ignorance forces people to think about the problem of social justice from an impartial point of view and implements a moral attitude and justice as fairness in people.[49]

Through the veil of ignorance people are supposed to always act rationally; that is, people will choose primary goods as the most important ones. And justice as fairness implies precisely the distribution of primary goods to the least well off in society. However, if the veil of ignorance places all individuals on an equal footing, then the individual appears to be completely disconnected and cut off from the materiality and circumstances in which other people are situated. Rawls later modified the concept of original position and veil of ignorance. He refined his perspective, arguing that citizens who hold opposing conceptions of equality in society can find a shared basis of "reasonable" agreement through an *overlapping consensus*.[50] Interestingly, "reasonable" for Rawls has to do with choosing the good for society that is the already established egalitarian distribution and the principle of difference. The individual is asked to act and speak in a reasonable way.

Let's think more closely about the implications of such a perspective for one's voice. Despite the terms of cooperation and the intent to ensure justice, Rawls' theory of the political reflects a mono-valent perspective of community and sharing. The idea of the veil of ignorance is emblematic of the artificiality of the context necessary for his intent to be distributed equally to everyone. Regarding this, critical legal theorists like Douzinas and Gearey write:

> *The temporary and heuristic destruction of identity in the original position attempts to place the self in a position of reversibility with others [. . .] Such a huge abstraction from what a real self is, and from how moral argument operates, is necessary in order to sustain the Kantian claim of the universality of the moral law. The subject of moral philosophy is not a real life person but a "generalised other;" someone we come across and relate to through public and institutional norms of formal equality and reciprocity. The other is a*

48 Rawls, *A Theory of Justice*, 12.
49 Lovett, *Rawls's A Theory of Justice*, 20.
50 John Rawls, *Political Liberalism* (New York: Columbia University Press, 1996).

> *representative of abstract humankind [. . .] The other person, the litigant who comes before the law, is stripped of what makes her a real self. Law silences her pain and anger, turns her into the instance of a rule or the example of a principle.*[51]

For Douzinas and Gearey, Rawls' theory also fails to account for the pain and vulnerability of people before law and justice, since law and justice appear to be concerned only with distributions, investments and returns.[52] The application of the Rawlsian theorization of the political in the welfare state of today's democracies appears also disconnected and cut off from the ambivalent and concrete community in which we live. For Johan Van der Walt, in Rawls' theory of fairness there is a sacrificial destruction of plurality; that is, plurality is dismissed through the use of "normative consensus."[53] While the social bond is constituted by dynamics of plurality, Rawls excludes those aspects from his theory and postulates the political in terms of exchange of resources, goods, welfare and thus calculation and sameness.[54]

Such a theorization reduces the political to some kind of One-ness and same-ness and produces a thinking of the subject as separation and cuts.[55] It suggests that we should be concerned with the efficiency of a community, in terms of control, production, distribution, mono-valence and One-ness. There seems to be no account of concrete and singular people living in the Rawlsian community. A person is only an individual with no unique face or body and no relationality, except for their relation to the principle of just distribution. The other is not even another but the same, to whom it is necessary to distribute goods, according to the established and normative difference principle.

Furthermore, Rawls' egalitarian distribution appears to depend on citizenship; that is, on a specific membership within a unitary conception of a people. People who are not citizens do not enjoy the distribution of welfare; they are completely unheard and excluded, possessing no voice, while the voice granted to those who are members or citizens is the institutionalized and already determined voice of a pre-defined liberalism.

Consequently, and although Rawls' theory appears to provide some sort of voice to people, his theory can be claimed to be structured on a *false choice*.[56] Slavoj Žižek explains how Rawls' freedom and liberty of choice are possible

51 Costas Douzinas and Adam Gearey, *Critical Jurisprudence: The Political Philosophy of Justice* (Oxford: Hart Publishing, 2005), 127.

52 Douzinas and Gearey, *Critical Jurisprudence*, 130.

53 Johan Van der Walt, *Law and Sacrifice: Towards a Post-Apartheid Theory of Law* (London: Birkbeck Law Press, 2005), 123, 148.

54 Van der Walt, *Law and Sacrifice*, 123, 148.

55 The capitalization of "One-ness" indicates a political experience decided by a sovereign center as opposed to the unique singularity in relationality involved in one's voice.

56 Slavoj Žižek, *Enjoy Your Symptom!: Jacques Lacan in Hollywood and Out* (New York: Routledge, 1992), 69–110.

only if one makes *the right choice*, which is the predicted choice of sameness and distribution. The "reasonable" choice is to accept the sacrifice of what is superfluous.[57] People who fall short of the subjectivity of the same are left unheard since the only possible choice is *the right choice*,[58] the only voice is the abstract and semantic voice of the liberal frame.

Regarding the voice, we can say that people can only speak with a general and generic voice rather than in their singular and corporeal voice. Paradoxically, in Rawls' liberal theory of fairness, there appears to be a voiceless possibility of speaking and being aware of oneself. His community results in being aphonic, because a precondition for speaking is knowing nothing of oneself, being blindfolded in a *veil of ignorance*, and talking only the language of what has been considered just. The justice system, advocated by Rawls, remains a system imposed from above that decides in advance the predicaments of the people. Rawls' resistance to law is imagined from within the legal structure and the liberal tradition. In the next section, I will explore the perspective on resistance articulated by Martha Nussbaum, who claims to diverge from Rawls' position, offering a voice to everyone.

1.2 Resistance and the good standard of human function

A more recent liberal approach to resistance has been offered by the capability theory of Martha Nussbaum. Her approach was used by the United Nations during the 1980s to adjust development concerns in so-called developing countries. Her approach counters in some ways the Rawlsian theory of justice focused on goods with an approach grounded on capabilities. Importance is given to capabilities rather than the mere acquisition and distribution of goods. The capability theory attempts to adapt liberalism to difference by organizing a set of capabilities that are beneficial for human functioning.

In his theory of justice as fairness, Rawls does not take into account the differences among human beings. Unlike Rawls, Nussbaum's theory presupposes that human beings differ from one another and people are contextualized in their material reality.[59] For Nussbaum, people live in different natural and social contexts and have specific personal characteristics, such as age, sex, and physical and mental abilities.[60] For her, such differences are important in enabling us to understand how inequalities are produced and sustained.

For instance, in the case of a disabled person who cannot "function" as a healthy individual, the capability approach helps to understand inequality and enables the

57 Žižek, *Enjoy Your Symptom!*, 69–110.
58 Slavoj Žižek, *Plague of Fantasies* (London: Verso, 1997).
59 Martha Nussbaum, *Sex and Social Justice* (Oxford: Oxford University Press, 1999).
60 Nussbaum, *Sex and Social Justice.*

best capability to function. Nussbaum claims that taking into account materiality, needs and vulnerability is helpful because those aspects are part of our human dignity and, therefore, they are not abstract ideas and should not remain in the realm of abstraction.[61] Through the system of good human functioning, the central question of politics becomes better adapted to personal needs. Difference is seen in relation to the standard, the capability to function. Capability is precisely the quantity of freedom enjoyed by a human being and the condition that allows good human functioning. The presupposition is that people have various needs, different resources, and diverse abilities to make these resources function or to access them.

The approach not only asks about distribution of resources and opportunities, but also attends to each individual in relation to the functions that are considered important.[62] Nussbaum claims that her approach considers people one by one rather than as part of an organic entity, such as, for instance, the family.[63] Her approach, therefore, does not focus only on the distribution of resources, but rather resources acquire value in promoting human functioning. She points out that human functioning is paramount in converting resources and giving them value. If a human being is unable to convert a resource into valuable functioning because of a disability, they are put into a position of inequality.

> *This approach [The Rawlsian approach] does enable us to criticise persistent inequalities, and it strongly criticizes the view that preferences are simply given rather than shaped by society's basic structure. But in one way the Rawlsian approach stops short [. . .] People have varying needs for resources [. . .] They also have different abilities to convert resources into functioning [. . .] Unlike the type of liberal approach that focuses only on distribution of resources, the capability approach maintains that resources have no value in themselves, apart from their role in promoting human functioning.*[64]

For Rawls, justice and equality among subjects are achieved through the distribution of goods and this is what is supposed to materialize his life projects, whereas for Nussbaum justice and equality are achieved when human beings reach a level of capability to function. This implies distribution but also the elimination of obstacles that impede good functioning. The aim is therefore to ensure that resources promote capacities and good human functioning. In a way, this allows the abstraction of liberalism to be accommodated to more practical human needs. We can say that by paying attention to the individual's access to human functioning, Nussbaum's theory raises more awareness of the economic injustices inflicted upon women and other vulnerable and excluded groups.

61 Martha Nussbaum, *Hiding from Humanity: Disgust, Shame and the Law* (Princeton: Princeton University Press, 2004), 334.
62 Nussbaum, *Sex and Social Justice.*
63 Nussbaum, *Sex and Social Justice.*
64 Nussbaum, *Sex and Social Justice*, 33–34.

For Nussbaum, the capability approach requires that we choose which capabilities are more central than others, which functions are to be considered necessary to live life fully. This means to have in mind a life where the dignity of the human being cannot be undermined by the absence of economic rights or other opportunities that are at the core of the capability to function.[65]

In *Women and Human Development*, Nussbaum is attentive to the needs and interests of women, who are treated unequally in many societies. They are often less nourished than men and more vulnerable to violence and abuses than men. That is to say, women do not benefit from the fundamental functions of a human life. Gender inequality is strongly correlated with poverty and this is a sign of the failure of the human capability.

According to Nussbaum, the case of women requires more than just simply distributing resources and goods: we need to provide them with the capacity to choose. Thus Nussbaum argues that her approach to justice offers not only better justice for women, but also a choice and a voice. It provides not the *what* but the *how*, not how many resources but precisely the capability to function.

At the core of Nussbaum's theory of justice or capability to function lies the universalism of equal worth of the individual.[66] The idea of dignity and equal worth means that all people equally deserve respect and this links to their liberty and to a liberal conception of life. *Each human being should be regarded as an end rather than as a means to an end.*[67] Nussbaum's theory of justice attempts to resist the inequality of the liberal theory. The goal of the idea of the capability to function is to treat people in a dignified and equal way. For Nussbaum, the universalism of liberal justice needs to be guided toward what is good for people; that is, toward basic human functions and capacities.

In her mind, good functioning does not exclude agency. The goal is to place people in a condition of agency, rather than pushing them into functioning.[68] In other words, Nussbaum thinks that universalism and standards are compatible with individual agency, because people would necessarily choose the good universalism and standards and direct their own agency toward the good goal.

> *Liberalism concerns itself with freedom and with spheres of choices [. . .] The choices that liberal politics should protect are those that are deemed of central importance to the development and expression of personhood [. . .] But the goal should always be to put people into a position of agency and choice, not to push them into functioning in ways deemed desirable [. . .] Rohima, quoted in the epigraphs to this volume, discovered that literacy was a powerful source of selfhood*

65 Martha Nussbaum, *Women and Human Developmsent: The Capability Approach* (Cambridge: Cambridge University Press, 2000), 32.

66 Nussbaum, *Women and Human Development;* Nussbaum, *Sex and Social Justice.*

67 Nussbaum, *Women and Human Development*, 32.

68 Nussbaum, *Sex and Social Justice*, 11.

> *and joyful expression, because for the first time she was using her capacities on her own hook rather than merely executing the will of others. It is this experiential idea of choice on which I rely in defending choice as a goal, and no argument has yet shown that there is any human being who does not desire choice so constructed.*[69]

Although Nussbaum appears to adjust some aspects of the Rawlsian theory, some critical legal theorists have underlined the problems in her approach. For instance, Karin Van Marle has argued that Nussbaum's approach contains a paternalistic viewpoint.[70] Despite Nussbaum's assertion of universalism not being incompatible with people's choice, the use of a standard shows no respect for the voice of people as agents, whereas for Loizidou, Nussbaum's theory of resistance presumes to know the needs and desires of others but in reality it affirms law's sovereignty over the voice of the people.[71]

The theory has attracted criticism from other scholars as well. For instance, Thomas Pogge argues that in Nussbaum's approach human diversity is conceived as vertical and this is incompatible with the ethos of human democracy, based on horizontal equality.[72] The specific political focus is thus always on a human being, who needs to be confronted with better standards of functioning and capabilities.

Furthermore, Persio Tincani has noted the deep similarity and interconnections between the two theories of Rawls and Nussbaum.[73] For Tincani, basic goods and capabilities are not alternative political concepts but diverse gradations of the same liberal argument.[74] Basic goods contribute, in fact, to the realization of capabilities. A theory of justice based on distribution makes sure that institutions provide individuals with a minimum amount of goods; whereas theories based on capability require instead that institutions guarantee people a minimum level of functioning. A theory of resources focuses on the constitutive aspect of justice, while a theory of capability underlines the operativity of justice.[75]

However, for Tincani, the approach of capability derives from the approach to goods and resources, since the capability of a person depends also on the goods that such a person is capable of possessing and using. Clearly, the politics of distribution, of standardization and regulation of voices, remains fundamental in both theories. The subject remains general and no account of one's singularity is available.[76]

69 Nussbaum, *Sex and Social Justice*, 11.
70 Karin Van Marle, "The Capabilities Approach, the Imaginary Domain and the Asymmetrical Reciprocity: Feminist Perspectives on Equality and Justice," *Feminist Legal Studies*, 11 (2003): 255–278.
71 Loizidou, *Judith Butler: Ethics, Law, Politics*, 165.
72 Thomas W. Pogge, "Can the Capability Approach Be Justified?" *Philosophical Topics*, 30(2) (2002): 167–228.
73 Persio Tincani, "I Beni Principali Come Capacitazioni," *Politeia*, 83 (2006): 21–44.
74 Tincani, "I Beni Principali Come Capacitazioni."
75 Tincani, "I Beni Principali Come Capacitazioni."
76 Tincani, "I Beni Principali Come Capacitazioni."

In Nussbaum's account, the singularity of the voice, as awareness of a specific corporeal experience, is sacrificed to the already established voice of the good standard of human function. The capability approach appears to be less normative than the one theorized by Rawls. Wealth and income are not in fact good on their own, but only insofar as they promote good human functioning. And yet, choice is always constrained by the choice of the standard of good human functioning and one is voiceless and one's voice is unheard. One may not be equalized and reach the good standard of human function.

It follows that the effect of Nussbaum's politically liberal theory is also a theorizing of an *unvoiced* subject in an abstract and *unvoiced* community: a subject whose voice has been taken away, buried and concealed behind law and rights. The speaking subject Nussbaum talks about is constructed through the logic of One-ness: one as a general and as a socio-linguistic subject. Heteronomy and needs are equated with one good standard and people are deprived of their unique corporeal specific voices. In such *unvoiced* conception of the political, people appear to speak using a voice which is just the general voice of the subject of philosophy and political theory. The possibility of speaking is already established by a reasonable conception of the political.

Both Rawls and Nussbaum take into account only one point of view, one perspective, even if this is a good and reasonable perspective. One's voice has been trimmed off all around, excluded, unheard, sacrificed and considered superfluous. In the next section, I am going to deal with a resistance theorized instead outside the liberal perspective that attempts to rearticulate identity, language and structures.

1.3 Resistance through critical ruptures in Judith Butler

Judith Butler is well known for having theorized a form of resistance as subversion of the subject against the normative system of forced choice, in which the subject itself is defined. It is important to acknowledge the Hegelian root of her subject and political theory in order to understand Butler's thought. This Hegelian root is especially evident in her first work, *Subjects of Desire*.[77] She also refers to Hegel in the book *Contingency, Hegemony, Universality*.[78] Butler is interested in the Hegel that discusses the subject, identity and otherness.[79] In particular, the theory of desire and recognition in Hegel and his dialectic constitute Butler's theoretical background.

Desire and recognition are fundamental aspects of Butler's performative politics, centered on the ecstatic self. "Ecstatic" in Greek means standing out and

77 Judith Butler, *Subjects of Desire. Hegelian Reflections in Twentieth-Century France* (New York: Columbia University Press, 1987).

78 Judith Butler, Ernesto Laclau and Slavoj Žižek, *Contingency, Hegemony, Universality: Contemporary Dialogues on the Left* (London: Verso, 2000).

79 Sari Roman-Lagerspetz, *Striving for the Impossible: The Hegelian Background of Judith Butler* (Department of Political Science, University of Helsinki: Academic Dissertation, 2009).

refers to being dependent on something outside of itself. In other words, a subject is standing out or is separated from itself and this appears to be a condition of the subject's existence. In Butler's theory, terms like woman, sexuality, gender difference and democracy are interpreted as being ecstatic. This perspective renders the Butlerian subject as being fundamentally dependent on the outside.[80]

It is necessary to mention Butler's reading of Hegel's *Phenomenology of Spirit*, where the subject's desire is central.[81] For Butler, the Hegelian subject wants to know itself and discovers alterity. Mediation is required for the self to know itself, and the Hegelian subject is essentially a reflective subject that necessitates a journey of discovery to find itself. However, the Butlerian reading of the Hegelian subject consists of an ecstatic journey of discovery of the fictitious construction of one's own subjectivity.[82]

The Hegelian desire appears to be a process of self-reflexivity, and as a consequence of this desire the Hegelian subject is precisely burdened by negativity. However, the negative moment is self-constitutive of the subject and produces effects on its identity, mainly because the subject is forced to remain in an ecstatic situation of externalization and cannot return to itself. But, at the same time, this desire constitutes the possibility of some identification, satisfaction and recognition. Butler appears to question the Hegelian metaphysical totality as being a finite system. She suggests one should read Hegel beyond such an interpretation. In *Subjects of Desire*, Butler shows that the ecstatic process of subjectivity formation produces an openness of the Hegelian phenomenology, an impossibility of closure of the metaphysics of presence and a sort of perpetual striving of the subject formation process.[83]

The ecstatic process of negativity can be neither negated nor resolved, but it is sustained in an open journey.[84] For Butler, the ecstatic process of subjectivity does not take any specific normative idea as a goal or a starting point. On the contrary, it suggests the possibility of a performative politics as a sort of Hegelian critical movement. Her gender performativity can be interpreted as a Hegelian moment of negation of the negation. Indeed, the Butlerian subject negates and preserves itself in a Hegelian way.[85]

In *Subjects of Desire*, the ecstatic character of the subject means that the subject repeatedly finds itself outside of itself and never returns to itself, to its initial form, but it transforms itself during the ecstatic process; that is, one discovers oneself-as-other. In the ecstatic process, one is forced out of oneself through the mediation of the socio-linguistic norms that decide on the visibility of subjects.[86]

80 Roman-Lagerspetz, *Striving for the Impossible*.
81 Butler, *Subjects of Desire*.
82 Butler, *Subjects of Desire*, 20.
83 Butler, *Subjects of Desire*.
84 Butler, *Subjects of Desire*, 12.
85 Butler, *Subjects of Desire*.
86 Butler, *Subjects of Desire*.

In Butler's theory, all identities necessarily fail, because all universal truths and normative linguistic structures, like law and justice, end up refuting the other and inevitably produce exclusion and abjection. Consequently, for Butler, all political terms need to be contested, questioned and subverted. It follows that the Hegelian recognition becomes an impossibility, a continuous process of struggle and, perhaps, a way of striving for the impossible. Butler's work can be understood as a form of resistance against the fixation of the ideological frame and the violence of subject formation. According to Butler, the subject appears as necessarily located within symbolic structures, always wholly connected with the dominating structures of socio-linguistic-cultural and legal norms, as in the case of sex or gender. The latter are seen as normative linguistic constructions of the body.

> *[. . .] sex not only functions as a norm, but is part of a regulatory practice that produces the bodies it governs [. . .]. If gender is the social construction of sex, and if there is no access to this sex except by means of its construction, then it appears not only that sex is absorbed by gender, but that sex becomes something like a fiction [. . .].*[87]

We could argue that, for Butler, the subject strives to achieve freedom in a sort of continuous repetition of the ideological and linguistic identity structures inside which it is forced to be. This is done by means of performing such identity structures. Through performativity and repetition of structures, some ruptures of the construction emerge and the excess, or what is abjected, excluded and refuted from subjectivity can arise, subverting existing categories. In other words, the disciplinary apparatus that produces discourses of subjection can generate by means of performativity the very conditions for subverting that same apparatus. In this, Butler's perspective partly resonates with an Austinian notion of speech act theory,[88] because in Butler speech does something beyond the intended semantic and syntactical meanings of language, opening up a space to consider the discursive forces involved in language and law.

In *Frames of War*, Butler writes five essays in response to war, where the themes of vulnerability and precarity and their denial become central. Butler argues that the linguistic and ideological frame not only regulates reality, but also participates in producing reality and thus materiality and our bodies.[89] An important point is that the frame leaves something cut away from it. Not all life is captured and recognized by the normative conditions of the frame. Rather, something exceeds the frame.[90] The linguistic and ideological frame is regulated

87 Butler, *Bodies that Matter*, introduction.

88 John Langshaw Austin, *How to Do Things with Words* (Cambridge: Harvard University Press, 1975).

89 Judith Butler, *Frames of War: When Is Life Grievable?* (London: Verso, 2010).

90 Butler, *Frames of War*, introduction.

by power and is able to dictate which bodies count as living beings and which people enjoy *livability*. We are made to apprehend some people as vulnerable and others as not. While some people are grievable and are apprehended as grievable, some others are reduced into *inert matter* and their numbers do not count. Consequently, Butler attempts to explore under which conditions grievability is made possible, or, in other words, how the norms allow recognition of vulnerability.[91]

The problem – explains Butler – is not to see whether people have the status of a person; rather, whether some linguistic and normative conditions for flourishing are possible or not. The issue is not life but the linguistic and normative conditions that sustain life, in the sense that what is at stake is the problem of life in relation to norms and the socio-linguistic and political frames. Vulnerability and precarity are seen in Butler as material aspects of our lives that are deeply interconnected with social and linguistic aspects. The latter differentiate and distribute vulnerability unequally within the frame.

There are moments when the frame is broken down and there is a certain release of control.[92] *Leakages* of the frame might show the excess, namely what is excluded and abjected by the frame.[93] By repeating normative structures through bodily and linguistic acts, it is possible to find moments of failure of the system of forced constructions and, therefore, enact change and also make vulnerability equally shared. The problem, for Butler, also becomes an ontological problem. There is a given ontological way of approaching the body that allows, or does not allow, the apprehension of its vulnerability.[94] For Butler, a different ontology that focuses on vulnerability can be used as a way to rethink our responsibility.

However, rethinking responsibility is a process always mediated by the frame, by the subject's ecstatic outside; namely, the socio-linguistic conditions and institutions. The Hegelian root of Butler's theory is evidenced by the fact that the *field of intelligibility* is ecstatic and it is necessary to rethink our responsibility through this process of externalization.[95] Ethical responsibility is precisely acting critically in the ecstatic process. If resistance begins from my body and the apprehension of its vulnerability, the mediating frame that allows for my responsiveness to be possible is necessarily involved. In particular, Butler suggests that to speak against and resist the process of abjection and exclusion by the normative frame, it is necessary that vulnerability and precariousness are apprehended and shared equally among us. It follows that we must, in any case, deal with those normative institutional frameworks if we want to rethink their terms in new ways.[96]

91 Butler, *Frames of War*.
92 Butler, *Frames of War*.
93 Butler, *Frames of War*.
94 Butler, *Frames of War*.
95 Butler, *Frames of War*, 33.
96 Butler, *Frames of War*, 145.

For Loizidou, Butler has brought two important contributions to the critical legal movement.[97] One consists of her attachment to a subject that, even though it is foreclosed by the linguistic and normative frame, always has the potential to counter the universality of law and to be an agent. The other contribution is that the subject, even if injured, is still able to be critical and to question the normative conditions. This also creates an openness in the inclusive-exclusive process at stake.[98] In conclusion, we can see in Butler an attempt to speak in one's own voice but the linguistic and normative frame makes such striving impossible, or only possible in different terms than one's singular voice. In the next section, I am going to investigate the resistance offered by one's own voice in Adriana Cavarero.

1.4 Resistance through the voice in Adriana Cavarero

Adriana Cavarero puts the voice at the center of her theory of resistance.[99] It is in the voice and more precisely in one's voice that she sees the possibility of resisting the metaphysical tradition of discourses. For Cavarero, the logocentric tradition of metaphysics insists on the already said, namely the normative and linguistic semantics of textual discourses.[100] Logocentric and metaphysical tradition insists on the *what is said* and does not attend to the *who is saying*.[101] The *who is saying* (a mouth and a voice) is regarded as inessential and superfluous and is excluded from the process of communication and signification.

> *As it develops in different forms over the centuries, the logocentric tradition of metaphysics continues to insist on what is Said and never asks after who is Saying. The tradition judges "the words of a language in front of a mouth that opens, coming from the one who speaks" to be inessential. [. . .] The aim is nevertheless not simply liberating ourselves from the system of signification in order to fall back on the meaningless, the irrational, or the nonsensical. Rather, the aim is to recuperate the "very significance of signification".*[102]

In her theory of resistance, Cavarero does not wish to avoid language and signification; on the contrary, she is searching for the very meaning of the already

97 Loizidou, *Judith Butler*, 165.
98 Loizidou, *Judith Butler*, 165.
99 Cavarero, *For More Than One Voice*.
100 Cavarero, *For More Than One Voice*, 29.
101 The voice Carol Gilligan talks about follows a different lineage. Her "different voice" (*In a Different Voice*, Cambridge: Harvard University Press, 1982) is the voice of the essentialized feminine that is already thought for us and presupposed to be caring and different and an alternative to the masculine voice. Thus Gilligan offers a constructed voice, whereas in Cavarero one's voice de-essentializes sexual difference: one's voice springs from a singular and corporeal body, male or female; it is not an essence or a construction but a vulnerable experience that happens during speaking to others.
102 Cavarero, *For More Than One Voice*, 28–29.

said and signification. For Cavarero, the voice cannot be cut out from what is said. Speaking in one's voice is a moment of radically singular materiality that begins from an awareness of oneself in relation to another. There is a radical proximity between unique beings that simply communicate without necessarily communicating something. Such uniqueness, founded on relationality, goes beyond signification and becomes instead the *significance of signification.* Cavarero's way of resistance emerges then as a reciprocal communication of unique voices.

The voice has an ontological valence that reverses the stereotypical and patriarchal tradition of meanings. The feminine in sexual difference comes into play as something excluded from the production of words and speech; whereas the voice allows the unfolding of the feminine by rooting speech in the body. Opening the vocal reconnects the subject to its injury: the injury of division through sexual difference and through the split between mind and body. Selfhood becomes an embodied uniqueness beyond sexual difference. As a result, the voice is rooted in the corporeal uniqueness of the speaker, entrusted in the body.

Consequently, while the voice has been associated traditionally with the feminine, Cavarero reverses the stereotype and shows that the voice belongs to everyone as singular and corporeal. Such an act of reversing is a common reading strategy for Cavarero; her previous work engaged with re-reading ancient philosophical texts in a way that detached them from the male philosophical and metaphysical tradition and offered an alternative voice to women. For instance, in her book *In Spite of Plato,* Cavarero re-reads classical texts to expose the masculine theoretical approach at work in philosophy.[103] Cavarero practices a sort of strategy of stealing figures from the classics to reverse the ontological script of Western civilization. She uses gendered stereotypes to unfold them strategically against themselves.

> *Here, a male subject claiming to be neutral/universal declares his central position, disseminating a sense of the world cut to his own measure and revealed in his own mythic figures. According to this perspective, even female figures have a place in reference to the male subject who is at the origin of their creation.*[104]

> *My tactic has the explicit intention to steal by leaning on theoretical axes that have already sought to dislodge themselves from their context through a radical shift in perspective.*[105]

In her book *Relating Narratives,* Cavarero begins to reveal her roots in the work of Hannah Arendt.[106] In *The Human Condition*, Arendt asserts that what

103 Adriana Cavarero, *In Spite of Plato: A Feminist Rewriting of Ancient Philosophy,* trans. Serena Anderlini-D'Onofrio and Aine O'Healy (Cambridge: Polity Press, 1995).

104 Cavarero, *In Spite of Plato,* 2.

105 Cavarero, *In Spite of Plato,* 5–6.

106 Adriana Cavarero, *Relating Narratives. Storytelling and Selfhood,* trans. Paul Kottman (London: Routledge, 2000).

counts in politics is not the *what* but rather the *who* of people; while speaking and acting, one reveals one's uniqueness.[107] Cavarero underlines the materiality and vulnerability of such singular human uniqueness, already commenced by Arendt. The core point of *Relating Narratives* is the ontology behind telling one's life story, a story necessarily exposed to others.[108] Life stories are always new and unique. They reveal a unique *who* beyond the *what*. Therefore, the ontology behind such a *who-ness* is an ontology that is anti-metaphysical and contingent. The self, who tells the story, is a narratable selfhood that is always changeable, never defined in an already said or narrated story. The focus on narration reveals one's uniqueness as opposed to the reproduction of universal language by traditional philosophy.

> *Narration, as is well known, is a delicate art – narration "reveals the meaning without committing the error of defining it." Unlike Philosophy, which for millennia has persisted in capturing the universal in the trap of definition, narration reveals the finite in its fragile uniqueness, and signs its glory.*[109]

The focus on uniqueness and singular corporeality suspends the metaphysical talking of fixed identities and opens unexpected spaces of resistance detached from the already narrated language of metaphysics. Cavarero's work is not about identity, or the individual, or the *what* – those are to be considered as only limited and constructed aspects of us that separate and cut out our uniqueness, singularity, corporeality and relationality. In this respect, we can consider the legal and normative subject as a cut subject, a subject that does not include the traits of *who-ness* and singularity that Cavarero reflects.

In her most recent book, *Inclinazioni*, Cavarero speculates on the Western philosophical subjectivity appropriated by law and rights, where the subject has been thought of since the beginning in terms of "homo erectus," as vertical, right, straight.[110] The verticality of Western subjectivity indicates a self-referential and isolated subject that stands up in the arrogant act of his own foundation, speaks with the voice of rectitude, rules and order. This subject is capable of engaging only with a multitude of other vertical and independent subjects.

To such a vertical ontology, Cavarero counterposes an ontology of inclination, where the subject precisely bends toward the other and engages in relations within a community of unique beings. However, such an inclined and relational ontology does not echo the horizontality of essentialized feminine subjectivity, but rather indicates our own constitutive inclination as unique living beings and

107 Hannah Arendt, *The Human Condition* (Chicago: Chicago University Press, 1958).
108 Cavarero, *Relating Narratives*.
109 Cavarero, *Relating Narratives*, 3.
110 Adriana Cavarero, *Inclinazioni: Critica della Rettitudine* (Milan: Raffaella Cortina Editore, 2013).

our relationality to others. An inclined subject is no longer straight, it bends in respect to the vertical axis. A subject characterized by inclination is also a subject that speaks in her own voice, that lives the material life with her unique body and is aware of her own vulnerability and that of others.

Yet, it is specifically in her work entitled *For More Than One Voice* that Cavarero emphasizes the primacy of the in-articulated voice, the coming of voice and the breathing from the mouth.[111] She detects in the voice a space of meaning independent from speech. The voice constitutes the unexpressed side of speech; it *generates and exceeds speech*. The voice, Cavarero says, communicates uniqueness beyond the contents of communication:

> *The voice indeed does not mask, but rather unmasks the speech that masks it. Speech can play tricks. The voice, whatever it says, communicates the uniqueness of the one who emits it, and can be recognized by those to whom one speaks. But it is not being recognizable that renders the voice unique. On the contrary, every voice is unique, and because it is unique, once it is known it can be recognized.*[112]

One's uniqueness is revealed in relationality. We become aware of our uniqueness in relationality with others. This can happen, for instance, by telling others our life story, as in *Relating Narratives*, but also through the voice, as in *For More Than One Voice*. Radical corporeal uniqueness is also connected to an exposure of vulnerability. Cavarero engaged closely with the theme of vulnerability in her book *Horrorism*.[113] Here Cavarero talks of vulnerability, referring often to the Latin term of *vulnus*.

> *The human being is vulnerable as a singular body exposed to wounding. There is not, however, anything necessary about the vulnus (wound) embedded in the term "vulnerable," only the potential for a wound to occur at any time, in contingent circumstances [. . .] As a body, the vulnerable one remains vulnerable as long as she lives, exposed at any instant to vulnus. Yet, the same potential also delivers her to healing and the relational ontology that decides its meaning. Irremediably open to wounding and caring, the vulnerable one exists totally in the tension generated by this alternative.*[114]

We are inevitably exposed to each other in our vulnerability. For Cavarero, we can choose to act toward others with care or by inflicting wounds. We can say that if one speaks as a subject constituted by language and norms, one speaks as a cut

111 Cavarero, *For More Than One Voice*.

112 Cavarero, *For More Than One Voice*, 24.

113 Adriana Cavarero, *Horrorism: Naming Contemporary Violence*, trans. William McCuaig (New York: Columbia University Press, 2009).

114 Cavarero, *Horrorism*, 30.

subject, separated from one's uniqueness, one's body and from others. From such a position, it is easy to react by inflicting wounds, with disregard for vulnerability, because the subject is cut and separated from self and others.

Whereas, if one speaks in one's voice, one is exposed to oneself and others, one is aware of one's vulnerability and that of others. Such an awareness pushes us toward responding to the *vulnus* with care and attending to the other with care. In Chapter IV, the book connects such a possibility of ethical response to a justice that springs from one's vulnerable voice, as opposed to the legal justice of resentment. The voice as awareness of singularity, corporeality and vulnerability leads in fact to an ethical response to vulnerability and, therefore, to choosing care. In this respect, Cavarero considers the newly born as an absolute example of vulnerability.[115] Our bodies are vulnerable, but it is specifically that of the newly born, defenseless and vulnerable, that requires an ethical response of care.[116]

In engaging with vulnerability, Cavarero does not deal with the mechanisms of intelligibility that belong to language; she simply focuses on the corporeal vulnerability of unique bodies and on the radicality of ethical responsibility that can be linked to such an experiential condition of life. On various occasions, Cavarero mentions the concentration camp of the Holocaust and goes back to the experience of it.[117] This is because the camp can be understood through the voice and the uniqueness behind it.

One's unique breath and voice have the potential to reconnect to life and a notion of the beginning, rather than death.[118] In the concentration camp, the separation between the voice and language, or speech, reached moments of extremity. The camp is an extreme example, where subjectivity was separated, injured and cut. For instance, in the camp nudity was used as a violation of uniqueness; life and death were decided in a second, thus there was extreme vulnerability; people were crowded in masses, and yet they were alone as relationality was destroyed.[119]

People were not allowed to speak to one another, so that there was no voice left to express awareness of the self, and thus there was no possibility of being human. Language contributed to the factual violence and evil as it was used to denigrate, or else it was used paradoxically: for example, happy songs such as "Rosamunda" were played, in contrast to the sad reality of suffering and death. Thus often language contributed to forcing prisoners into a subhuman condition.[120]

Cavarero cites Primo Levi, who argued that in order to survive after the camp he had to speak in his own voice the trauma, the account of himself, the

115 Cavarero, *Horrorism*, 21.
116 Cavarero, *Horrorism*, 21.
117 See Cavarero, *Horrorism*, 210–211.
118 Cavarero, *For More Than One Voice*, 32.
119 Primo Levi, *Survival in Auschwitz and the Reawakening*, trans. Stuart Woolf (New York: Summit, 1986).
120 Levi, *Survival in Auschwitz and the Reawakening.*

vulnerability as felt by himself.[121] And how then could he resist the frame of the camp by speaking in his own voice? Levi experienced precisely the inadequacy of language to express the cuts and the injuries to his subjectivity. Nevertheless, he tried to speak in his own voice so as to reconnect with the living wounds of his body and subjectivity and to put the pieces of himself back together.[122]

Cavarero talks also of Hurbinek, cited by Levi, a boy perhaps born in the camp, who died early unable to articulate language comprehensibly.[123]

> *Primo Levi recounts that, in the days, that followed the liberation and the first transfers of the survivors, there appeared in the "big camp" of Auschwitz a child of about three years of age who could not speak and had no name [. . .] Now, as for the communication of a content, or the comprehension that comes from sharing a language, Hurbinek's is a nonlanguage that sinks into the abyss of the nonman, or underman. However, as far as the reciprocal communication of uniqueness goes, it is an act that – in Hurbinek's sonorous articulations – already intones the truth of a voice that is destined to speech and that is thus peremptorily human.*[124]

From the point of view of the frame, Hurbinek is a non-human, incapable of articulating language. But from the point of view of a bodily awareness of the self, there was language in his non-meaningful sound and uniqueness. Cavarero notes how although his voice did not reach the level of the semantic, it was characterized by a certain musicality and human intonation.[125] The voice Cavarero talks about is the voice that springs from breathing and the passing of air in one's throat, a voice that is radically corporeal and unique.

Through denial of the separation from uniqueness that operated in the camp, we can see in Cavarero a theorization of an ontology of the body that opposes and resists such a separation. The focus on the voice reflects such a diverse ontology. Cavarero points to the methods used in the camp to destroy uniqueness. She is not trying to make of the subject a better normative and sovereign subject, but she is only emphasizing the non-sovereign and non-normative aspects of being. This is congruent with the unique *who-ness* theorized by Arendt. And, as Zerilli comments, the problem of freedom in the Arendtian conception of *who-ness* is shifted outside the subject-frame and the traditional way of understanding agency in terms of sovereignty.[126] Usually, in the concept of freedom, agency is identified

121 Cavarero, *For More Than One Voice.*

122 Anna Bravo and Federico Cereja, *Intervista a Primo Levi, Ex Deportato* (Turin: Einaudi, 2011); Levi, *Survival in Auschwitz and the Reawakening.*

123 Levi, *Survival in Auschwitz and the Reawakening*; Cavarero, *For More Than One Voice*, 211.

124 Cavarero, *For More Than One Voice*, 211.

125 Cavarero, *For More Than One Voice*, 212.

126 Linda M.G. Zerilli, *Feminism and the Abyss of Freedom* (Chicago: The University of Chicago Press, 2005), 16.

with sovereignty, and thus with a type of politics without plurality, whereas plurality is at the core of both Arendt's and Cavarero's *who-ness*.

Inevitably, for Zerilli, feminism has worked on the same model of agency, attempting to provide more agency to women and thus more sovereignty.[127] On the contrary, the focus on *who* someone is, rather than the *what* of identity and subjectivity, indicates that feminism can make use of a different type of agency, other than that of sovereignty, that does not require mastery of others and, moreover, can suspend – even if for a short time – the sovereign frame. The *who* – on which both Arendt and Cavarero focus – excludes the sovereign subject because there is no substance so it is impossible to say *who* someone is. The *who-ness* is only exposed or revealed through one's voice or actions and in a condition of relationality and plurality. One's voice cannot be reduced or metabolized into sovereign discourses. If one's voice is just any voice, then one's voice is general and can be easily predicted. There are no predictions about one's unique voice. Thus one's voice is a rupture with the very logic of signification assigned to the current *unvoiced* subjectivity and ideologically sovereign framework.

Subsequently, I argue that there is also a diverse understanding of ontology at stake in Cavarero. This is not ontology as metaphysics or presence of things, truths or norms. Rather it is singular, material, contingent, changeable and corporeal. Cavarero's voice is never the same as anyone else's – my voice is never your voice. The space for speaking or acting in plurality is contingent, not defined or fixed. Rather it is shaped during the journey of experience. Relationality is made up of corporeal and unique communication between people and this is ontologically empty – it does not contain fixed truths – but it is an ontology in the sense of a way of thinking and theorizing life and being in life with others. Arendt's action is always an action in plurality, revealed in the public space; Cavarero's unique voice is always revealed during speaking with others, in relationality.

Therefore, for Cavarero, as for Arendt, the community is not originated or guaranteed in law. For both, the community of unique beings lies in a space that is revealed, or appears, precisely when we focus on the voice or we act unpredictably; that is, when we speak and act from a radical awareness of ourselves and others, in the human condition of corporeal vulnerability, in which we are all inevitably situated.

In this book, I work with a notion of resistance that draws on the approach of Adriana Cavarero that is rooted in that of Hannah Arendt. We can say that uniqueness and *who-ness* are revealed in the voice during speaking or acting and consist of a sort of awareness of oneself. Such an awareness suspends and dislocates one from the normative and constituted subject. *Who-ness* means, then, having an awareness of oneself; an awareness of oneself that is foreign to the sovereign and

127 Zerilli, *Feminism and the Abyss of Freedom*, 1–33.

ideological frame and that reflects an empty ontology. From this perspective, there is no more appropriation of linguistic structures to be able to speak, but only exposure of one's voice and *who one is*. In the next section, I will explore the awareness of oneself that springs from speaking in one's voice.

1.5 The Arendtian root of awareness of oneself and Butler's ethical approach

In this section, I will show that the awareness of oneself in Cavarero reflects the Arendtian way of resistance. First of all, it is necessary to say that although some of Arendt's work cannot be characterized as anti-liberal – for instance she was a defender of constitutionalism and fundamental human rights – it would be a mistake to evaluate Arendt's thought in terms of the traditional categories of liberalism. My argument is that the main points of Arendt's theory of resistance can be found in her idea of action in relation to the awareness that one has of oneself and the reflection on judgment.

Arendt's theory of action is deeply connected to the voice as the ability to speak from oneself and thus in awareness. Central to Arendt's theory is the idea that *one needs to think what one is doing*.[128] In her prologue to *The Human Condition*, Arendt wrote: "*what I propose, therefore, is simple: it is nothing more than to think what we are doing.*"[129] Thinking what one is doing means being aware of one's actions. For awareness to happen, one needs to begin from within oneself in exposure to others.

Action is the fundamental Arendtian category of the human condition.[130] Action allows freedom and resistance. In Arendt's work, freedom and resistance are not seen as the liberal possibility of choosing from a given subjectivity and normative frame, but rather they are the capacity to begin from oneself and in plurality. Such capacity to begin from oneself is connected to natality and birth, and consequently to a human condition that must be intended also as corporeal and vulnerable.

Therefore, despite the fact that Arendt seems to ground her thought in abstract ideas, there is also an Arendtian body, a body marked by its mortal destiny and the vulnerability of the human condition; a body of the animal *laborans* that reminds human beings of their material struggle for existence and against decay.

When Arendt talks of human life, however, she does not focus on death but on natality, intending it also as starting something anew and responding with new actions. For Arendt, resistance becomes precisely the capacity to be aware of oneself and to begin. Beginning springs precisely from the self and happens in

128 See: Bernard Bergen, *The Banality of Evil: Hannah Arendt and the Final Solution* (Oxford: Rowman & Littlefield, 1998).

129 Arendt, *The Human Condition*, 6.

130 Arendt, *The Human Condition*.

interaction with others, that is, in plurality. Political action, for Arendt, is this possibility of acting in plurality and, therefore, of speaking and acting from oneself in plurality. In a way, to speak one's voice is to act and to begin to produce something new, not the repetition of the sovereign and normative frame. Her subject refuses to be constructed as an identity by the frame, to be immobilized in splits, cuts and injuries; instead, her subject begins from herself with others.

I think that resistance in Arendt is this continuous making of new beginnings. One begins to become aware, then one speaks and acts in the sharing world, then one fails or succeeds and begins again and again. Speaking is acting and acting is speaking from oneself in relation to others, through the awareness of oneself. Such an ability to begin can bring unexpected results. Only the fact that a person is capable of action or speaking can make her actualize something unexpected, as in the case of natality.

The Arendtian goal is to break with the sovereign subject that repeats the same sovereign linguistic utterances in a Cartesian isolation from others and in separation from oneself. Action, in Arendt, happens always in the public sphere of appearance, where politics is conceived and concretized. However, by acting in the appearance of the public sphere, we reveal our uniqueness, *who we are* and, subsequently, an awareness of ourselves. Arendt opposes who one is to what one is or the identity in which one gets construed.

Being a *who* rather than a *what* entails awareness of one's human condition of vulnerability and detachment from the frame. Such a position of speaking through action can produce new ways of acting politically. In my view, this is the crucial point of Arendt's thought that demarcates her from a liberal notion of the public sphere of appearance and identity politics and connects her to the Cavarerian voice. It is Arendt's argument of one's unique *who-ness* beyond appearance which is identified with awareness of oneself.

Awareness of oneself implies resistance in terms of suspension from the frame and constituted normative subjectivity. The space of Arendtian resistance suddenly becomes counter liberal; it becomes a space of connection to oneself that is not made of external linguistic and normative rules and roles, but of oneself. The space of resistance to the divided and separated subject of liberalism consists of the unique *who-ness* of each one of us in the sharing world.

This special, private and vulnerable moment allows one to speak and act in the public space of political life but it is also always revealed by means of one's acts and speech. Narratives of action and speech reveal *who someone is*. The public space of appearance of the public normative subject cannot exist without our *who-ness* in speech and actions. There are then associations between the focus on the voice in Cavarero and Arendtian thought.

The voicing of uniqueness in Arendt also has ethical implications for justice. In *The Human Condition*, Arendt links action to forgiveness.[131] Forgiveness is a special

131 Arendt, *The Human Condition*.

action, which is boundless and potentially capable of healing the multiple divisions produced by violence between people. For instance, Arendt says:

> *Without being forgiven, released from the consequences of what we have done, our capacity to act would, as it were, be confined to one single deed from which we could never recover; we would remain the victims of its consequences forever [. . .] Trespassing is an everyday occurrence which is in the very nature of action's constant establishment of new relationships within a web of relations, and it needs forgiving, dismissing, in order to make it possible for life to go on by constantly releasing men from what they have done unknowingly.*[132]

Forgiveness is an action that surely springs from within one's *who-ness* and thus from an awareness of oneself and one's vulnerability. I argue Arendt's conceptualization of action and forgiveness-as-action reflects a deep awareness of one's vulnerability and the vulnerability of others, incorporating a materialist perspective. I forgive because I can see the vulnerability of another self behind the wrong action, the vulnerable doer behind the deed. It is only by being aware of one's own vulnerability and the vulnerability of the other that one can attempt to enact forgiveness.

Forgiveness is, for Arendt, an example of producing something new through our actions, something unexpected, natality, something that sets us apart from the sovereign frame and from the justice of law, an expression of one's voice. Forgiveness is linked to promise and natality and thus to an ability to respond ethically to vulnerability. On the other hand, the justice of law is projected toward further divisions between people, and rests on resentment and retribution. Justice appears to be a righteous reaction to an injury and this reflects the general voice of law.

For Lisa Guenther, forgiveness, as something new and an expression of natality, is a gift for the other; it springs from a non-sovereign grounding of oneself and requires hospitality and the passing of air without belonging.[133] There is a suspension and an interruption of sovereign normativity. Awareness of vulnerability calls for an awareness of oneself in relationality to others, and an ethical responsibility toward vulnerability. Forgiveness allows precisely a shift away from the endless repetition of violence. Scholars see in actions such as forgiveness the possibility of keeping human relatedness open, as opposed to a righteous vengeance that shuts down and pushes away the relation to others.[134] Forgiveness can thus be seen as a courageous act that opens up a non-violent political space of resistance but only

132 Arendt, *The Human Condition*, 213, 216.

133 Lisa Guenther, *The Gift of the Other: Levinas and the Politics of Reproduction* (Albany: State University of New York Press, 2006); Lisa Guenther, "Being from Others: Reading Heidegger After Cavarero," *Hypatia*, 23(1) (2008): 99–116.

134 Craig Calhoun and John McGowan, *Hannah Arendt and the Meaning of Politics* (Minneapolis: University of Minnesota Press, 1997).

if it springs from one's voice, from within, and in the awareness of vulnerability. I will explore this possibility of ethical response in Chapter IV.

There is another aspect of Arendt's theory that I find particularly important for the purposes of this book: her theory of judgment and the banality of evil.[135] The latter relates also to an ethical response and equally emphasizes the importance of an awareness of oneself, that is, of one's voice. In the Arendtian theory, in order to fight the banality of evil, awareness of oneself is necessary.

When Arendt presents her argument on the banality of evil, it is implied that we could all be Eichmann and enact evil if we were posited in different historical conditions.[136] Arendt holds in her theory of the banality of evil that while Eichmann's identity appears to be anchored to an end (being an SS officer), in his trial in Jerusalem he was unable to escape the frame of his identity, unable to say anything new about himself, to be aware of himself and of *who he was.* Violence is easily enacted if we are constructed as subjects cut and separated from ourselves.

I can interpret Arendt's argument as consisting again of the need for awareness of oneself in the sharing world; or, in other words, that *one needs to think what one is doing.* "*He merely, to put the matter colloquially, never realized what he was doing.*"[137] As Bergen notes, it seems that Arendt finds the significance of the final solution in the banality of *who one is* and in an awareness of oneself in relationality.[138] The corporeal experience of oneself is different from the linguistic experience of oneself. Arendt knew, from her theory of action, that it is paramount to *think what we are doing*, that resistance is the experience of refusing oneself as being spoken by the sovereign frame, refusing oneself as a cut and divided subject. To put it in Cavarero's terms, in order for one to resist, one needs to speak in one's voice, to begin from oneself. Resistance is my experience of action through my awareness, and only this makes me think and act anew, unpredictably.

Identity is neither the end point nor the point of departure. The point of departure is the moment in which we reveal our uniqueness, *who we are*, outside our identity and subjectivity. Thus there are unforeseen directions and ways to grasp the banality of evil. Evil becomes the understanding of a person through the frame and the effect of general speech, whereas the experience of oneself as unique can protect us from such evil.[139]

From the Arendtian root of the Cavarerian voice, I can conclude that central to the juridical question of this book is the thinking of an ontology of oneself and one's body, where the body is experienced, rather than thought of or spoken linguistically; the voice comes from one's body and from a unique awareness of

135 Hannah Arendt, *Eichmann in Jerusalem: A Report on the Banality of Evil* (New York: Penguin Books, 1994).
136 Bergen, *The Banality of Evil*, IX–XVI.
137 Arendt, *Eichmann in Jerusalem*, 287.
138 Berger, *The Banality of Evil*, IX–XVI.
139 See: Berger, *The Banality of Evil.*

oneself in relationality. One's voice is more than a means to an end. One's unique voice exposes one's material singularity and allows one to speak through an awareness of oneself that originates in the corporeal specificity and uniqueness of one's body. One's voice is the experience of oneself lived through one's body and not the voice of legal and political representation and discourses.

Similarly to Arendt, Cavarero works on the dimension of the self that escapes the level of normative and linguistic appearance. Cavarero focuses on the dimension of the voice that reveals *who one is* and provides an account of oneself. The voice is a speaking action and reflects, in some ways, the theory of action in Arendt. Cavarero's ontological approach that is rooted in the Arendtian theory of action stands opposite to the subject of the current legal and political frame, which has no voice and no body as it speaks only to itself, resembling the Cartesian rational subject.

The voice one can speak as a Cartesian subject is the voice of the mind; the linguistic voice of the semantics and discourses already decided for one. Such a voice, it is argued, is not one's voice but the abstract general voice that has been cut out from one's corporeal voice as sound. In contrast, one's own voice represents what is excess and superfluous to the legal and normative framework and, thus, a form of resisting law by being foreign to it. The voice contains an ontology other than law, an ontology that escapes the generality, universality and sovereignty of law. Vocal ontology is deeply related to one's vulnerability and, as such, calls for actions that become ethically responsible for such vulnerability. Arendtian forgiveness is an example of such an ethical response.

We have seen that Cavarero's ontological approach of the voice leads to an awareness of oneself and this thinking is rooted in Arendt. *Who someone is* provides awareness of oneself. Such an awareness is revealed in our voice but also in action. Awareness of oneself is a special way of intending one's agency outside the economy of return and the idea of agency as sovereignty.[140] Drawing on Cavarero and Arendt, ethics requires speaking in one's voice or acting anew, producing a response in terms of an ability to respond with response-ability to the vulnerability of others. The relation to others, as perceived here, goes beyond the linguistic agent-subject relation, because it suspends the *said* of language and works on the unpredictability of the saying, and toward the vulnerability of others.

Butler also attempts to deal with the problem of ethics but she poses a different ethical question.[141] Unlike Cavarero's and Arendt's *who-ness*, the Butlerian subject is integrally involved in social, cultural and legal norms. Life, for Butler, cannot escape its fundamental linkage to subjectivity and identity. It is in relation to norms and intelligibility that life is taken into account. Accountability is accountability to the norms. The agent in Butler is a subject who knows she cannot both account fully for herself and fully speak for herself. And yet it is precisely this

140 Zerilli, *Feminism and the Abyss of Freedom*.

141 Judith Butler, *Giving an Account of Oneself* (New York: Fordham University Press, 2005).

fallibility and lack of self-coherence that allows an acknowledgment of the limits of self-understanding and provides a sort of ethical critical agency.[142]

I can argue that the Butlerian life contains materiality and specificity even though conceived through the frame.[143] Life is brought into being, not as a general and abstract subject but as a specific and embodied subject, whose possibility to act is limited by the contingent context of action and by the normativity of the symbolic order. For Butler, life and the potential to speak can only be enacted through the forms of the linguistic sovereignty. By performing speech acts and normative identities, the subject can find ruptures and thus achieve new ways of expression and livability in relation to the normative space.

But again, what is important to note in relation to agency, as Loizidou notes, is that Butler takes the debate on ethics in a different direction and shows that the subject is constituted in language and, therefore, agency consists of this possibility of acting and speaking within the normative and linguistic frame.[144] For Butler, being the subject, a public and social subject, one has to speak within the terms that make oneself intelligible, more or less livable. The subject is able to undo the way it is constituted precisely through language.

In Butler's terms, if one wants to act ethically there is no inner subject, aware of oneself and relating to others. There is instead a struggle with the un-chosen conditions of life and it is precisely those conditions that make agency possible. This subject can act ethically by acknowledging the limits of not being able to be aware of oneself. The subject in Butler seems to reach an impossibility – she cannot speak for herself. Ethics, for the Butlerian subject, is precisely this not being able to ever be aware of oneself; it is rather the possibility of being critical of oneself as constituted by language. The impossibility of being fixed and essentialized in schemas, identities and subjectivity is the only possibility that one can have of being aware of oneself.

Agency in Butler becomes inevitably and paradoxically the acknowledgment of the impossibility of speaking in one's own voice, since one cannot experience things through one's body without the medium of language and norms. A search for awareness of oneself would in fact mean, in Butler's terms, going back to new essences and forced fixed choices for our being. Rather, the subject in Butler must avoid this ontological closure and be critical.

Returning to the Hegelian root of Butler's perspective, the relation to the other in Butler is ecstatic. This means that the subject finds itself outside itself. When encountering the other, there is transformation and the subject cannot return completely to itself. This mediation that happens outside oneself also exemplifies

142 Butler, *Giving an Account of Oneself.*

143 Judith Butler, "How Can I Deny that These Hands and This Body are Mine?" in *Material Events: Paul De Man and the Afterlife of Theory*, eds Cohen, T., Cohen, B., Miller, J. and Warminski, A. (Minneapolis: University of Minnesota Press, 2001), 254–276.

144 Loizidou, *Judith Butler.*

the relation between subject and language. Responding ethically then requires the medium of such an ecstatic outside, the linguistic and normative frame through which we can perform our subjectivity and be critical of this performance.

Kathy Dow Magnus has accurately pointed to some problems in Butler's understanding of agency, as well as its strengths.[145] She suggests that, while Butler's earlier books reflect a restricted notion of agency, *Giving an Account of Oneself* offers an adjusted type of agency.[146] For Magnus, Butler's agentic subject prior to *Giving an Account of Oneself* does not adequately explain how the subject determines its own desire and purposes.[147]

Agency in Butler is intended as the possibility of countering the linguistic and normative frame that constitutes the subject itself and does not consist of choosing but of opposing one's own constitution. There is therefore a negative understanding of agency.[148] Seen as the ability to repeat and perform the subject's own linguistic and normative formation, agency is reduced to counter-resistance.[149] For Magnus, Butler discounts the full range of the subject's potential, not taking into consideration a wide range of other possible actions such as reflective and intersubjective agency.[150]

By being entangled in the web of relations, the subject is never able to have an awareness of oneself, to touch one's origin and reach *who one is; one is never available to oneself.*[151] However, this unavailability of oneself does not foreclose ethics for Butler. To the contrary, such unavailability of the subject becomes the moral enquiry itself. Ethics is precisely the impossibility of having awareness of oneself. To be ethically responsible is to admit one's limits and to completely justify oneself through an action. Consequently, for Butler, ethics means being critical of the linguistic, social and normative conditions that produce us as subjects.

We can therefore argue that, for Butler, ethics is exercising critique. Responsibility takes the form of relating to others by being a stranger to oneself. Being a stranger to oneself constitutes an ethical connection to others. However, according to Magnus, later in *Giving an Account of Oneself* agency becomes, for Butler, intersubjective and more reflexive. The subject seems to be participating more in the discursive processes that constitute her life, even though intersubjective and reflexive relations happen always through linguistic and social media.[152]

145 Kathy Dow Magnus, "The Unaccountable Subject: Judith Butler and the Social Conditions of Intersubjective Agency," *Hypatia*, 21(2) (2006): 81–103.
146 Magnus, "The Unaccountable Subject."
147 Magnus, "The Unaccountable Subject."
148 For the negative understanding of agency in Butler, see also: Catherine Mills, "Efficacy and Vulnerability: Judith Butler on Reiteration and Resistance," *Australian Feminist Studies*, 15(32) (2000): 265–279.
149 Magnus, "The Unaccountable Subject."
150 Magnus, "The Unaccountable Subject."
151 Magnus, "The Unaccountable Subject."
152 Magnus, "The Unaccountable Subject."

To conclude, the limits of law's reforms and institutions suggest that it is necessary to think beyond law reforms and institutions themselves as well as beyond the ideas of universal justice and value (Rawls and Nussbaum). The critical legal movement has shown how unsatisfactory it is to approach jurisprudence as restricted jurisprudence and instead suggests a more general approach.[153] Thinking beyond law is inevitable if we want to focus on the voice, on a singular and material level beyond the universal and normative level of law.

Rawls, Nussbaum, Butler and Cavarero are all interested in resisting the current liberal approach. However, we can identify three opposing attitudes. Rawls and Nussbaum – although not insensitive to difference – continue to maintain the framework of universal subjectivity, choice and voice in their engagement with legal liberal institutions. Both Rawls and Nussbaum accept the notion of political liberalism as a good framework.

Butler and Cavarero, however, are arguably more critical of universalism and strive to account for what is cut out, made superfluous and exceeds law. In comparing Butler and Cavarero, both begin from positions of radical materiality and acknowledgment of vulnerability. Butler employs the linguistic and normative framework as integrally connected to materiality, emphasizes Hegel's ecstatic outside and shows the necessary struggle of the subject outside itself. For Butler, it is important to be critical of such an outside, while at the same time one is inescapably immersed in it. The possibility of speaking is precisely this impossibility of speaking and this opens the ethical struggle of the subject and a diverse sense of justice beyond law. The subject becomes a self in a continuous becoming and the notion of a subject as fully present is rejected.

On the other hand, Cavarero joins Butler in her critique of the subject as being forced and separated from singularity as the result of the identity formation process, but follows the Arendtian root of an awareness of oneself. The subject in Cavarero is rather characterized by inclination, that is, by leaning out; the linguistic subject moves in some ways outside the vertical and linguistic direction in which it has been conceived and relates to others through dependence. One's voice is the moment when one ecstatically escapes the verticality of the subject and becomes aware of inclination. Through one's voice, one's vulnerability is exposed to oneself and others. This opens an ethics of a singularity-in-relatedness that can act in totally unpredictable ways and poses new paths for justice beyond law. For both Butler and Cavarero there is a break with the legal subject of resistance, whereas for Rawls and Nussbaum their argument of setting up good standards appears to weaken their position, in terms of voice and resistance, and their theory of the legal subject of resistance remains within the notion of reformation.

The theoretical framework of this book, drawing on the work of Adriana Cavarero on the voice and its Arendtian developments, employs an ontology of

153 Douzinas and Gearey, *Critical Jurisprudence*.

singularity and materiality that leads to ethical insights beyond the thinking of law. The next section deals with the methodological question of the resistance offered by the voice. The voice allows a moment of suspension from the textual and from the semantics of law. However, what needs to be examined is whether such a suspension is continual, arbitrary and completely disconnected from the semantics. In other words, it appears to be necessary to analyze the methodological approach to resistance offered by the voice.

1.6 The voice's engagement with and disengagement from law

This section is concerned with resistance and its methodological approaches. Despite the fact that I see one's voice as a moment of suspension and disengagement from language and law, it is necessary to think how it can relate methodologically to law and its institutions. I will explore how a general jurisprudence (within the critical legal tradition) opens the way to resistance through the voice. As has been shown earlier, a general jurisprudence consists of a theoretical and philosophical approach to law that goes beyond law, since it does not focus exclusively on a resistance that takes place solely in the legal framework. It rather opens up the symbolic, transforms the shared meanings of the world and re-orients law's ethical values. The focus on a resistance through the voice is intended within such a wider critical legal approach. In contrast, a narrow jurisprudence perspective often ends up excluding and dissociating extra-legal elements from its legal rules, norms and procedures.

After having analyzed some theories of resistance – those of John Rawls, Martha Nussbaum and Judith Butler, as well as Cavarero's approach to the voice – I need to explore how the voice can methodologically resist law and legal institutions. In other words, the possibilities of resistance offered by the voice vis-à-vis law and legal institutions need to be examined. What type of resistance is provided by the voice? Does the voice disengage or engage with legal institutions? Where does the voice situate itself in relation to contingency and determinacy?

I have argued that the voice – as awareness of oneself – implies some form of suspension from the semantics and, therefore, from the normativity of law. The voice reconnects somehow to those corporeal, unique and relational aspects of ourselves that exceed law and are excluded by its normativity. When one focuses on the voice rather than on the signification of words, one can reconnect to the unique sound of oneself, one's vibrations and other corporeal aspects that are exposed to one's interlocutors. The voice contains meanings that go beyond the semantic. The focus on the voice calls for a signification beyond signification and suspends – even if only for a moment – the conventional signification of speaking. Thus inherent in the voice is a form of resistance other than the one of language and law.

Furthermore, the voice opens up ethical spaces of resistance beyond the current thinking of justice. The focus on the voice is linked in fact to an exposure of vulnerability. When I speak to others, vulnerability is necessarily revealed.

Consequently, I become aware of vulnerability and such an awareness pushes me toward choosing to care for the exposed vulnerability. By doing so, the voice opens up a space for justice that suspends the parameters of law, in a space beyond law itself. If law requires the punishment of the perpetrators within a logic of righteousness and verticality, one's voice leads rather to an awareness of vulnerability when speaking with others and a logic of inclination. I will reflect on such a suspension of conventional justice related to one's voice in Chapter IV. For the moment, I am more interested in the methodological suspension from law and conventional justice that is derived from one's voice.

It may in fact be impossible to permanently suspend law and its institutions and remain beyond the law or to take a completely non-juridical stance when resisting the law. In other words, it may be impossible to resist law through a complete dissociation from any reference to its language, rules, procedures or norms. Consequently, I am reflecting on the necessity of looking into the wider engagement with law while focusing on one's voice. The methodological issue of resistance to law and its institutions is central to the critical legal movement's thought and such a relation has always been ambivalent.[154] I will explore the methodology of resistance to law within the critical legal movement framework and discuss how some scholars, such as Walter Benjamin, Adriana Cavarero and Hannah Arendt, have methodologically approached resistance. Then I will open up the possibility of resistance through the voice.

Various critical legal theorists have speculated on the terms of resistance within the critical legal movement. Peter Goodrich notes, for instance, *a paradoxical or unwitting commitment to legality.*[155] For Goodrich, the critical legal scholars' relation to legal institutions is contradictory. He describes it as a relation of *love* and *hate* that brings the critical legal movement into a space somehow beyond the law.[156] Goodrich notes the rapid transition from resistance to law to the theorization of its renewal, from confrontation with law to a conformism to the law.[157] He remarks how:

> *the analysis of judicial reasoning [of the critical legal movement] was based in theoretical critique of the process and ultimately the form of judgment and so in the end engaged more closely with linguistics and philosophical hermeneutics than with substantive law.*[158]

This confirms a paradoxical critique and resistance of law that evades methodologically substantive law and disengages from the legal doctrine but at the same

154 Peter Goodrich, "The Critic's Love of the Law: Intimate Observations on an Insular Jurisdiction," *Law and Critique*, 10 (1999): 343–360.
155 Goodrich, "The Critic's Love of the Law."
156 Goodrich, "The Critic's Love of the Law."
157 Goodrich, "The Critic's Love of the Law."
158 Goodrich, "The Critic's Love of the Law," 348.

time teaches and reproduces law. For Goodrich, this disjunction between the resistance operated by critical legal theory and the practical reason of law can also be understood as indifference to the substance of law and an expression of identity crisis; essentially, as the expression of a desire for a better world:

> *Critical legal studies has not transformed the legal institutions, it has not dramatically changed the law school curriculum nor has it had any great impact upon the legal profession. It has only indirect and hesitant effects upon law because it has not studied or engaged with law nor even endeavoured explicitly and self-consciously to rethink the curriculum or the pedagogic relationship. The law that is taught, the doctrine that is repeated and through repetition reproduced is not written by critical legal scholars nor challenged in its substance by their castigations of its form.*[159]

On the contrary, Goodrich calls for a diverse methodological approach to law and its institutions. For Goodrich, what is needed is *some sustained critical and collective self-reflection and renewal.*[160] More significant than its relation with the legal institutions is the need for the critical legal movement to take institutional power seriously, which means that the critical legal movement has to think about and deal first with its own institutional structuring in order to avoid repeating the same structural and relational violence of law.

In *Politics, Postmodernity and Critical Legal Studies* both Peter Goodrich and Costas Douzinas argue for an ethicality in the critique and resistance to law and the necessity of opening a space for a diverse ontology or being within the legal institutions.[161] In the introduction to their book, it is argued that escape from legal institutions and the positivized system of legal governance remains impossible.[162] There is an inescapable double bind of belonging to the legal and political tradition and desiring disengagement. However, precisely this unhappy consciousness of the critical legal movement opens up a resistance in terms of ethics and justice. Ethics and justice become the distinguishing characteristic of resistance and its methodological way of proceeding.[163]

For both Douzinas and Goodrich, the status of resistance in terms of being an outsider is not the only possible space – there is also the space of responsibility for the reproduction and transmission of law.[164] Law is precisely reproduced through a politics of texts, such as the reporting of judgments and case law. Therefore, resistance consists also of an ethics of writing and a critique of discourses. In other

159 Goodrich, "The Critic's Love of the Law," 359–360.

160 Goodrich, "The Critic's Love of the Law," 358.

161 Costas Douzinas, Peter Goodrich and Yifat Hachamovitch, *Politics, Postmodernity and Critical Legal Studies: The Legality of the Contingent* (New York: Routledge, 1994), 131.

162 Douzinas, Goodrich and Hachamovitch, *Politics, Postmodernity and Critical Legal Studies,* 1–31.

163 Douzinas, Goodrich and Hachamovitch, *Politics, Postmodernity and Critical Legal Studies,* 1–31.

164 Douzinas, Goodrich and Hachamovitch, *Politics, Postmodernity and Critical Legal Studies,* 1–31.

words, it implies the necessary task of reading but also re-writing the text of law.[165] Therefore, if resistance implies a return to the legal institutions, it is with the aim of revealing what is repressed and discovering diverse ways of speaking and having a voice. It also calls into question the legal subject who speaks as well as a different ontological understanding of law and its institutions.[166]

In Goodrich and Douzinas, there is a concern with the legal text, the symbolic structure of the law and legal governance.[167] What becomes important is the focus on that which has escaped the legal text and has been marginalized and rendered superfluous. Such a space of resistance – as a focus on the excess – stresses also the contingencies and weaknesses of law and the distance between law and justice. As both scholars argue, it is necessary to think of the justice of the contingent in terms of the uniqueness of life experience. On the other hand, the law comes into being through judgments, operated according to similarities and differences, and makes of them a rule or distributes a norm. In order to oppose this, resistance needs to be ethical so as to be able to hear voices and speeches not heard by the administration and distribution of law.[168]

In other words, Goodrich and Douzinas find that resistance is not so much about being outside law and its institutions but more about thinking about the way of escaping certain normative and narrow mechanisms of law and institutions, recuperating the excess and life, and thus going beyond law, approaching jurisprudence as *prudence* of the law.[169] This means recuperating an ontological and ethical space that we need to keep in mind together with law.[170] In this respect, Elena Loizidou is right to perceive resistance as going *up against order and through ethics.*[171] She stresses that life cannot be caged completely in legal institutions and suggests a possibility of resistance that consists of living life in parallel with law.[172] The critical legal movement seems to suggest that the moments of disconnection from law and institutions cannot be permanent, and thus a way of connecting, in terms of ontology and ethics, appears necessary.[173] Since it is impossible to permanently detach from the legal system, it is necessary to find new forms of being for the legal subject and thus an ontological thinking that both engages with law and contributes to a rethinking of law itself – remaining parallel to law.

165 Douzinas, Goodrich and Hachamovitch, *Politics, Postmodernity and Critical Legal Studies.*
166 Douzinas, Goodrich and Hachamovitch, *Politics, Postmodernity and Critical Legal Studies.*
167 Douzinas, Goodrich and Hachamovitch, *Politics, Postmodernity and Critical Legal Studies.*
168 Douzinas, Goodrich and Hachamovitch, *Politics, Postmodernity and Critical Legal Studies.*
169 Douzinas, Goodrich and Hachamovitch, *Politics, Postmodernity and Critical Legal Studies.* See also: Douzinas and Gearey, *Critical Jurisprudence.*
170 Douzinas, Goodrich and Hachamovitch, *Politics, Postmodernity and Critical Legal Studies.*
171 See: Elena Loizidou, "This Is What Democracy Looks Like," in *How Not to Be Governed. Readings and Interpretations From a Critical Anarchist Left*, eds Klausen, J.C. and Martel, J. (Lanham: Rowman & Littlefield, 2011), 167–187.
172 Elena Loizidou, "Before the Law, Encounters at the Borderline," in *New Critical Legal Thinking. Law and the Political*, eds Douzinas, C., Stone, M. and Wall, I. (New York: Routledge, 2012), 181–197.
173 Douzinas, Goodrich and Hachamovitch, *Politics, Postmodernity and Critical Legal Studies.*

In this regard, I think Walter Benjamin's insights could be of relevance to a methodological analysis of resistance. Benjamin offers a model of resistance that detaches and suspends law, uncovers the origin of authority and the violent ground of law, and theorizes outside the parameters of an institutionalized philosophy, although is not completely disconnected from it. His essay "Critique of Violence" is precisely an essay on law and justice concerning the position of resistance.[174] Benjamin shows how the sovereign, or the state, maintains a binding status on its subjects. In Benjamin's terms, the violence of subjectivity formation works through continuous mechanisms of law-making and law-preserving violence.[175] I could say that for Benjamin the outcome is a subject posited as injured, cut and split from materiality, and a legal and political system that produces an ongoing violence on the subject in different ways.

Benjamin understands all violence as either law-making or law-preserving, where law is perpetuated through mechanisms of binding and accountability to its institutions. Judith Butler explains accurately how this prevents subjects from developing a critical perspective on the legal system.[176] For Butler, subjects are construed as accountable to law and its institutions and end up being defined by such a legal accountability.[177]

Benjamin attempts then to sketch a politics of pure means and a theory of not positing, a theory of resistance of not binding and being accountable. His theory can be interpreted as one of suspension: it is a theory that exposes the violence of positing, while it breaks with the domination of forms and disrupts mechanisms of cognition. In Benjamin's words, a destruction of violence is necessary. Such a destruction or resistance, for Benjamin, cannot happen within the frame, the mechanisms, of law-making and law-preserving violence – it cannot be part of the elaboration of a positive law. Rather, such destruction of violence needs to destroy the basis of positive law and of the sovereign symbolic frame. He then looks for another form of resistance, one that is non-coercive and non-violent, one that does not posit or impose violence; Benjamin, rather, perceives the general strike of the proletariat as a way to paralyze the violence of the state.

For Werner Hamacher, Benjamin's justice belongs in a space distant from law and violence.[178] Hamacher perceives Benjamin's example of the proletarian general strike as a non-violent means of annihilating legal violence: it is located outside any

174 Walter Benjamin, "Critique of Violence," in *Reflections: Essays, Aphorisms, Autobiographical Writings,* ed. Demetz, P., trans. Edmund Jephcott (New York: Harcourt Brace Jovanovich, 1978), 277–300.

175 Walter Benjamin, "A Critique of Violence."

176 Judith Butler, "Critique, Coercion and Sacred Life in Benjamin's Critique of Violence," in *Political Theologies,* eds De Vries, H. and Sullivan, L.E. (New York: Fordham University Press, 2006), 201–219.

177 Butler, "Critique, Coercion and Sacred Life in Benjamin's Critique of Violence."

178 Werner Hamacher, "Afformative Strike," in *Benjamin's Philosophy: Destruction and Experience,* eds Benjamin, A. and Osborne, P. (London: Routledge, 1994), 113–163.

means–end relation and cannot be understood with a logic of positing, because it is entirely non-violent; it is something beyond the order of positing. Therefore, for Hamacher, Benjamin's approach does not pose but deposes. This means that it does not produce, but instead it interrupts the sovereign mechanisms of production; it is also *afformative* in the sense that it exposes an event.

What we can conclude from Benjamin's methodological insights is that resistance is not made possible by actions that are accountable to institutions and bound by law itself. Rather, resistance needs to be thought of as a moment of separation from law and institutions. The general strike engages in non-violent actions that are pure means. The intention of the general strike does not simply lie in the modification of the sovereign semantic frame, but it pushes for radical transformations of the sovereign semantic frame. Resistance becomes omission, failure to comply and perpetuate the law of the state and the sovereign.

However, as Judith Butler stresses, it is necessary not to see Benjamin's resistance as an anarchic moment completely disconnected from the linguistic and normative frame and, consequently, separate from the institutional structures.[179] For Benjamin, the general strike is linked to the written commandments of the Hebrew Decalogue, which limit, through divine violence, law-making violence. Similarly, the transformative violence of the general strike opposes violence with a different kind of violence, becoming an ethical space of resistance that goes beyond the framework of legal accountability.[180] Thus the divine commandments offer a way to link the general strike to law and its institutions while maintaining simultaneously a space of resistance beyond law. The commandments do not bind and do not require accountability to legal violence; they do not require the form of justice that necessitates law, namely, punishment and revenge. The commandments, as Butler emphasizes, leave open the modes of their applicability and refusal.[181]

Following Butler's reflection, and connecting this with the reflection made by the critical legal movement, resistance in Benjamin cannot be reduced to the anarchic moments of the general strike. Rather, resistance resides in the responsibility to respond in ethical ways that are beyond law-making by focusing on what remains unbound by law, on that which is not part of the positive law but that comes into terms with the law. In this regard, the Benjamin of the *Theological-Political Fragment* refers to an inner man whose responsibility remains radically distinct from the accountability to law and its institutions, since the latter cannot fully address or adjust the conditions of human suffering.[182]

In an attempt to associate Benjamin's critique of violence with the voice, I could argue that speaking in one's voice and being aware of one's uniqueness

179 Butler, "Critique, Coercion and Sacred Life in Benjamin's Critique of Violence," 203.

180 Butler, "Critique, Coercion and Sacred Life in Benjamin's Critique of Violence."

181 Butler, "Critique, Coercion and Sacred Life in Benjamin's Critique of Violence," 203.

182 Astrid Deuber-Mankowsky, "Walter Benjamin's Theological-Political Fragment as a Response to Ernst Bloch's Spirit of Utopia," *The Leo Baeck Institute Year Book*, 47(1) (2002): 3–19.

and corporeality in relationality means refusing, in Benjamin's words, to instate and preserve violence. This, in turn, implies the withdrawal of one's compliance with the law, and the need to occupy a space (fragile or strong) that fails to preserve the law but it is, rather, capable of beginning law's resistance. Benjamin's inner man illustrates the need of such an awareness of oneself, a unique and non-generalizable moment that has the potential to remain detached and to paralyze the basis of the sovereign frame. The inner man of Benjamin signifies a going on strike with the imposed voice of a subjectivity separated from one's body that addresses things only through the semantic. Both the commandments and the inner man lead to a space beyond the current justice system and to a release of the anger that circulates in the frame through revenge, punishment and justice as resentment.

We can say that the methodological approach proposed by Benjamin connects with that of the critical scholars in the critical legal movement, in that both focus on resisting laws by searching for those aspects that are not accounted for within or accountable to law; both offer an ethical relationship of being and acting beyond law. Furthermore, in Benjamin as in Cavarero, accountability cannot be accountability to the legal frame and norms. Rather, accountability must come from an awareness of oneself, and resistance requires an awareness of oneself. Awareness of oneself is not to be intended as recognition of subjectivity, or linguistic identity, a form of naming, but rather as awareness of the voice as one's voice, body, vulnerability, of that which is not included in the violence of our formation as legal subjects, and which escapes the violence of one's naming and the positing of law.

Similarly to the critique offered by the critical legal movement and Benjamin, the Cavarerian voice requires detachment from the normative frame and calls also for an ethical way of approaching justice. A focus on the voice means an emphasis on what exceeds law and an ethical responsibility to choose care toward vulnerability. The voice calls for an ontology of a selfhood in flesh and blood, unique and relational. While exposing the contingency of one's body, the voice implies a diverse ethical ontology unlike the normative ontology of law, and such ontology remains parallel to law, opening a space of resistance. However, escaping the semantics is not completely possible; it is not possible to stay permanently outside law and institutions, but it is necessary to pay attention to the relationship between law, institutions and people. Therefore, the focus is on ethical thinking and acting. For Cavarero, this can lead also to acting strategically.

When asked about resistance and institutions, Cavarero seems to be well aware of the cage of language and normativity, and the subsequent fact that we are forced into the master's house, and she argues that we must necessarily use the master's tools strategically.[183] The voice becomes a strategic means as it suspends

183 Adriana Cavarero with Elisabetta Bertolino, "Beyond Ontology and Sexual Difference: An Interview with the Italian Feminist Philosopher Adriana Cavarero," *differences: A Journal of Feminist Cultural Studies*, 19(1) (2008): 128–167, 153–154.

language and goes beyond language, expressing that which is extra-linguistic in a selfhood. The dimension of the voice cannot be codified by law and we could perceive it as a space that runs parallel to law, opening ethical possibilities for rethinking the relationships to law and justice.

The voice reflects both the contingency of the passing of air and the breathing of a corporeal and unique body, and finds itself to be at the same time a means for the production of words. The voice, as moment of resistance, can be said to be a link between one's uniqueness and the bounded symbolic in which we are immersed, between life and law. The voice – as some scholars have noticed – can be seen as the possibility of freedom from the normative and sovereign subject of law.[184] The voice can be said to be a moment of awareness of one's singularity that interrupts, even if only for a moment, the instituted symbolic order, and radically opens new possibilities not pre-established by the legal and institutional frame, or by the more general linguistic and political frame in which law is rooted.

As Cavarero makes clear in her interview, resistance cannot be exhausted in the moment of suspension from the pre-established order.[185] The voice opens spaces for politics, but it is necessary also to strategically use law and its institutions, and the master's tools, with *cattive intenzioni* (bad intentions) to radically push toward contingency and ethics in a community of relational and unique selves.[186] We can say that Cavarero derives such a way of resisting from the feminist thought of the early movement of women's collectives in 1980s Italy that looked for an alternative feminist politics, such as Diotima in Verona.[187] Rather than accommodating their political thought within male-dominated institutional politics, or comparing their work to that of male subjects, women's groups in Italy creatively organized new spaces in which to find a new politics.

Cavarero's thinking draws on the work of the Italian feminists who created women's centers, bookshops and libraries as places of detachment from existing dominating institutions, where women could separate themselves from masculine systems of thought. Those centers were spaces where they could experience independence and freedom from the sovereign subjectivity and symbolic order. What is important is that they emphasized a politics of difference among women themselves rather than an emancipatory politics of equality between women and men. Drawing on such a legacy of Italian feminism, Cavarero offers, via the voice, an approach to resistance that suspends the normative institutional framework.

We can also explore the Arendtian roots of the Cavarerian resistance via the voice; that is, the voice in terms of action and natality. Natality is to be intended as people taking initiative and acting unexpectedly, by virtue of birth. Such a

184 Zerilli, *Feminism and the Abyss of Freedom.*

185 Cavarero with Bertolino, "Beyond Ontology and Sexual Difference," 137.

186 Cavarero with Bertolino, "Beyond Ontology and Sexual Difference," 137.

187 In relation to autocoscienza, see Paola Bono and Sandra Kemp, *Italian Feminist Thought: A Reader* (Oxford: Basil Blackwell, 1991).

capacity of acting for Arendt is rooted precisely in the fact of natality. Cavarero's resistance through one's unique voice is deeply connected to this Arendtian politics of transformation and newness of unique actions. The notion of new beginnings and the idea of action are central to understand Arendt's methodology of resistance. Resistance in Arendt's view is about breaking with the established, the passive, the predictable, and creating one's freedom by acting something that did not exist before, newness and natality.

And yet, Arendt also had to confront her resistance to existing law and institutions and find a way to do it. Scholars view Arendt's relation to law and institutions in different ways. Andreas Kalyvas, for instance, reflects on the shift in thinking about freedom in Arendt and the necessity of dealing with law and institutional frameworks.[188] For Kalyvas, in *The Human Condition* Arendt appears to see resistance as a non-institutionalized moment of uniqueness revealed by acting and beginning something new.[189] While Arendt recognizes the necessity for public spaces bounded by law, she also maintains the need for a politics that cannot be exhausted by those legal and institutionalized spaces. For Kalyvas, resistance in Arendt is understood as a moment that suspends and interrupts the institutional and legal politics and as a politics of the extraordinary because there is an existential understanding of resistance in terms of natality, beginnings and newness that is contingent and appears to be arbitrary ***and disconnected from the established order.***

However, Kalyvas notes how later in her writings, for instance in *On Revolution*, Arendt shows that the extraordinary moments of beginnings, although they are not ignored, need not to be understood as a total revolutionary rupture with the institutional political and legal framework.[190] Therefore, in *On Revolution*, Arendt focused on the relationship between the extraordinary moments of rupture and authority, and her thought becomes a search for a balance between *liberty and order, the constituent and the constituted power* and between the politics of the extraordinary and ordinary politics.[191]

For Martel, one can find in Arendt two different approaches.[192] One is a kind of pure resistance as detachment from law and the sovereign and the other is a form of resistance that engages with law and authority. In her conflicted relationship with sovereign power and authority and her attempts to work within the confines of the state as a basis for politics, Arendt seems to direct herself toward non-governance as a form of detachment and the only possible way of resistance.

188 Andreas Kalyvas, *Democracy and the Politics of the Extraordinary: Max, Weber, Carl Schmitt and Hannah Arendt* (Cambridge: Cambridge University Press, 2008).

189 Kalyvas, *Democracy and the Politics of the Extraordinary.*

190 Kalyvas, *Democracy and the Politics of the Extraordinary.*

191 Hannah Arendt, *On Revolution* (Harmondsworth: Penguin Books, 1973).

192 James Martel, "The Ambivalent Anarchism of Hannah Arendt," in *How Not to Be Governed: Readings and Interpretations from a Critical Anarchist Left*, eds Klausen, J.C. and Martel, J. (Lanham: Rowman & Littlefield, 2011), 143–155.

Martel concludes that precisely this ambivalent and conflicting approach to sovereign law and authority allows one to find in Arendt's work a special way of understanding resistance that "neither forgets its originary vision (as appearance), nor shrinks from contending with 'facts on the ground' of our time."[193] Martel reads Arendt's ambivalence as a complex and sophisticated form of resistance that attempts to overcome the traps of an impossible resistance. Rather, her resistance to law and authority becomes conceivable precisely because it is neither institutionalized nor a pure detachment from institutions.

Vikki Bell argues that Arendt gives up the willing self of liberalism for an acting self.[194] An acting self can surprise with unexpected actions that cannot be decided in advance by the frame but, rather, happen unexpectedly and involve us in new ways that are not deliberate or intended. The whole of liberalism rests upon both its general promises and the specific promises of those in power. These mechanisms are premised upon a calculable self, who needs to calculate. On the contrary, for Arendt beginning anew implies leaving behind this calculable self, based on the "I will," and embracing the "we can" that leads us to act in non-calculable ways.[195]

Some other scholars have theorized more specifically on Arendt and the law. For Michael Wilkinson, for instance, law *comes into being* by means of *production* rather than as action.[196] This means that law is an enclosed border that functions in terms of exchange rather than as a relationship and, as such, if law is to engage with Arendtian resistance, limits would be placed on actions and the exercise of political freedom theorized by Arendt.[197] For Johan Van der Walt, it is law that is incapable of participating in the Arendtian space of appearance, as law is not a phenomenon and cannot appear.[198] Law is already fully apparent and cannot grasp the political and phenomenological truth of the world of appearance. No political institution can reflect the full truth of human existence.[199] Appearance requires a multiplicity of actions, whereas law has a finite perspective and inevitably causes harm. Actions, such as forgiveness, can be said to be in the space of appearance and thus escape the finite perspective of law. Van der Walt links this to the banality of evil in the case of Eichmann, where law's only interest consisted of confronting Eichmann's mind with the objective standard of the reasonable person's state of mind.[200] In this case, law showed its own limits and finite

193 Martel, "The Ambivalent Anarchism of Hannah Arendt," 144.

194 Vikki Bell, "The Promise of Liberalism and the Performance of Freedom," in *Foucault and the Political Reason*, eds Barry, A., Osborne, T. and Rose, N. (London: UCL Press, 1996), 81–97.

195 Bell, "The Promise of Liberalism and the Performance of Freedom."

196 Michael A. Wilkinson, "Between Freedom and Law: Hannah Arendt on the Promise of Modern Revolution and the Burden of the Tradition," in *Hannah Arendt and the Law*, eds Goldoni, M. and McCorkindale, C. (Oxford: Hart Publishing, 2012), 35–61.

197 Wilkinson, "Between Freedom and Law."

198 Johan Van der Walt, "Law and the Space of Appearance," in *Hannah Arendt and the Law*, eds Goldoni, M. and McCorkindale, C. (Oxford: Hart Publishing, 2012), 63–97.

199 Van der Walt, "Law and the Space of Appearance."

200 Van der Walt, "Law and the Space of Appearance."

perspective. Whereas speaking in one's voice and acting anew, as with forgiveness, reveal the uniqueness of the person and show the appearance beyond law.

Despite those positions, the point that needs to be stressed here is that both Arendt and Cavarero seem to acknowledge – in different ways – the impossibility of remaining radically outside the institutional framework and the necessity of compromising in some way with authority. Both scholars reveal in their way of resisting the paradox that is intrinsic to freedom and revolution. Such a paradox can be said to consist of the fact that after a moment of awareness and revelation of one's uniqueness and *who-ness*, one has necessarily to engage with forms of authority and representation and speak and act in a context of ordinary politics. In the end speaking and acting both engage with forms of an ordinary context and resist such an ordinary context. And therefore one's voice and actions need to be thought of in relation to their linguistic and normative contexts, while resisting them.

We could say that in dealing with such a paradox, the two scholars suggest that both speaking and acting necessarily need to be in concert and relationality with other people. Precisely, this space in-between people is unlikely to be caged in representation and calls for an ontological and ethical rethinking of the relationship between people and institutions, beyond law. This space constitutes a parallel way of approaching reality to that of approaching law and authority. Both Arendt and Cavarero see the space of plurality as necessary:

> *Action, the only activity that goes on directly between men without the intermediary of things or matter, corresponds to the human condition of plurality, to the fact that men, not Man, live on the earth and inhabit the world. While all aspects of the human condition are somehow related to politics, this plurality is specifically the condition – not only the condition sine qua non, but the condition per quam – of all political life.*[201]

> *There is dependence on others that passes through a plural connection of mouths and ears. Unlike what Plato believes – when he inaugurates the metaphorical voice of the soul – speaking is not at all a thinking that expresses itself out loud, nor is it merely vocalised thought, nor is it an acoustic substitute for thinking. The phenomenology of speaking possesses an autonomous status in which the relationality of mouths and ears comes to the fore.*[202]

In addition, one's voice consists of an empty ontological space, because there is no fixed truth in it, but only a transient and singular voice. Such an empty ontological space of one's voice can represent a parallel ontology to the one of law. As Loizidou affirms we can make use of law, not forgetting about life.[203] One's *who-ness* and uniqueness will always and inevitably escape law.

201 Arendt, *The Human Condition*, 10.
202 Cavarero, *For More Than One Voice*, 174.
203 Loizidou, "Before the Law, Encounters at the Borderline," 185.

Conclusion

The argument of this chapter has been threefold. Firstly, I have attempted to connect the theme of the voice with the concern for the deconstruction of the legal text within the critical legal movement. Critical legal scholars, such as Goodrich and Douzinas, have opened up the meanings of legal texts and argued for a postmodern jurisprudence which reveals forms of reasoning and displays the excess of the texts of law; that is, what is not included in the substance of law. Similarly, the focus on the voice shows the excess that is not included in the linguistic system and in the pre-established normative order. The voice consists of breathing, a passage of air, and suggests a singularity, a notion of unique self. It thus opens a space of resistance against the metaphysics of presence and the sovereign. The voice also implies awareness of oneself and one's body, rather than the positing of law.

Secondly, I have analyzed and compared some literature on resistance, namely the perspective on resistance offered by John Rawls, Martha Nussbaum, Judith Butler and Adriana Cavarero. I also presented Adriana Cavarero's reading of Hannah Arendt's work. Both Rawls and Nussbaum acknowledge that there are inequalities and injustices and want to make law and justice more equally distributed. Rawls theorizes resistance in terms of justice as fairness, understood as the distribution of goods to the least well off in society. This, however, assumes a universalizing approach that perceives people as being essentially the same. Such an account fails to recognize difference, differing contexts and differing power positions, and so people are necessarily viewed as opting for a sort of reasonable consensus.

On the other hand, Nussbaum argues for the importance of considering the differences among people. She also argues for a law and justice that allow people to reach a good standard of capabilities and functioning. In her view, such a standard would be defined and negotiated by people themselves, since everybody desires to improve their own conditions in life. Both Rawls and Nussbaum open possibilities of resistance by theorizing within the liberal legal and political framework. As a consequence, they ground their arguments on normative notions of universal rights, of dignity and worth of human beings and attempt to adjust inequality by adopting good criteria that respect those universal values.

Resistance is theorized in terms of reformation of the law and institutions and remains within the institutional politics of the ordinary. It also rests on the same ontological thinking of law and rights founded on normative views of what is just for everybody. Equality is perceived as a universalizing, normalizing sameness. Individuality and singularity are covered up by a standard or notion of a "general person" that is found to be at the core of law and its institutional practices.

Next, the chapter discussed Judith Butler's theory of resistance: a theory that aims to include difference and excess in the ideological mechanisms of the established order by being critical of normative and ideological intelligibility and through subverting practices that cause ruptures within the system.

The perspective is complex and cannot be seen as an adjustment to the same legal and institutional thinking of liberalism. It is a theory of critical re-articulation of the symbolic and normative order. Her work points to a notion of resistance that necessarily passes through the contextual linguistic and normative frame, since the latter cannot be dissociated from any form of excess and materiality. Difference and excess can only emerge through, within and against those linguistic and normative structures.

Finally, the chapter introduced Adriana Cavarero's theory of resistance – a theory which, as I have argued, constitutes the main theoretical approach of the book. The focus on the voice shifts the emphasis onto the excess and on what is excluded from the normative and linguistic frame. More specifically, the voice, as a conceptual tool, is used in order to reflect upon one's uniqueness, corporeality and also the possibility of plurality and relationality of our being in the world. Those are all aspects of ourselves that are perceived to be superfluous and are thus excluded by legal subjectivity. There is a different ontology at stake for Cavarero. The voice signifies an empty and contingent ontology of a singular body, always changeable, never the same. Thus ontology in this chapter signifies something other than the ontology of the metaphysics of presence; it is an ontology that reverses ontology itself and shows the excess and what has been made superfluous and excluded.

The voice also reflects upon the possibility of becoming aware of a self that stands outside the symbolic and normative order. The awareness of oneself provides the possibility of resistance through interruption and suspension, rather than accommodation, even if such a suspension can only be temporary and some form of relation to the system is necessary or inevitable. Such an awareness of oneself extends beyond linguistic recognition and becomes then the locus of new possibilities and of an ethical opening beyond law and its legal and normative institutions. The voice unfolds in fact the current political and legal construction of the subject, which is tied to an economy of return. One's voice allows awareness of oneself from within and in relationality to others and thus transforms the current construction of the subject into a foreign experience because one's vulnerability is exposed. The awareness of oneself derived from speaking in one's voice calls for ethical responses toward vulnerability – I will deal with this in Chapter IV.

I have concluded by exploring the possibilities that are opened up when thinking through the voice. Speaking in one's voice can signify the possibility of a politics outside the ordinary, a politics of the extraordinary that allows interruption and suspension; a form of resistance that does not require negotiation or compromising with the existing institutions and ideological framework. Here Benjamin's theory on resistance has been employed only methodologically, together with further methodological reflections taken from Arendt and Cavarero.

All political theorists discussed in this chapter agree that moments of suspension and interruption involve some forms of interaction and relationship with the normative and linguistic frame, in the sense that we are immersed in such a frame and that a complete anarchic detachment may not be possible. The critical legal movement, and in particular critical legal theorists such as Goodrich and Douzinas, propose a rethinking of such a relationship with law and its institutions by shifting the focus toward the ethical and the political aspect of law.

We can conclude by arguing that this book continues the critical legal discourse on the possibility of resisting the linguistic and normative imposition of law by focusing on the voice rather than on signs and texts. It attempts to contribute to the tradition of critical legal studies by expanding in a different direction to the postmodern critical interpretation and reading of legal texts. The book suggests various paths of resistance through one's voice: the path that resists the linguistic and normative aspects of law by taking account of one's materiality and singularity; the path that opposes the liberal ideology in law made up of standards and based on an autonomous subject of rights; and the path that resists the violence of separation, of a subject cut and divided from her uniqueness and material vulnerability, constructed through stereotyped forms of sexual difference and disconnected from the community.

By following those interconnected paths of resistance, this book contributes also to a rethinking of ethics and justice, also opening up paths of resistance for feminism. It does this by rooting the voice in something unexpected, unpredictable, and in ambivalence as well as in the vulnerability revealed by speaking in one's voice. The Arendtian action of forgiveness reveals these unexpected and unpredictable aspects of speaking in one's voice and implies awareness of vulnerability, uniqueness and relationality. The action of forgiveness becomes linked to one's voice. This is not a moralized turn nor an understanding of forgiveness in terms of an institutional move or as expression of a standard or a righteous subject. It is rather a forgiveness that comes from awareness, from within in relationality to others, that happens on a level in which one is vulnerable and dependent on a community.

This also has implications for feminism, in that feminism often looks for paths of action that follow the empowered and righteous subject of the woman. Such paths of resistance repeat the violent mechanisms of the sovereign subject. A focus on the voice suggests rather that there are other possible ontological and ethical actions that can be enacted. This argument is developed in Chapter IV. This book thus contributes to a further reflection on the ontological background of the voice.

I also seek to substantiate my arguments through two gendered contexts, or case studies, in the following two chapters. The two case studies provide a critique of the law in relation to FGC and objectification in sex work. I will take into consideration statutes but also case law such as those of *Re MB* (1997) and *R v Gary Lee Cole and Stephen Kevin Barik* (1993) as well as the articulation of other elements that may be revealed by speaking in one's voice. Through the case studies I will attempt to juxtapose the experience of one's voice with that of law to further explain and bring alive this book's theory on the voice. The case studies suggest how one's voice may constitute a radical means of resistance for women and other groups of people that suffer discrimination in our society, such as homosexuals, transsexual people or migrants, in that one's voice constitutes a radical critique of the construction of the subject in law and imagines a different selfhood.

In the next chapter I employ the voice, as theorized by Cavarero, in order to rethink critically the practice of cutting the female genitals. I depart from the position of the legal subject of resistance, characterized by the principles of consent and the integrity of the body. Law views FGC as being a priori unlawful and constructs women as mutilated in opposition to the idea of the intact and whole legal body. I argue against such a mono-valent and limited legal perspective as it reflects upon a cut subject. A cut subject indicates that mind and body are essentialized through sexual difference and then separated, whereas the body is treated as a general idea. On the contrary, the ontology of one's voice is open to ambivalence in the understanding of events and allows for a reconnection of self and body. In addition, one's voice overcomes the essentialized sexual difference dichotomy and grounds the possibility of a subject characterized by inclination rather than by verticality.

Part II

The voice beyond sexual difference

Chapter 2

The ambivalence of wounds, consent and the integrity of the body

> *The voice as a phenomenon is directly corporeal and non-textual. My intention was to underline precisely this, that the voice in the logos, the word, is the directly corporeal element. I have not examined this in the text because it is already well known. The voice has an immediate emotional and affective impact and provokes emotional and affective reactions [. . .] What interests me most in the corporeality of the voice is that the voice is unique, in other words, the voice indicates the singularity of the body, which is one of the things I insist on.*[1]

This chapter and the next consist of two case studies, in which I attempt to apply the theoretical perspective of one's voice to female genital cutting (FGC) and objectification in sex work.[2] Both cases exemplify processes of physical or psychological separations and cuts that may happen in the life of a woman and that also mark the cuts and separations operated on the subject by an essentialized perspective on sexual difference. One's voice is meant precisely to resist these disjunctions. According to the essentialized sexual difference perspective, the masculine subject is construed as dominant, whereas the feminine is understood as less than a subject, peripheral and associated with bodily traits. As a result, the subject is cut and divided in two essentialized positions. As Cavarero says in the passage above, it is interesting to confront the voice with contextual situations, where one can find unique emotional, affective and corporeal reactions. Thus in the following case studies I reflect on statutes and case law but also on the living experience of people from the point of view of one's voice; that is, from a non-separated and non-cut perspective, a voice that comes from within oneself in relationality with one's vulnerability and that of others. I shall begin in this chapter with the case study of FGC.

1 Adriana Cavarero with Elisabetta Bertolino, "Beyond Ontology and Sexual Difference: An Interview with the Italian Feminist Philosopher Adriana Cavarero," *differences: A Journal of Feminist Cultural Studies*, 19(1) (2008): 128–167, 135.

2 I shall use the term female genital cutting (FGC) rather than female genital mutilation (FGM) as talking in terms of cut is more neutral and allows ambivalence in the understanding of the practice.

Drawing on Adriana Cavarero's insights, I argue that one's voice can resist the reasonable consent, the *intactivism* of the principle of integrity of the body deployed in law to stop FGC as well as law's mono-valent thinking.[3] Firstly, I assume that consent can be said to represent the legal voice in situations when one wants to undergo body cuts. And yet consent is inconsistent, since it is part of the myth of the autonomous, rational and independent legal subject that is cut and divided from the start and thus unable to deal with the cuts that FGC makes to the body. In particular, I see the legal subject – that speaks through consent – as a rational and neutral subject that has been already divested from the materiality of the sexed selfhood. Whereas according to law an adult needs to be competent to be able to consent and consent needs to be informed, competence becomes denied to adult women undergoing the surgery of FGC, even though it is accepted, for instance, in situations of surgery for cosmetic reasons. For the purpose of my speculation on consent and one's voice, I am going to deal only with FGC in relation to adult women who choose to undergo the practice and I will not involve cases of children undergoing the practice because this would require a different approach.

The perspective of adult women who choose to undergo FGC might show that the very concept of consent, which is supposed to provide one with autonomy and a voice within the legal system, is trapped in a phallocentric register. As a result, it produces a differential treatment in the specific case of adult women who undergo FGC. I will discuss the issue of competence in consent with reference to the case law of Ms MB, a case of alleged incompetence in cesarean section.[4] Although the case does not deal with FGC, it demonstrates the problematics of consent and of the dominant ideology of the liberal rational individual and of individual choice.

I will then proceed to a critical exploration of the ways in which the legal principle of the integrity of the body reflects a vision of *intactivism* of the body. I argue that in cases where consent to the cut is allowed (such as in cosmetic surgery) the integrity of the body in law is construed differently from cases where body cuts are ascribed to patriarchal discourses of gender subordination and are thus ruled to be a priori unlawful, such as in the case of FGC. In these latter cases, women's agency is excluded, legal consent to the cut is denied and the body is understood as lacking integrity.

This is the result of the fact that legal discourse perceives the body in abstraction, as generic, often tied to an identity discourse, instead of engaging with a unique and singular body. The legal body no longer reflects one's body or voice.[5] Against this tendency, one's voice reconnects ontologically the separations and cuts in the

3 Mono-valent refers here to a way of seeing things only from the perspective of the vertical axis that constitutes the subject.

4 *Re MB* (Caesarean Section) [1997] 8 Med LR 217.

5 Here the term "generic" is intended in the sense of abstract, and as opposed to a specific singular corporeality.

subject and body operated by law. For Cavarero, the problem of the generic body is the outcome of a vertical thinking of the subject, of the *homo erectus*, who by standing up erect also looks up toward the truth and the good, thus forgetting his corporeal origins.[6] This man has today become a self-referential ego; he has elaborated a theory where rectitude, rightness, correction and verticality concur.[7] He has become arrogant of his own foundation by displacing both the inclination of the body and of the relational aspects of his life and by focusing only on the verticality of his actions.[8] In particular, this man with a masculine valence expresses the absolute pretence of denoting the whole of mankind. Being uprooted from his body, nature, and matter or *physis,* this man produces metaphysics, in complete disregard of his fleshy and corporeal existence.[9]

I argue that law insists precisely on such an uprooted and vertical understanding of the self and the body and treats the issue of FGC in a mono-valent and biased way. Both the notions of consent and the integrity of the body are reflections of the vertical and normative gesture of such a subject. As a result, FGC is ruled to be unlawful simply from the legal point of view, and there is a failure to recognize other perspectives at work behind the practice.[10] The legal discourse treats the body as general and appears also to be biased against non-Western approaches of the body.

Conversely, according to Cavarero, the focus on one's voice implies a subject that is rooted in her unique body, inclined, one that bends toward others, renounces the gestures of autonomy and independence and the pretence of owning the truth and takes account of the ambivalence in events, thus disturbing the solipsistic foundations of the system. It should be noted that this is not the traditional asymmetrical and unbalanced figure of the mother, who provides care, but rather the structural posture of all of us who experience vulnerability and inclination in different ways during life and are confronted with different ambivalent events.[11]

This book argues for an approach to FGC through one's voice. One's voice reflects an attitude of inclination toward one another and implies also starting from oneself in relationality to others, becoming aware of vulnerability, understanding events through ambivalence, perceiving others as agents of their lives

6 Adriana Cavarero, "Recritude: Reflections on Postural Ontology," *Journal of Speculative Philosophy*, 27(3) (2013): 220–235; Adriana Cavarero, "Inclining the Subject: Ethics, Alterity and Natality," in *Theory After Theory*, eds Elliot, J. and Attridge, D. (New York: Routledge, 2011), 194–204.

7 Cavarero, "Recritude," 221; Cavarero, "Inclining the Subject," 195.

8 Cavarero, "Recritude"; Cavarero, "Inclining the Subject."

9 Adriana Cavarero, "Demeter," in *In Spite of Plato: A Feminist Rewriting of Ancient Philosophy,* ed. Cavarero, A., trans. Serena Anderlini D'Onofrio (Cambridge: Polity Press, 1995), 57–90.

10 I refer here to perspectives that consider FGC as a cultural expression and also to the ambivalence of the practice. I will explore the following perspectives: Renata Salecl, "Cut in the Body: From Clitoridectomy to Body Art," in *(Per)versions of Love and Hate*, ed. Salecl, R. (London: Verso, 1998), 141–168; Bruno Bettelheim, *Symbolic Wounds: Puberty Rites and the Envious Male* (London: Thames and Hudson, 1995).

11 Cavarero, "Recritude," 233.

and moving beyond identity discourses that tend only to equalize one body with another. It is precisely one's voice (a voice leaning out from the subject) that can help us understand the paradoxes of consent and the principle of integrity of the body deployed in law, as well as the limits to the legal subject of resistance. One's voice allows a suspension of identity discourses and brings up forms of resistance that both engage with law and disengage from it. The focus on one's voice questions the vertical approach of the legal subject of resistance and redirects its axis of thinking through ambivalence and inclination, not in an attempt to correct the vertical legal ontology but rather in order to stress the gap between verticality and inclination.[12] In the next section, I will deal with the paradoxes involved in the concept of consent; that is, the impossibility of having a voice within law.

2.1 Law and the impossibility of consent

Law's verticality is visible in the paternalistic and sovereign approach toward FGC, precisely when law is biased in its use of the principle of consent and the integrity of the body with reference to FGC. Although consent and integrity constitute an expression of the vertical and autonomous subject, in the case of women and FGC, consent for adult women – that is, choosing to undergo the practice of FGC – is deemed to be impossible by law, mainly because their consent is perceived to be forced by cultural and patriarchal imperatives. Hence, women seem to lack true autonomy.

In this section I will deal with consent, whereas in Section 2.3 I will take into consideration the principle of the integrity of the body. In the specific UK context, for instance, the British parliament felt that the unlawfulness of the practice needed to be put beyond doubt by the introduction of a special statutory legislation, The Female Circumcision Prohibition Act 1985, which was then changed to The Female Genital Mutilation Act 2003.[13] Such statutory legislation reflects a fixed and mono-valent feminist way of understanding FGC, perceived as barbarism against women with its only aim to control and offend women and their sexuality.[14] Consequently, law assumes that it is not possible to ascribe any autonomy to those who undergo the practice, because of a cultural context intertwined with patriarchal coercion, manipulation and lack of better alternatives; a combination that makes consent appear impossible.[15]

12 Cavarero, "Inclining the Subject."

13 See R.D. Mackay, "Is Female Genital Circumcision Unlawful?" *Criminal Law Review* (November 1983): 717–722; Kearns Hayter, "Female Circumcision. Is There a Legal Solution?" *Journal of Social Welfare Law*, 6 (1984): 323–333.

14 Efua Dorkenoo, *Cutting the Rose: The Practice and its Prevention* (London: Minority Rights, 1994); Patricia Broussard, "The Importation of Female Genital Mutilation to the West: The Cruellest Cut of All," *University of San Francisco Law Review*, 44 (2009–2010): 787–824.

15 The Prohibition of Female Genital Circumcision Act was enacted in 1985. In 2003 a new Female Genital Mutilation Act was drafted. This newly enacted Female Genital Mutilation Act 2003 became law in 2004. The 2003 Act contained a revised terminology; the naming of the practice

Despite the fact that there have been no prosecutions against FGC, the statutory legislation communicates a clear message of inadmissibility and intolerance toward FGC as a non-Western cultural modification of the female body. As a result, law's position is paradoxical because it contradicts the liberal approach that is grounded on freedom of choice and the autonomy of the individual. I argue that the approach is biased since it refutes the possibility of consent in the case of FGC, but accepts it in relation to other cultural modifications and surgeries of the body that are unavoidably conditioned by Western society and culture.[16]

In cosmetic surgery procedures such as breast implants, liposuction and facelifts, there are health risks that can be considered similar to those associated with FGC, such as blood loss, hematoma, pulmonary edema, infections, deep vein thrombosis, wound healing problems, scarring, and even death. Despite those risks, patients who choose cosmetic surgery are treated in most cases at self-regulating private clinics where few safeguards are offered by the law to patients.[17]

Some scholars view critically such a legal approach in favour of cosmetic surgery. Melanie Latham suggests, for instance, that informed consent based on individual choice is not sufficient to protect patients against the patriarchal cultural pressure to comply with certain standards of beauty or normality and that it is necessary instead to respond with an understanding of all aspects that lead to those choices.[18] Shelly Sheldon and Stephen Wilkinson interpret the present legal situation in the UK as ethically unsustainable because the ban on FGC is unjustified and it should apply equally to certain types of cosmetic surgery.[19]

Moira Dustin indicates some ambiguities in relation to the different treatment of FGC and cosmetic surgery found within the statutory provision against

changed from female circumcision to female mutilation; it also imposed more severe penalties and added the concept of extraterritoriality. The Act states that a person is guilty "if he excises, infibulates or otherwise mutilates the whole or any part of a girl's labia majora, labia minora or clitoris." Exceptions are considered when the procedure is done by a professional and is necessary for the woman's mental or physical health. However, the Act specifies that cultural or traditional norms cannot be taken into account when determining whether the procedure should be done for mental health reasons.

16 Regulation of the private cosmetic surgery sector has been part of a general schema of reforms of the healthcare professions such as The Care Standards Act 2000 and the Health and Social Care (Community Health and Standards) Act 2003, The National Health Service Act 2006 and The Health and Social Care Act 2012, which received Royal Assent on 27 March 2012.

17 Carolyne McLeod and Susan Sherwin, "Relational Autonomy: Feminist Perspectives on Autonomy, Self-Trust, and Health Care for Patients who are Oppressed," in *Relational Autonomy: Feminist Perspectives on Autonomy, Agency and the Social Self*, eds Mackenzie, C. and Stoljar, N. (Oxford: Oxford University Press, 2000), 259–279.

18 Melanie Latham, "The Shape of Things to Come: Feminism, Regulation and Cosmetic Surgery," *Medical Law Review*, 16 (2008): 437–457.

19 Shelly Sheldon and Stephen Wilkinson, "Female Genital Mutilation and Cosmetic Surgery: Regulating Non-Therapeutic Body Modification," *Bioethics*, 12 (1998): 263–285.

FGC itself.[20] Delays in passing the previous 1985 Act against FGC appear to have been caused by a disagreement over cases of women developing anxiety about the shape and size of their external genitalia that resulted in legal surgical modifications of a cosmetic nature. The final wording of the Act allows such an exception, but only if necessary for the patient's physical or mental health.[21] Consequently, as Dustin notes, the procedure is allowed only if one is a British adult consenting to modify one's genitals for mental health reasons, but not in the case of an adult woman from a minority group who consents to modify her genitals for mental health reasons caused by her culture.

But what would be the position of law, if the statutory provision on FGC was abolished or were not in place? Would the position of law still exclude consent in relation to FGC? The latter question requires an examination of the criminal and medical law. Under criminal law, consent is not a defense to all crimes; it is necessary to look at various aspects, for example whether the victim truly consented and was responsible, the type of harm and the rationale for consent as defense.[22] Whereas, in medical law, for a procedure to be lawful, the patient has to consent in advance of the procedure, or the procedure must have been carried out because of necessity, in emergency circumstances.[23]

From the case law, it follows that in the absence of any statutory intervention and under common law cosmetic surgery and FGC would both be regulated by the law of assault and battery.[24] In view of the injury to health caused by FGC and the

20 Moira Dustin, "Female Genital Cutting in the UK: Challenging the Inconsistencies," *European Journal of Women's Studies*, 17 (2010): 7–23.

21 Such an exception is also reproduced in the current 2003 Act.

22 C.M.V. Clarkson and S.R. Keating, *Criminal Law: Text and Material*. Seventh Edition (London: Sweet & Maxwell, 2010), see: section on consent. The two leading cases on consent are those of *Attorney General's Reference* (No. 6 of 1980) and *R v Brown* [1994] 1 AC 212 (House of Lords). But also *Airedale NHS v Bland* (1993) AC 789 (House of Lords).

23 Emily Jackson, *Medical Law: Texts, Cases and Materials*. Third Edition (Oxford: Oxford University Press, 2013), 165–284.

24 From the case law of *Attorney General's Reference* (1980), *R v Brown* [1994] and *Airedale NHS v Bland* (1993), consent appears to be a defense in reasonable and proper surgical interferences. In fact, in *Attorney General's Reference* (1980), the majority in the Court of Appeal approved the dictum of Lord Lane and held that consent was not a defense. It was decided that it is not in the "public interest" that people inflict on each other actual bodily harm for no "good reasons." Lord Lane also affirmed that the legality of reasonable and proper surgical interference is not to be doubted because it is in the public interest. In *R v Brown* [1994], it was decided that consent can be a defense to common assault but that it is not generally a defense to an assault occasioning actual bodily harm or to an unlawful wounding. In particular, Lord Templeman affirmed that there are exceptions to this general rule, based on policy and public interest, such as in the case of surgery, ritual (male) circumcision, tattooing, ear-piercing and rough sport. In those exceptions, where the injury is a foreseeable incident of a lawful activity in which the person injured is participating, consent is allowed as a defense. Lord Templeman also added that criminal law restrains practices which are regarded as dangerous and injurious to individuals and harmful to society generally. In *Airedale NHS v Bland* (1993), Lord Mustill affirmed that bodily invasions in the course of proper medical treatment stand completely outside criminal law and that the consent of the patient is essential to the propriety of

absence of medical benefits, the courts would probably declare the practice unlawful and contrary to the public interest even in the absence of the statutory provision.[25]

In reference to this, Sheldon and Wilkinson suggest that in the case of absence of the statutory provision the court could then consider taking a holistic approach to the injury produced by surgical interferences.[26] In the FGC context, it would be necessary to consider that a woman may gain social and psychological benefits that would outweigh the direct physical harm. The two scholars suggest that courts could refer to the law regulating the removal of organs from live donors, where the benefit to the donor has been described in terms of wider gains such as social, psychological and emotional benefits.[27]

Nevertheless, while consent to FGC in the case of adult women would still be refuted by common law outside the statutory provision, the idea of consent itself remains generally problematic. This is because, according to law, consent must be grounded on certain pre-arranged criteria concerning both the context and the agent. The individual is supposed to be able to make a free, autonomous and non-coerced choice and be capable of consenting, which means that the individual must be competent.

"Competent" means rational and of sound mind and implies that consent must be informed, which means that the individual must be in possession of sufficient information about what is at stake. But consent is not attributed to those whose autonomy is impaired. It should be noted that many cases of women, and specifically those cases that have to do with women's bodies, seem to be perceived through the lens of lack of competence and of impaired autonomy.[28] I explain this by the fact that one's body and one's emotional traits and desires continue to be associated with the essentialized feminine subject and are thus excluded from the vertical and independent image of the dominant subjectivity. As Cavarero says:

> *[. . .] Every inclination unbalances it [the subject] and displaces the internal barycentre on which the autarkic and self-sufficient figure of the Kantian moral*

medical treatment. In *R v Brown*, Lord Mustill made similar comments, stating that proper medical treatment that requires consent as a prerequisite can be said to be a category of its own. Thus under civil law it is accepted that the intentional harm or wounding that is inflicted on the patient by doctors is exempted from criminal liability on the grounds that its therapeutic purposes are in the patient's best interests and that therefore there is a good reason for harm to be caused.

25 Support for this potential outcome is provided by the case of *Adesanya* (1974), where a mother was found guilty under S. 47 OAPA 1861 for carrying out a ritual scarification of the cheeks of her sons. *Adesanya* (1974), *The Times*, 16 and 17 July.

26 Sheldon and Wilkinson, "Female Genital Mutilation and Cosmetic Surgery."

27 This is what happened in cases such as *Strunk v Strunk* (1969) and *Re Y* [1996], where the removal of an organ from a live donor incapable of giving valid consent was allowed on the grounds of psychological, emotional and social benefits, such as renewed meaning in life and an enhanced position in the family context.

28 *St George's Healthcare NHS Trust v S* (1998) 3 All ER 673; *Norfolk and Norwich Healthcare NHS Trust v W* [1996] 2 FLR 613; *Tameside and Glossop Acute Services Trust v CH* [1996] 1 FLR 762; *Rochdale Healthcare (NHS) Trust v C* [1997] 1 FCR 269.

I as well as the various historical samples of the philosophus erectus species are constructed.[29]

Body, emotions and desires unbalance precisely the straight line of the consenting rational individual, revealing what has been cut out and made superfluous in the construction of our subjectivity. Thus I argue that the idea of consent is also part of an understanding of the individual as being vertical, rational, autonomous and independent and therefore divided and cut; whereas any type of inclination and vulnerability of the subject makes consent fragile. In the understanding of consent in terms of such a vertical subjectivity, one's voice is denied. It is in reference to this argument that I will now analyze the case of Ms MB, followed by a critical discussion of the principle of the integrity of the body.[30] The case of Ms MB, although it does not deal with FGC, shows clearly the problematic nature of consent. Consequently, Ms MB's case is of help in supporting the argument that law's approach denies the voices of adult women who undergo FGC. I will now analyze Ms MB's case and provide some critique.

2.2 The case of *Re MB* (Caesarean Section)

Often, in matters of life and death, the easiest way to reach a pro-life decision involves declaring a patient as incompetent. In *Re MB* (Caesarean Section) [1997],[31] a competent patient, aged 23 and 40 weeks pregnant, was declared temporarily incompetent because of her fear of needles. When Ms MB was admitted to the hospital, she signed the consent form for the cesarean section but refused more than once to undergo a venepuncture because she was suffering from a needle phobia. After several attempts, the hospital sought a court order, which was emitted in a few hours.

In *Re MB*, the court took into consideration the criteria that need to be met in order to declare the incompetence of the patient, while affirming the standard rights of the individual to consent:

A mentally competent patient has an absolute right to refuse to consent to medical treatment for any reason, rational or irrational, or for no reason at all, even where that decision may lead to his or her own death [. . .] Medical treatment can be undertaken in an emergency even if, through a lack of capacity, no consent had been competently given, provided the treatment was a necessity and did no more than was reasonably required in the best interests of the patient.[32]

29 Cavarero, "Recritude," 226.
30 *Re MB* (Caesarean Section) [1997] 8 Med LR 217, 9.
31 *Re MB* (Caesarean Section) [1997] 8 Med LR 217, 9.
32 *Re MB* (Caesarean Section) [1997].

On a theoretical level, a refusal to consent, according to the court, was valid, whether rational, irrational or made for no reason at all. However, those principles did not apply to the case of Ms MB and the question of capacity emerged. At this point, the court took into consideration previous law cases and concluded:

> *Every person is presumed to have the capacity to consent to or to refuse medical treatment unless and until that presumption is rebutted. A competent woman who has the capacity to decide may, for religious reasons, other reasons, for rational or irrational reasons or for no reason at all, choose not to have medical intervention, even though the consequence may be the death or serious handicap of the child she bears, or her own death. In that event the courts do not have the jurisdiction to declare medical intervention lawful and the question of her own best interests, objectively considered, does not arise. Irrationality is here to be used to connote a decision which is outrageous in its defiance of logic or of accepted moral standards that no sensible person who had applied his mind to the question to be decided could have arrived at it [. . .]*
>
> *A person lacks capacity if some impairment or disturbance of mental functioning renders the person unable to make a decision whether to consent to or to refuse treatment. That inability to make a decision will occur when*
>
> *a) The patient is unable to comprehend and retain the information which is material to the decision [. . .]*
> *b) The patient is unable to use the information and weigh in the balance as part of the process of arriving at the decision [. . .]*
> *c) The "temporary factors" [. . .] (confusion, shock, fatigue, pain or drugs) may completely erode capacity but those concerned must be satisfied that such factors are operating to such a degree that the ability to decide is absent.*
> *d) Another such influence may be panic induced by fear. Again careful scrutiny of the evidence is necessary because fear of an operation may be a rational reason for refusal to undergo it. Fear may also, however, paralyse the will and thus destroy the capacity to make a decision.*[33]

The court considered that Ms MB consented to a cesarean section and that what she refused was only the prick of the anesthetist's needle and that capacity to consent is commensurate with the gravity of the decision to be taken. The court then pointed out that Ms MB could not undergo the accepted cesarean section due to her fear of needles. "*At the moment of panic [. . .] her fear dominated all.*" (My emphasis.) The court considered fear as a mental impairment which makes the person unable to make a decision and that Ms MB's fear of needles dominated her thinking, making her incapable of

33 *Re MB* (Caesarean Section) [1997].

considering other factors.[34] It was also noted that the best interests of a person are not limited to the best medical interests. In the case of Ms MB, her best interests were related to whether she would suffer significant long-term damage if the child was born with a disability or died, and the fact that she would not suffer long-term harm from anesthesia and the child would also be safely delivered.

Therefore, despite the fact that Ms MB was a competent patient, she was rendered temporarily incompetent by her needle phobia, since her needle phobia was understood to dominate the whole event and to stifle her belief in the information provided to her, and thus Ms MB was considered to be unable to weigh information. On this ground, the court ruled that Ms MB was incapable of making a decision and that medical intervention was in her best interest. Even though the court recognized the theoretical possibility that fear of an operation may be a rational reason, fear was instead considered, in the second possibility given by the court, as an element capable of paralyzing the will of Ms MB, making her incompetent.

From what has been described, I would like to stress that Ms MB was declared incompetent due to an emotional element, such as fear, that cannot be contained within the rational identity of the liberal subject of resistance. My point is that despite the theoretical lines drawn by the court, fear is removed and is cut out from the way the identity of the subject is constructed, namely in liberal terms. If one fears medical interventions, one becomes incompetent to consent and thus one is not allowed a voice regarding one's body. The fact that fear is cut out shows that consent is very much part of the myth of the legal subject and its divisions.

For Ian Kennedy, "fear" is far too loose a term to constitute a mental impairment in the case of Ms MB. Ms MB was not incapable of making a decision; she made one and decided to refuse a needle prick.[35] In his comments on the case, Kennedy also notes the uncertainty in relation to the concept of incapacity as a whole. Incapacity becomes very much related to a decision that has already been decided for one by a sovereign agent, according to criteria of supposed rationality.

> *The two, the patient and the decision, are inextricably intertwined. The trouble is that the moment we admit this, that the content of a patient's decision is relevant in the determination of capacity, we face the problem of autonomy simply being overwhelmed by paternalism. Disagree with your medical adviser and ipso facto you are incompetent, at which point, well-meaning (and they are) others will decide for you.*[36]

Kennedy argues that the fundamental flaw in the current legal approach on consent is that it does not take into account the singular "individuality" of

34 *Re MB* (Caesarean Section) [1997].

35 Ian Kennedy, "Commentary to Re MB (Medical Treatment) Consent: Adult Refusal of Consent, Capacity," *Medical Law Review*, 5 (1997): 317–328, 324.

36 Kennedy, "Commentary," 321.

each person.[37] Respect for autonomy requires that even when someone is incapable of being autonomous, consideration for her individuality is ensured.[38] On the contrary, it is as if the right to consent must be submitted to someone – the doctor – who has unchallengeable power to decide whether one can exercise such a right.[39] Kennedy concludes that law can be accused of paternalism since in this case, despite the principle of autonomy, the final decision is taken *for* rather than *by* Ms MB and the patient's voice is completely disregarded.[40] Although Ms MB consented to the cesarean section, she did not consent to anesthesia by injection; she desired to have a cesarean section to avoid risks for the baby but did not want to endure a needle prick and her reasoning cannot be taken for irrationality leading to incompetence and, therefore, to a forced cesarean section.

For Elizabeth Wicks, the real question is whether the ineffectiveness of consent derives from the patient's incompetence or whether the incompetence derives from the refusal to consent.[41] A refusal to accept doctors' recommendations can easily become evidence of mental incapacity. Therefore, despite the general principle on consent affirmed by the court, the refusal of consent can be easily interpreted as a symptom of unsoundness of mind or, in other words, irrationality or loss of reason, and may become a symptom of incompetence.

Sabine Michalowski has underlined alternative ways that could have been considered before acting in the alleged best interest of the patient.[42] For instance, it could have been possible to weigh the possible risks of anesthesia on the patient and the effects of undermining the patient's autonomy and trust, or to think about alternative forms of anesthesia or to help Ms MB overcome her needle phobia.[43] I could thus conclude by saying that even if the current legal frame assumes that everyone who is adult and competent can theoretically enjoy the possibility of consent and thus speak as an equal agent – this has for instance been confirmed already in the case of *Airedale* and *Re T [1993]*, where the principles of autonomy of the current subject were affirmed – yet the court seems to betray itself in some situations when applying competence and consent principles.[44] Despite its theoretical commitment, in practice law makes consent an incoherent liberal principle.

37 Ian Kennedy, *Treat Me Right* (Oxford: Clarendon Press, 1998).

38 Kennedy, *Treat Me Right*, 57–58.

39 Kennedy, *Treat Me Right.*

40 Kennedy, "Commentary," 323.

41 Elizabeth Wicks, "The Right to Refuse Medical Treatment under the European Convention on Human Rights," *Medical Law Review*, 9 (2001): 17–40.

42 Sabine Michalowski, "Court-Authorised Caesarean Sections – The End of a Trend?" *Modern Law Review*, 62 (1999): 115–127.

43 Michalowski, "Court-Authorised Caesarean Sections."

44 In *Airedale NHS v Bland* (1993), Lord Mustill affirmed that bodily invasions in the course of proper medical treatment stands completely outside criminal law and that the consent of the patient is essential to the propriety of medical treatment. Lord Goff stressed that the principle of self-determination should be given priority, which means that respect must be given to the wishes of the patient of sound mind, however unreasonable their reason. Similarly, in *Re T* (Adult Refusal of

The case of MB exemplifies the problem with consent and indicates how both the subject and the consensual voice are cut and divested of any singularity. In addition, while the court has confirmed that the autonomy of the female patient is not to be reduced by the pregnancy, in practice this clashes with the principles of autonomy and consent of pregnant women. Overall, it seems that consent remains the expression of a general liberal individual, a vertical and standard subject, who speaks and authorizes his own discourse and offers no space for one's singular, unique and vulnerable experience.

The principle of consent, as it is used in legal practice and defined in terms of competence as sound and rational mind, allows for unfair treatment and there is much inconsistency in its application. It is difficult to draw a line between irrational decisions which must be taken into account and irrational decisions that are tantamount to evidence of incompetence.[45] Competence can end up being decided on presumptions and prejudices about people. In addition, the individual capable of consent reflects a general standard of autonomy and reasonableness within the essentialized sexual difference divide.

When it comes to a particular situation, the standard appears to be far away from the needs and the level of vulnerability of one's bodily life. For Alison Young, the body is, for instance, always divided by a regime of sexual difference, always split and doubled, with the feminine body being the one that interrupts the neutral legal mask of the masculine.[46] "Masculinity," Young says, "is the only knowable term of the couplet of sexual difference and this makes [for instance] criminology a struggle to know the unknowable."

> *The problem with criminology is never simply its representations of woman as biologically determined, or as unequal to men, or as innately law-abiding (and therefore uninteresting). Rather, the problem of criminology is one of sexual difference, in that Woman is required to function as an abyss against which masculinity can be comprehended [. . .] Criminology exists in a constant state of struggle with Woman, continually returning her to the closet from where traces of her repression trickle out, demanding attention. Woman is constantly "coming out" through feminist interventions in the discipline, which, in turn, is compelled to return Woman to its closet.*[47]

We can argue that the idea of consent reflects such a masculine subjectivity, grounded in reasonableness and the mind, while sexual difference is essentialized and associated with the feminine traits and the body is cut out, excluded and pushed into the closet. In reality, consent appears to remain impossible in some

Treatment) [1993], all three judges in the Court of Appeal confirmed the principle of autonomy of the competent adult, regardless of the irrationality of the decision and of the circumstances.

45 Wicks, "The Right to Refuse Medical Treatment," 27; Kennedy, "Treat me Right," 336.

46 Alison Young, *Imagining Crime* (London: Sage, 1996).

47 Young, *Imagining Crime*, 46–47.

contexts for a woman and the theory of consent becomes more fragile in the case of incapacitated patients. Women may appear more likely than men to be incapacitated because of pregnancy and other bodily and emotional aspects with which they are associated. Law's refusal to deal with the fear of Ms MB signifies perhaps another fear: that of the legal subject for the female body and desire, which are cut out from the standard rational subjectivity of law.

Adriana Cavarero has also focused on the patriarchal perspective of the legal and political subject and, in particular, on how it produces the erasure of birth and invades women's life.[48] Cavarero explains this by discussing the Greek myth of Demeter in her book *In Spite of Plato*. Demeter represents the act of regeneration, birth and a feminine genealogy, but when her daughter Kore is abducted by Hades, Demeter reacts by no longer generating, threatening sterility. Hades then sends Kore to her mother for certain periods of time during the year and fertility returns during such times.

The male subject in the myth invades the feminine space and appropriates birth, making it death. The coming of sterility signifies that birth, life, are possible only within a reciprocal visibility and contact between a mother and a daughter, within a natural gaze, which is different from the one imposed by masculine normativity and order. In Cavarero's reading of the myth, the natural exchange of gaze between mother and daughter is forcibly interrupted by a male figure and birth becomes a function to be controlled by such a masculine gaze, whereas death is counter-opposed to birth. Such violence, Cavarero explains, is still perpetrated on women.

> *The man snatches the daughter from the mother and takes her to his home. His is the house of unbearable death [. . .] Mother and daughter are now separated from each other and alone. Their gender can no longer take root and spread in their reciprocal gaze. Exiled to a masculine order, Kore is no longer Demeter's daughter, but Hades' wife [. . .] The violence of the myth is not unusual or remote: the codes of modern society still carry it and inscribe it.*[49]

> *This order relocates women in a place that assigns them roles and functions at the service of the fathers' realm. This is a place where women are "shadowy nurses." [. . .] In this place, birthing, rearing, caring for, and feeding children are no longer acts inscribed in a feminine symbolic order capable of embracing them as secret passed down through female genealogies; nor are they aspects of common experience inscribed in a feminist horizon. On the contrary these acts are inscribed in an alien symbolic order that controls them, and paradoxically, identifies them with the nature of the feminine.*[50]

48 Adriana Cavarero, *In Spite of Plato: A Feminist Rewriting of Ancient Philosophy*, trans. Serena Anderlini-D'Onofrio and Aine O'Healy (Cambridge: Polity Press, 1995), 57–90.

49 Cavarero, *In Spite of Plato*, 65.

50 Cavarero, *In Spite of Plato*, 66.

For Cavarero, then, women's body becomes appropriated and controlled by the masculine order and women are constructed in an essentialized way that the masculine order considers necessary. Karin Van Marle underlines precisely Cavarero's refusal to take up and occupy places assigned to both men and women by the patriarchal order and the possibility she sees of recreating a space for politics through the revealing of one's uniqueness.[51]

Patrick Hanafin emphasizes how the model of true logic of the current law is abstract and invasive and how women's role in reproduction and birth is by-passed by the male thinking that characterizes law today.[52] The power of a person to decide is taken from the individual in the name of an abstract idea of life and such an invasion is repeated by law each time a corporeal being comes before the law with her desires and fears. In both Demeter and Ms MB, woman's power of giving birth is erased and framed within a law that is instead obsessed with death.

More specifically, Hanafin underlines how with the myth of Demeter Cavarero suggests that we are inheritors of a masculine Greek classical society characterized, in Cavarero's words, by an ignorance about genetics; a society that is built upon the idea that the father alone has the power to generate and the mother is only a host and the fetus a guest. Hanafin wants to view the law otherwise and for this purpose he turns to Cavarero and the gaze between mother and daughter – a gaze that has been stolen and directed toward the vertical and abstract gaze dominated by the masculine subject. The patriarchal gaze, as Cavarero says, erects itself toward an abstract truth and looks away from others and from inclination.[53]

In reference to FGC, if law's position appears inconsistent and constitutes an expression of a cut subject, divided by a patriarchal and essentialized sexual difference perspective that characterizes the masculine order, for Cavarero winning back both birth and the gaze between mother and daughter means allowing one to speak in one's voice, thus grounding politics in the reciprocal speech of sexed but also unique bodies, in defiance of the patriarchal construction and its vertical mono-valent perspective of reality.

Having shown the limits of legal consent, in the next section I am going to deal briefly with another legal construction, that of bodily integrity.

2.3 Law and the idea of bodily integrity

The idea of consent is in fact linked to the integrity of the body. In the liberal legal ethos, consent allows us to maximize the right to personal integrity by

51 Karin Van Marle, "Introduction: Towards a Politics of Living," in *Sex, Gender, Becoming: Post-Apartheid Reflections*, ed. Van Marle, K. (Pretoria: Pretoria University Law Press, 2006), VII–1.

52 Patrick Hanafin, "A Voice Beyond the Law: Reading Plato, Reading Cavarero," in *Feminist Encounters with Legal Philosophy*, ed. Drakopoulou, M. (Oxon: Routledge, 2014), 9–19. See also: Maria Drakopoulou, "Introduction: Reading Law, Reading Woman," in *Feminist Encounters with Legal Philosophy*, ed. Drakopoulou, M. (Oxon: Routledge, 2014), 1–8.

53 Cavarero, "Recritude."

denying others access to our body. However, the integrity of the body means little when consent is not backed by competence, as in the case of Ms MB discussed in Section 2.2. Bodily integrity is a concept that refers to the inviolability of the material body and it stresses at the same time the importance of individual autonomy and self-determination of one's body. Violation of bodily integrity is an unlawful and unethical infringement. I would like to emphasize here that the idea of the integrity of the body in the legal discourse reflects an imaginary body that is proper and intact, a sort of "intactivism" of the body.

Such legal *intactivism* seems to be employed in biased ways that support liberal principles.[54] A first point to consider is that *intactivism* itself becomes possible for the liberal subject insofar as other subjects are construed as non-intact and mutilated. Juliet Rogers has underlined a similar concept by writing that for law the mutilated subjects-bodies are construed as others, in contrast to the law's proper legal subjects.[55]

The legal Western subject is a non-mutilated subject capable of remaining *intact* and maintaining all the body parts as whole. The wholeness of the legal subject includes also the integrity of the genitals; the body is wholly present, *intact*, proper and non-mutilated. Juliet Rogers has outlined how the UK Parliament changed the Female Circumcision Prohibition Act 1985 into the Female Genital Mutilation Act 2003 so as to emphasize precisely the message of *mutilation*, thus producing the proper legal subject and her (or his?) others.[56] The assumption is that when there is agency, choice, and thus when true consent is possible, women would not submit to such harmful practices. On the contrary, FGC implies an impossibility of consent; it suggests an incapacity and incompetence to make a choice and consent. Law enables precisely such a production of a consent-less victim and a mutilated body.

We can trace the idea of the mutilated body in the symbolic violence deployed by the mono-valent anti-FGC campaign in its efforts to eradicate the practice. During the 1990s, there was a great deal of righteous thinking against the barbarism of FGC and this resulted in the necessary construction of some women as mutilated. For women who have undergone the practice, this might have caused conflicting messages regarding one's body and sexuality and internal struggles with respect to the integrity and *intactivism* of the body proclaimed by law. In law, FGC stands as a priori monolithic evidence for sexual dysfunctions and repression of women. One's singularity is made invisible as one is made to feel lacking in legal integrity and one feels the imposition of a body as proper and normative.

54 For legal intactivism, I intend the insistence of the law on the concept of the integrity of the body. The idea of the integrity of the body in the legal discourse reflects an imaginary body that is proper and intact, a sort of "intactivism" of the body, or legal body intactivism.

55 Juliet Rogers, "Flesh Made Law: The Economics of Female Genital Mutilation Legislation," in *International Law and Its Others*, ed. Orford, A. (Cambridge: Cambridge University Press, 2006), 197–220.

56 Rogers, "Flesh Made Law."

Similarly, Renata Salecl suggests that the modern idea of human rights that advocates bodily integrity is an expression of the lack of integrity, of a deep cut within our subjectivity, that cannot be resolved by symbolic evocation.[57] In other words, human rights proclaim respect for bodily integrity precisely because humans do not enjoy bodily integrity, since the body is culturally inscribed.

> *The modern idea of human rights is based on the Kantian subject. And, especially in the case of human rights, we usually invoke the idea of respect. Human rights concern some parts of the subject's inner freedom, which the community or other people have no rights to violate. (And here freedom is also meant as protection of the subject's bodily integrity. From this perspective, those who criticize clitoridectomy rightly point out that this practice contradicts the idea of human rights) [. . .] The inner freedom of the subject that human rights protect concerns nothing other than the lack that marks the subject when he or she becomes a speaking being. And when we respect the bodily integrity of the subject, this actually means that we avert our gaze from the fact that the subject actually does not have a naturally given bodily integrity, since this integrity comes into being only when the subject undergoes symbolic castration.*[58]

A second point to be emphasized here is that the notion of the legal integrity of the body and its *intactivism* becomes more paradoxical in relation to the very Western surgical modification of the body for non-medical reasons; that is, cosmetic surgery.[59] In cosmetic surgery, people often modify their bodies lawfully through expensive and often health-damaging interventions to appear beautiful and comply with Western cultural and social standards – a practice that is not perceived to be contradictory to the idea of the integrity of the body.

In this respect, Andrew Sharpe explains how surgical interferences with the body can either discursively restore the body to its integrity or mutilate its integrity, and that there are different interpretations of integrity.[60] In some cases of manipulation of the body, as in cosmetic surgery, the body is not seen as lacking integrity but rather as achieving integrity. Despite the fact that the body is manipulated, cut, wounded and physically modified, even in irreversible ways, the body does not seem to be losing its integrity, but rather improving it. In this case, the subject is perceived through a liberal lens, an authorial subject backed by the law, an agent with autonomy that is able to consent to surgical modifications of her body.

In such cases, modifications through surgical operations are constructed as a path to bodily integrity, and bodily modifications become a tool for normalizing one's own body, whereas in the case of FGC, manipulation of the body does not

57 Salecl, "Cut in the Body."

58 Salecl, "Cut in the Body," 148, 149.

59 Susan Orbach, *Bodies* (London: Profile Books, 2009).

60 Andrew Sharpe, *Transgender Jurisprudence: Dysphoric Bodies of Law* (London: Cavendish, 2002).

reflect dominant Western views of the proper intact body and the principle of autonomy appears not to be involved. As a result, the surgical intervention of FGC is considered as mutilating and destroying the integrity of the body. I think that those biases and paradoxes in the construction of integrity show that in both accounts of the body, cosmetic surgery and FGC, the body is treated as an idea and in relation to a standard; it is not one's unique body but something provisional, immaterial, tractable and thus metaphysical. In both cases, where notions of consent and integrity are at play, the body is treated as general and without a voice. There is no concern for one's voice and awareness; instead the body is perceived only through rules and discursive identity constructions.

In the case law of Ms MB, the cesarean cut was seen as necessary from the liberal point of view, in the sense of achieving the legal norm and safeguarding the life of the baby. It was for the law to decide how to perform the cesarean cut on her body. In relation to FGC, the body is also understood from the point of view of the liberal subject as already lacking integrity and needing to conform to the standard of the intact body of law and of the liberal subject itself. Thus, both the concept of integrity and that of consent contain the paradox of a subject constructed in a certain way where the body has been excluded and cut out, to be included only in terms of an abstract, intact body.

In the remaining part of the chapter, I will revolve the discussion around the need for speaking in one's voice, showcasing my argument by applying it to FGC. I will also connect one's voice to an opening of ambivalence, which opposes the understanding that the cuts on the body are operated by the legal principles of consent and integrity of the body. The legal principles proceed in fact through standards. In particular, in the next section, I will discuss FGC in relation to the subject as it has been theorized by John Rawls and Judith Butler.

2.4 The cut in relation to the subject

Despite its liberal principles of autonomy, consent and integrity, in ruling a priori FGC to be unlawful, law appears to disconfirm the significance of agency and its legal subject of resistance does not recognize women who have undergone FGC as agents who negotiate their lives creatively, resisting sovereign discourses under various constraints and in some ways expressing themselves. Yet it is important to view actions through agency. Agency and the capacity of a selfhood to act upon one's own circumstances are central in understanding the reasons why women decide to undergo the operation despite its negative health consequences and suffering.

In my opinion, focusing on women's agency, when dealing with FGC, does not deny the limits within which a decision could have been made; neither does it minimize the damage which accompanies certain decisions, but it allows women to keep a voice. In this section, I will start by presenting the reasons why some women consent to the modification of their bodies through FGC. This will allow an account of women's agency and work toward an understanding of the practice of FGC through ambivalence. It is my belief that the shift from identity thinking toward one's voice takes place precisely through ambivalence.

Various cultural justifications are reported to be the reason for the choice of FGC, such as increased marriageability within one's community, protecting virginity, discouraging female promiscuity, making women faithful, purification of the genitalia, belief that the female genitalia is ugly and needs to be trimmed, feeling pride in having made it clean and having gone through suffering without screaming, emphasizing women's maternal qualities rather than sexuality, and showing compliance with other religious beliefs.[61] In some narratives, FGC is believed to be a ritual that enriches women, providing them with the capacity to exercise self-control, take charge of their sexual desires against scarce resources and economic circumstances and bring into play power in daily affairs.[62]

Patriarchy alone would not explain the practice of FGC and women's persistence in practicing it. As Renata Salecl argues, FGC cannot be adduced solely to patriarchy, given that women are active agents in keeping the ritual.

> *The problem is not simply that women live in patriarchal societies in which they have no power to express their disagreement with rituals. Many cultures that perform clitoridectomy are not classical patriarchies – in some cultures men are even perceived as quite powerless and considerable authority is in the hands of older women, who are cherished as father-like figures and as guardian of traditions, which is why they are entrusted with the task of carrying out clitoridectomies.*[63]

Consequently, women do not appear to be passive victims of discursive traditions. Rather, they seem to be able to actively engage with cultural discourses. What women say in support of FGC often expresses autonomy, agency and conduct that shows maintenance of conventions but also personhood, kinship identification, loyalty, bonding and solidarity; that is, values and choices that are different from autonomy, consent and the integrity of the body in law.[64]

As a consequence, some women might perceive FGC in terms of benefits rather than as a violation of rights and, thus, the criminalization of the law might have little legitimacy among them.[65] Therefore, if from the Western perspective

61 Guyo Jaldesa, Ian Askew, Caroline Njue and Monica Wanjiru, "Female Genital Cutting Among the Somali of Kenya and Management of its Complications," *USAID* (2005); Rogaia Mustafa Abusharaf, "Virtuous Cuts: Female Genital Circumcision in an African Ontology," *differences: A Journal of Feminist Cultural Studies*, 12(1) (2001): 112–140.

62 Abusharaf, "Virtuous Cuts."

63 Salecl, "Cut in the Body," 144.

64 Abusharaf, "Virtuous Cuts."

65 As reported, for instance in the UK there are adult women who ask to be re-infibulated after childbirth even if this is illegal. In addition, the FGC criminalization might also result in culture clash and isolation among minority groups who find themselves striving to balance their different cultural identities and subjectivity with realities of Western citizenship and subjectivity. See on

FGC is an act that mutilates women's bodily integrity and is thus in violation of law and human rights, for those who embrace FGC the absence of it signifies a lack of values.[66] Renata Salecl explains the ambivalent feelings about FGC of people who practice it in the West:

> *From a Western point of view, it is shocking that clitoridectomies are performed in democratic societies. It is also surprising that the development of capitalism in third world countries has not contributed to its extinction; on the contrary, in some countries this practice has become even more widespread in recent years. How can we explain this fact? Women from ethnic groups that practice clitoridectomy usually claim that it forms part of their ethnic identity and has been performed for generations; and that by continuing to practice the ritual they are essentially contributing to the survival of their community's traditions. When members of such ethnic groups migrate to the West, they insist on their right to preserve their identity by means of clitoridectomy.*[67]

For Renata Salecl, the dilemma of why women support the ritual has to do primarily with the position of the subject within culture and the community and the identity discourses that are employed.[68] Salecl compares the current situation of FGC with some forms of contemporary body art and finds similarities between the cut in the body performed by some artists and the cut of FGC. In some forms of contemporary body art, the body is considered as the ultimate point of the subject's identity, *the only remaining realm over which an individual has retained power.*[69] Through surgery, one can transform one's body into language as the flesh becomes word, one can impose control over one's body and resist dominant ideologies.

For instance, the French artist Orlan, known for her work with plastic surgery, aims at reinventing herself through cuts on the body, celebrating and accepting difference and fighting against discrimination.[70] In particular, she claims that her body transformation increases her body power and does not diminish it. She has undergone several surgical operations on her body because she believes that cutting her body is a powerful work of art.

> *No, my goal was to be different, strong; to sculpt my own body to reinvent the self. It is all about being different and creating a clash with society because of that. I tried to use surgery not to better myself or become a younger version of myself, but to work on the concept of image and surgery the other way around.*[71]

this: Comfort Momoh, a specialist midwife in the field of FGC and public health who has reported on women giving birth in the UK and then asking to be re-infibulated – www.forwarduk.org.uk.

66 Salecl, "Cut in the Body," 144–147.

67 Salecl, "Cut in the Body," 142.

68 Salecl, "Cut in the Body," 155.

69 Salecl, "Cut in the Body," 160.

70 Stuart Jeffries, "Orlan's Art of Sex and Surgery," *theguardian.com* (1 July 2009).

71 Jeffries "Orlan's Art of Sex and Surgery."

Salecl seems to suggest that we can approach in a similar way adult women who insist on undergoing FGC, since they claim they become actually empowered by the cut. Thus, for Salecl, it seems that both body artists who cut their body and women who decide to undergo FGC attempt to challenge a stable identity desired by the authority – the cut in the body challenges precisely the idea of an identity in the body. Both artists of the body and women who undergo FGC try to find in the body some "reality," something that can be manipulated from inside oneself. Indeed, Salecl explains how, for Orlan, behind the search for meaning in the cut what remains constant is the voice, the voice as a drive for action, the voice as "real" in the performance.

> *The voice [. . .] always undermines the subject's identity. Orlan tries to show with her art how she can play with her identity, but her voice nonetheless remains the real, what is in her more than herself (her plastic self).*[72]

Thus one's voice and one's *who-ness* can be seen beyond the performance of the cut and any identity discourse that the cut wants to achieve. The voice, as Salecl says, represents the *real* or, we can say in Cavarero's words, one's unique voice.

Any decision to cut one's body presents, then, complex and ambivalent meanings rather than fixed, general and mono-valent readings. Any apparent absence of resistance needs to be approached skeptically rather than in terms of a moral perspective. Consequently, there appears to be a discrepancy between the way law resists FGC, denying consent and perceiving the body as lacking integrity, and the way in which some women relate to FGC, through agency and with the attempt to have a voice. While law requires women to accept as dominant identity the rationally consenting patient who wants to remain intact, a woman may want, as Salecl suggests, to insist on cutting and manipulating her own body so as to break with fixed constructions of dominant identities.

The legal approach also appears to follow standards of reasonableness through consent and the principle of integrity which apply unequally to FGC and cosmetic surgery. Where it concerns FGC, law excludes women's agency for reasons of gender subordination. Thus law denies consent in relation to the integrity of the body. It could be argued that the reasonableness and the paternalism of the legal position resembles the subject as theorized by John Rawls.[73] In *A Theory of Justice* Rawls contextualizes individuals within an *original position*. The original position is a hypothetical situation that is supposed to replace the state of nature. In the original position choice is made through a *veil of ignorance*, which deprives people of information, thus forcing people to select in an impartial and rational way.[74] For Rawls, the condition of *tabula rasa* in the

72 Salecl, "Cut in the Body," 162, 163.

73 John Rawls, *A Theory of Justice* (Cambridge: Harvard University Press, 1971).

74 Rawls, *A Theory of Justice*, 420.

original position allows people to develop rational plans, which is what is good for people themselves.

People's happiness depends upon their capacity to follow through those rational plans. On the contrary any desire that may impede rational plans from being accomplished becomes supported by irrational and incorrect beliefs. Thus Rawls suggests that there is something false about those desires, precisely because they make rational plans impossible. He writes in chapter VII:

> *[K]eeping in mind that our overall aim is to carry out a rational plan (or subplan), it is clear that some features of desires make doing this impossible [. . .] The same thing holds for desires that depend upon our having incorrect beliefs [. . .] Nevertheless, the desires that these beliefs support are irrational to the degree that the falsehood of these beliefs makes it impossible to execute the plan, or prevents superior plans from being adopted. [. . .] Awareness of the genesis of our wants can often make it perfectly clear to us that we really do desire certain things more than others. As some aims seem less important in the face of critical scrutiny, or even lose their appeal entirely, others may assume an assured prominence that provides sufficient grounds for choice.*[75]

Seen from Rawls' perspective, the rational plan of Ms MB fails because her irrational desires and fears derive from incorrect and irrational beliefs. The rules of law and justice assume an accurate knowledge of the subject's wants, in the case of Ms MB having her baby delivered healthily. Doctors and judges are thus able to ensure grounds for choice.

Following his own theorizing of an *original position* where people are blindfolded with a *veil of ignorance* and are assumed not to know their own good, Rawls' strategy consists of focusing on certain rational principles to orient people in their decision-making, despite their fears or desires. Yet we could argue that similarly to law's attitude to women who undergo FGC (being perceived as consent-less and lacking integrity), Rawls' conception is shown to be equally paternalistic, assuming people's needs without listening to their voices; even more, the law seems to be legitimized to choose on behalf of those who are unable to decide rationally.

Critical legal scholars Costas Douzinas and Adam Gearey have underlined the *reflective equilibrium* that results in such a way of theorizing.[76]

> *[Reflective equilibrium] consists in selecting some of our strongest moral convictions and trying to discover the most consistent set of principles that can justify them. This set is then refined and adjusted to match and explain other beliefs and intuitions, some of which are revised or abandoned in the process if they are*

75 Rawls, *A Theory of Justice*, 420.

76 Costas Douzinas and Adam Gearey, *Critical Jurisprudence: The Political Philosophy of Justice* (Oxford: Hart Publishing, 2005), 128.

> *found to be distorted or irregular [. . .] In these "well-ordered" societies, law and the institutions impose their sense of justice on people.*[77]

It could be argued that in the liberalism of John Rawls, law exercises authority over its citizens. If one fails to obey or to choose rightly, law dictates the right choice. And this does not conflict with human freedom and autonomy. Authority is justified, in that one has in some ways given one's tacit consent to it a priori, and thus the value of human life is constrained by the principles of justice.[78] One's voice must submit to the general principles of justice and to rational plans already decided upon as the good choices for people. We can see how the individual in Rawls reflects a subject construed totally on the rational side of the human possibility that marks the sexual difference divide. Under Rawls' theory, FGC would also be deemed impossible because it is not in accord with individuals' (supposedly) rational plans and with the principles of justice in legal liberalism.

On the contrary, for Salecl there is now a different relation of the subject toward the symbolic order.[79] The subject returns to rituals such as FGC, or other forms of body cuts and surgeries, to resist paternalistic impositions of identities because individuals' understanding of authority has changed, with the latter being seen as just a fiction.[80] Under Rawls or current legal liberalism and the modern subject, those who do not identify with authority are misguided by incorrect knowledge, considered perhaps incompetent or psychotic. However, contemporary approaches to body cuts suggest that people may be searching for imaginary identity roles and may want to change their body, seeing in the inscription of the body a way to re-establish the lost authority of their own voices, to resist and to guarantee an alternative to dominant forms of identity.[81]

Judith Butler offers some further reflections on such a struggle of the subject.[82] According to Butler, the subject acknowledges itself to be a construed fictitious self that has to survive in the necessary authority of the symbolic order out of which it emerges. The Butlerian subject does not believe in authority and only repeats and recites identities and bodily inscriptions. If the subject merely does this, repeating and reciting roles, then the subject does not accept the constructed identities but merely performs them. Performativity helps the subject to question identities and roles and search for more suitable means of representation.

Performativity breaks with the gender identity divide because it makes gender a simple repetition of acts and un-grounds the ground of its identity. Transformation and the breaking of tradition and fixed identity schemes are fulfilled by the

77 Douzinas and Gearey, *Critical Jurisprudence*, 128.
78 John Simmons, "Tacit Consent and Political Obligation," *Philosophy and Public Affairs*, 5 (1976): 247–291.
79 Salecl, "Cut in the Body," 159, 167.
80 Salecl, "Cut in the Body."
81 Salecl, "Cut in the Body," 153.
82 Judith Butler, *Gender Trouble: Feminism and the Subversion of Identity* (New York: Routledge, 1990).

acts of repetition of the tradition itself, since the latter unfolds the fictitious construction of the authority and reveals its points of failure. The repetition of the rituals or of legal body *intactivism*, like the repetition of gender, reveal in Butler's terms the regulatory authority of culture and law over the body and cause it to lose its fixed identity meaning.[83]

When the subject repeats and questions authority and norms, she questions simultaneously herself and her subject formation that passes through the same authority and norms. Recognition always implies recognition of another, which means that to know herself the subject must exist outside herself in an ecstatic process of recognition. In this context, one can clearly see Butler's Hegelian roots and can thus understand better the process of repetition of rituals and body cuts in relation to identity formation. In *Giving an Account of Oneself*, Butler writes:

> *The norms by which I recognize another or, indeed, myself are not mine alone. They function to the extent that they are social, exceeding every dyadic exchange that they condition.*[84]
>
> *Other readings of Hegel, however, insist that the relation to the other is ecstatic, that the I repeatedly find itself outside itself, and that nothing can put an end to the repeated upsurge of this exteriority that is, paradoxically, my own.*[85]

Applying Butler's perspective to women who insist on FGC, this could be understood as a way to repeat the cut on the body, to perform it and search for identities that oppose the normative symbolic order. Such a performance might transform the normative legal identity by uncovering its hidden masculinist approach, looking for new bodily expressions and performing new acts. In this sense, FGC would also question the truth of any newly formed identity and thus allow a transformation of the self.

2.5 One's corporeal voice

I argue for one's voice as a form of resistance that begins with oneself and one's corporeal body, a singular experience and awareness of oneself when one is not yet structured into subjectivity. As Salecl suggested, one's voice shows the "real" of one's body, undermining any performance of identity, any *what* or construction on the body. One could argue that the cutting of the body establishes a membership by tying one wounded body to another, leading to an ordering that equalizes one body with another. An identity discourse is tantamount to disconnection and cutting oneself from one's body. Forms of body cuts, as Salecl suggests, respond precisely to a search for new forms of identity,

83 Butler, *Gender Trouble*, 192.
84 Judith Butler, *Giving an Account of Oneself* (New York: Fordham University Press, 2005), 24.
85 Butler, *Giving an Account of Oneself*, 27–28.

where the involvement of the body testifies to the need to reach a "real" beyond identity.[86]

Law also treats the body as general and in terms of identity through principles such as consent and integrity, where one is forced to act within the just principles of liberalism. For instance, in the case of Ms MB, her body was not treated as singular, her voice was not heard and she was dealt with as part of a collective identity. It was decided that it was good for her, her baby and the community that her body underwent a cesarean section enabled by injection. It was as if her body was not material and corporeal but imagined by the law of the community, a body turned over to the imagination of others. Women's bodies that undergo FGC are perceived as a generic body by the law, and FGC is a priori made unlawful, with bodies and selves being constructed as consent-less and lacking integrity. The legal subject of resistance can only resist within its cut construction and mono-valent understanding of events.

The voice instead reverses the way of resistance by beginning within one's singularity and corporeality. The voice reconciles the cracks and fractures of the legal subjectivity constituted through the paradoxes of consent and integrity, as well as through the essentialized sexual difference divide. Both the construction of consent and the integrity of the body reflect in fact the male monopoly of the production of knowledge and construction of subjectivity. In "Disobedience Subjectively Speaking," Loizidou underlines a similar type of resistance, one operated through actions and the body of one as singular, noting also how disobedience and resistance cannot be articulated within the limits of law.[87] Yet, in arguing this, Loizidou criticizes the way civil disobedience of a singular embodied subjectivity might have been dismissed by Arendt. According to Loizidou, in her essay "Civil Disobedience" Arendt appears to disregard the political valence of a singular subjective experience, since, for Arendt, subjective experience often serves particularistic interests.[88] In "Civil Disobedience," as Loizidou notes, Arendt seems to emphasize only a form of collective resistance made by a plurality of singularities, which comes together in the sharing of the world of politics. In addition, in the essay Arendt appears also to consider law as just and objective.

On the contrary, what emerges from Cavarero and her interpretation of Arendt is that the voice signifies a singular experience of disobedience and resistance which always occurs in relation to the plurality of voices that constitute the community. As has been argued in Chapter I, Cavarero's focus on the voice is rooted in Arendt's work and both Arendt and Cavarero theorize resistance through the notions of uniqueness and plurality.

86 Salecl, "Cut in the Body."

87 Elena Loizidou, "Disobedience Subjectively Speaking," in *Disobedience: Concept and Practice*, ed. Loizidou, E. (Oxon: Routledge, 2013), 108–124.

88 Loizidou, "Disobedience Subjectively Speaking"; Hannah Arendt, "Civil Disobedience," in *Crisis of the Republic: Lying in Politics*, ed. Arendt, H. (Harmondsworth: Penguin Books, 1973), 49–102.

Despite contradictions in some of Arendt's writings, both Cavarero and Arendt are interested in a core theoretical point: one's uniqueness; that is, the *who one is* rather than the *what*. The *who* is precisely the question that allows an opening for the voice.[89] The *what-ness* represents instead the subject of identities and social roles, constructed with reference to a standard and as belonging or membership.

The voice resists any manipulation of the body as alienation from one's body or strategies to achieve new identities, and sustains instead actions that are decided from an awareness of oneself, always exposed to others, always touching upon one's own and another's vulnerability. Indeed, speaking in one's voice connects one to one's vulnerability and that of others. Thus through speaking in one's voice one would approach one's body as connection rather than disconnection. One's voice puts forward *who speaks*, the flesh of her throat, the passage of the air in her throat, the vibration, the saliva, and it does this by means of exposure. All this unique corporeality undermines any discourse on identity and subjectivity.

> *The voice, which is embodied in the plurality of voices, always puts forward first of all the who of saying. As a faithful testimony to the uniqueness of the one who emits it (as Calvino says) "from a throat of flesh," the voice not only dethrones the "subject" of traditional metaphysics, but it renders this subject ridiculous.*[90]

And when the voice meets the plurality of voices, the sense of plurality reveals a different sense of the community; not a community as a standard, as a dominant identity everyone needs to be made equal to, but rather a community as relationality of corporeal selves. This approach of one's voice overcomes the fictitious binding together of liberal individuals as it appears in Rawls' theory and in the current legal subject of resistance:

> *The voice not only announces this relation, but it announces it as corporeal, material, and rooted in the always embodied singularity of an existent that convokes the other with the rhythmic and sonorous breath of his or her mouth. Actively and reciprocally communicating their uniqueness, the speakers above all make heard a mutual dependence on a voice that is invocation, no longer autonomous or self-sufficient individuals in search of something that binds them, but already "tied" (to use Nancy's term) by an acoustic dialogue that takes its cadence from the very rhythm of breath. Their logos is oriented toward resonance, rather than toward understanding.*[91]

89 Adriana Cavarero, *For More Than One Voice: Toward a Philosophy of Vocal Expression*, trans. Paul Kottman (Stanford: Stanford University Press, 2005).

90 Cavarero, *For More Than One Voice*, 30.

91 Cavarero, *For More Than One Voice*, 200.

The voice reflects a selfhood that is inclined, able to bend toward others in relationality. Inclination in Cavarero is intended as the structural configuration of ourselves that overcomes the dualism of both verticality and horizontality in thinking about the subject.[92]

> *What we are focusing on, in fact, is the inclined posture of an "I" that leans out of itself, that is to say, the inclined line that constitutes the axis of the relational geometry within this framework. In substance, within this framework equally freed from verticality and horizontality, "mother" is therefore simply the name of a necessary configuration, an indispensable inclination.*[93]

Such an account of oneself and the body breaks away from a notion of consent and integrity of the body that depends on the rationality of the normative standard subject. Rather, consent and integrity would mean reconnection with one's vulnerability and the body and with the vulnerability of others around us. The awareness of my body and of its physical sensations, from which my voice springs, can be said to represent a new form of awareness that does not arise from the discursive rational mind.

By approaching reality through one's voice and an ontology of inclination and relationality, one has the opportunity to experience oneself as a body in relation to other bodies. My mind inhabits my body and it is important to start with my body since my body allows me to be alive, to be situated in the world. From the voice rather than language, one can have a different sense of reality and perform different actions. Firstly, one can connect to one's body, resist sovereign impositions and then one can connect to others. There are always many possibilities and different responses and actions. But responding needs the re-establishing of the roots of my mind in my unique corporeal body and its world of experience.

For a woman who has undergone FGC or has modified her body through other types of cuts for non-medical reasons, a voice as such means that one speaks with one's living selfhood, one's throat, chest, with the air passing through one's body, with vibrations of sound in the throat, saliva, one's body in flesh and blood, and one acts by being aware of the vulnerability of oneself and others. What matters for the voice is precisely what generally is not perceived as significant in the discursive narratives of identity and subjectivity: the vital and non-ruled uniqueness of one. There is thus a suspension and break from the cut, the fragmented imagination of the vertical subjectivity of law, a subject disconnected from the body; rather, instead of verticality one's voice implies inclination. Moreover, the ontology of one's voice brings about ambivalence in the understanding of events, which allows one's voice to bring together mind and body.

92 Cavarero, "Recritude," 233.
93 Cavarero, "Recritude," 233.

Howard Caygill, for instance, indicates that it is necessary to approach an alleged near-zero condition of resistance with skepticism and ambivalence.[94] In this respect, Caygill points out how the human capacity to resist survived even the experience of total domination.[95] During the Nazi occupation, there was resistance even without engaging with the organized forms of resistance.[96] Rejecting Arendt's questioning of the absence of Jewish resistance against Nazism in her book *Eichmann in Jerusalem*, Caygill argues that such an argument would imply a symptomatic absence of a theory of resistance in Arendt herself.[97]

Taking a different path from Loizidou's analysis of Arendt's conceptualization of civil disobedience, Caygill concludes that, in Arendt, resistance against total domination can be located in the individual conscience, in the *who-ness* and spontaneity.[98] Caygill argues that during Eichmann's trial, Arendt appeared to emphasize the singular actions of a Jewish person who actively resisted the Germans, as opposed to the absence of resistance by the Jewish people as a group.[99]

Caygill invites ambivalence in the understanding of events and notes how the actions of such a singular person, cited by Arendt, needs to be located within a plurality of collective resistance. His actions of disobedience were possible given the contribution of a collective capacity to resist of many other Jewish people. In her theory of resistance, for Caygill, Arendt misses the ambivalence through which events can be understood; she assumes exceptions to be resistance, rather than looking for processes of defiance and considering obedience to be the normative exception.[100]

A similar understanding takes place when speaking in one's voice. Speaking in one's voice allows a perception through ambivalence, through the ontology of inclination, the agentic intention behind an event; furthermore, it allows one's defiance of body disconnection and discursive cuts and transforms collective resistance into a polyphonic community of voices. One's voice is capable of producing not only singular moments of rupture and suspension, but also collective actions of defiance against cut subjectivities and identities.

2.6 The ambivalence in the cut

The discourse of ambivalence produces a different approach to FGC. The focus on the voice opposes the dismissal of women's agency in the name of gendered subordination and offers a more critical and strategic engagement with FGC that

94 Howard Caygill, *On Resistance: A Philosophy of Defiance* (London: Bloomsbury, 2013), 158–165.
95 Caygill, *On Resistance*, 158–165.
96 Caygill, *On Resistance*, 158–165.
97 Hannah Arendt, *Eichmann in Jerusalem: A Report on the Banality of Evil* (London: Penguin Books, 1994).
98 Caygill, *On Resistance*, 158–165.
99 Caygill, *On Resistance*, 158–165.
100 Caygill, *On Resistance*, 158–165.

adopts ambivalence instead of self-righteousness and certainties. Therefore, while the practice of female genital cutting has been generally seen by Western discourses in its negative mono-valences (FGC has been perceived by feminists and Western law as the reflection of patriarchal power, a systematic way of controlling women's body, the expression of the negative male desire to dominate, keep women's body intact and control entrance to and exit from the body), the focus on the voice reverses such an approach since the body is one's body, not the general and rational body but changeable and alive.

Anthropologists have also drawn attention to the necessity of maintaining a relativist attitude toward genital cuts, suggesting that difficulties in discussing genital cutting have stemmed from mono-valent understandings of it.[101] Genital cutting has been seen to be essentially about sex or women's control, stressing castration and subordination and associating women of other countries with negative stereotypes. However, an ambivalent approach might downplay the physical, sexual and psychological damage cited by opponents of the FGC practice and facilitate instead a cross-cultural dialog that requires neither its condemnation nor its acceptance. Moreover, such an anthropological approach indicates that ambivalence in the understanding of events may be of help.[102]

Approaching FGC in terms of negative mono-valence has not allowed much space for resistance. The practice of wounding and cutting the female genitals might carry, in some ways, positive ambivalence in itself, not only in terms of achieving new identities that can possibly resist those that are dominant, but also in the sense of producing a different psychological perspective and point of view. In respect to the latter point, Bruno Bettelheim has approached FGC through a psychological perspective that has underlined some positive ambivalence in the practice itself.[103]

Bettelheim argues that the basis of the cut and wound is a male envy of the female genital apparatus and of what the reproductive female functions might hide. In other words, he argues for a fundamental male envy and fascination for female genital and bodily functions. He contests that too much attention has been paid to destructive elements in relation to FGC, as well as to the damage that the practice provokes to the genitals. Discourses on the cut have chosen to focus mainly on the idea of destruction of life; it is then no surprise that the law has ruled a priori inadmissibility of consent and of bodily integrity for women that choose to undergo the practice.[104]

Bettelheim reverses this type of thinking and considers the cut as the result of some constructive desire, such as the male desire to participate in women's

101 Janice Boddy, "Gender Crusade: The Female Circumcision Controversy in Cultural Perspective," in *Transcultural Bodies. Female Genital Cutting in Global Context*, eds Hernlund, Y. and Shell-Duncan, B. (London: Rutgers University Press, 2007), 46–66.

102 Boddy, "Gender Crusade."

103 Bettelheim, *Symbolic Wounds*; see also Marie Bonaparte, *Notes on Excision* (New York: International University Press, 1950).

104 Bettelheim, *Symbolic Wounds*.

pregnancy and in new life. Rather than interpreting it as a sign of the man's fear and dislike of the clitoris and of men's control of the vagina, Bettelheim suggests another possible psychological origin of the practice; that is, a deep human need of procreative functions, man's desire to make women bleed, to participate in the bleeding of women and wanting to acquire similar functions to those of women.[105]

The cut is seen then as a desire to participate in the activities and enjoyments that normally belong to the other sex. Such a different understanding projects the bodily cut to a new life rather than toward the destruction of it and opens up the ambivalence of the cut. Bettelheim's perspective shows that the male desire does not aim necessarily at acquiring, possessing or enjoying an object but that it can aim also at a subjective trait; the focus is on "to be" rather than on "to have." His perspective suggests that at the root of the cut of the female genitals might be something quite different than patriarchal control of female sexuality, for example a desire to participate. The cut might originate not by intents and emotions of subordination, exclusions and hates but rather from the wish to help, replace and be another. This is confirmed also by anthropological studies:

> *In drawing attention to the importance of masculine envy of female reproductive activity and sexual functions, Bettelheim does much more than merely indicate another important element which must be noted. He shows that if this envy is to be systematically taken into account, some drastic revisions are necessary in psychoanalytic interpretations of circumcision, subincision and puberty rites.*[106]

Such a reading of FGC, while not excluding the limits of the cut, also calls for other ways of approaching, understanding and dealing with the cuts. FGC may remain a non- desirable practice; nevertheless, Bettelheim stresses its positive rather than negative ends and allows the possibility of newness in liberating the practice from past negative mono-valence and opening it up to the possibility of one's voice. Confronting the physical modification of genitals with a positive ambivalence, along with listening to one's voice as awareness of one's vulnerability and that of others, might produce a different approach to the cut that escapes sovereign impositions of universal truth and promotes newness from inside, thus allowing people to be confident of themselves, of their bodily truth, to speak their own experiences and break the silence of taboos or other cultural and normative conditioning.

Through ambivalence and one's voice, it is possible to resist the metaphysical construction of the cut that exists before the body (body as the imaginary product of a community, body as an idea). This book argues for a resistance that begins from within, from the awareness of one's body as singular, corporeal and vulnerable. The ultimate goal is thus not to metabolize the sovereignty of imposed

105 Bettelheim, *Symbolic Wounds.*

106 David M. Schneider, "Book Review: Symbolic Wounds. Puberty and the Envious Male by Bruno Bettelheim," *American Anthropologist* 57(2) (1955), 390–391, 390.

discourses or accommodate oneself to norms. Rather, it is to break the violent cycle of foreign discourses through one's voice.

Having said that, we can take into consideration the ambivalence of contemporary body art. In contemporary body art, the subject is allowed to cut the body as an artistic practice, because people are seen today as subjects who can freely choose their own identity and resist dominant ones. Yet this is not just creation of new subjective identities but also creation of a bodily and corporeal identity through cuts in the body. As outlined by Salecl, the fact that the body becomes the site of resistance indicates a mistrust for mere words and for everything changeable and a desire to see what is behind, touching the real beyond the symbolic.[107]

> *The cut in the body thus appears as an escape from the imaginary simulacra that dominate our society. Young people usually explain their obsession with tattooing and body piercing as a way to escape the pressures of the dominant fashion industry. The media constantly bombard them with images of beauty, and one of the ways to oppose this enforced identification is to perform a real action – to mark the body in a way that cannot be changed [. . .] The body does appear as the ultimate point of the subject's identity.*[108]

Consequently, together with a search for new identities, a cut in the body means also going back to one's body. For Salecl, behind this search for meanings one's voice remains constant as the drive and the "real" that stays the same throughout the performances.

> *For Orlan, what is finally unchangeable is the voice. With the help of her voice, she tries to provide explanations for her art: she thus reads from theoretical texts as her face is cut and comments on the surgical procedure. But behind this search for meaning for her changeable face, her voice remains constant. Orlan's voice is the drive, i.e. the real, that stays the same throughout her performances.*[109]

Conclusion

In this chapter, I have tried to reflect on a resistance offered by the voice in relation to FGC. Cuts, such as in the case of FGC, are ruled unlawful by law and FGC is thus made an impossible choice. Consent, as a way to have a voice within the law, is not allowed when one decides to undergo FGC and the principle of the integrity of the body constructs women who have undergone FGC as lacking it and as mutilated bodies in need of help. Both the case law of Ms MB and

107 Salecl, "Cut in the Body," 152.
108 Salecl, "Cut in the Body," 160.
109 Salecl, "Cut in the Body," 162.

Cavarero's myth of Demeter show how law has appropriated a masculine gaze upon the body and how the body is treated as a norm, a generality and understood through an essentialized sexual difference perspective.

It is in Rawls' theory that one can find an explanation of the position of law with reference to FGC. In Rawls, rational plans are supposed to override any human desire. What counts is the principle of the just, whereas people are construed within the condition of the veil of ignorance. The subject of Rawls shows similarity with the "erectus" and vertical subject explained by Cavarero that stands upright looking toward the good and the just and has vertical contacts within a multiplicity of other "erectus" and vertical subjects.[110] Such a subject approaches events with a mono-valent attitude, since he lives life solipsistically and autonomously.

Unlike Rawls, Butler offers a perspective that has some points in common with Salecl's position in relation to contemporary streams of body art. Salecl mentions the French artist Orlan who has herself undergone several body cuts in search of new identities that resist dominant identities.[111] Those forms of body art, where the body is tattooed, pierced or literally cut, suggest a way to resist the fictitious identity required by authority. Authority is radically questioned and writing on the body represents a search for new identity.[112] Similarly, for Butler, the subject is essentially a questioning subject that is critical of the fiction of identity and norms and seeks new ways of performing reality and thus new identities in a continuum. Yet one's voice can constitute a form of resistance that suspends the level of identity and reaches one's body and one's awareness of vulnerability.

It has been argued that speaking in one's voice implies awareness of one's body and reconnection of the cuts between the self and the body. Thus the alienation and disconnection from one's body that characterize discursive identities are avoided. The voice allows for the possibility of a singular and corporeal resistance that also becomes collective resistance. Moreover, this chapter has stressed the necessity of approaching cuts to the genitals with ambivalence. Bettelheim, for example, reverses the negative thinking of the cut and links it to positive ambivalence. He suggests a reading of FGC in terms of an attempt by the male members of the community to participate in female reproductive functions. In this way, he liberates the cut from solely negative explanations and opens up its understanding to new possibilities of resistance. In Cavarero's thought, one's voice speaks of a self, characterized by inclination rather than verticality; a self that relates to others by bending, considering the other's needs and vulnerability, approaching events through ambivalence. Indeed, speaking in one's voice implies an ontological level of a body that is unique and singular, aware of one's vulnerability and that of others, capable of reconciling the cracks and cuts of the legal subject of resistance.

110 Cavarero, "Inclining the Subject"; Cavarero, "Rectitude."
111 Salecl, "Cut in the Body."
112 Salecl, "Cut in the Body."

The next chapter develops the voice in relation to the theme of sex work and objectification. Objectification in sex work is also the result of a subject thought of as cut and separated from the body, associated with feminine subjectivity. As a result, law reproduces a moralistic legal approach toward sex workers. One's voice, instead, enables one to speak beyond moralizing discourses. The voice also excludes the possibility of objectification in sexual interaction because the ontology of uniqueness that is exposed through the voice is grounded in relationality, vulnerability and reciprocity.

Chapter 3

Objectification and voice in sex work[1]

The notion of derivatization [objectification] is, after all, grounded in the recognition of embodied sexual difference, and it is underwritten by an ethics of sexual difference. It therefore follows that sexual attitudes, choice, experiences, orientations, behaviour, etc., are deeply interwoven with identity [. . .] Indeed, traditional constructions of femininity, I would argue, alienate women from their own sexuality, precisely insofar as they construct it as something with which to barter. Sex work is not the only place where sexuality is traded for something else: women, especially young women, are constantly encouraged to use their sexuality to garner illusory power, affection, prestige, attention, economic security, etc.[2]

The question of how sexual difference has been perceived is central for the understanding of the objectification of women in commercial sex. The cuts and separations implicit in the construction of subjectivity appear to reflect the divisions in operation in the process of objectification of selves and bodies in commercial sex. The case study of this chapter attempts to show how Cavarero's voice offers alternative approaches of resistance to both the moralizing position of law and the objectification of women in commercial sex. My aim is to show how the focus on one's voice has precisely the potential to come alive when considering the objectification of women in sex work. One's voice reconnects the disjunctions opened up by essentialized sexual difference subjectivity, forcing law to reflect on the significance of its legal subject. At the same time, one's voice requires an exclusion of objectification in human interaction and sexuality.

Historically, law has openly objectified sex workers by increasing their vulnerability instead of protecting them and improving their conditions.[3] More

1 The argument of one's voice and sex work has been developed also in the following paper: Elisabetta Bertolino, "Pasolini, le Lucciole and the Law," in *Rileggendo Pasolini. Il Diritto dopo la Scomparsa delle Lucciole*. Vol. 2, eds Contu, E., Guerrieri, A. and Romano, G. (Ariccia: Aracne Editrice, 2016), 255–264.

2 Anne Cahill, *Overcoming Objectification: A Carnal Ethics* (New York: Routledge, 2011), 122.

3 Julia Laite, *Common Prostitutes and Ordinary Citizens. Commercial Sex in London 1885–1960* (London: Palgrave Macmillan, 2012); Helen J. Self, *Prostitution, Women and the Misuse of the Law: The Fallen Daughters of Eve* (London: Frank Cass, 2003).

recently, the international legal debate on the sex industry has provided a turning point and has focused on the issue of trafficking for sexual exploitation and the vulnerability of the victims. The international legal perspective has also informed law at domestic levels. And yet, as we shall see, scholars such as Vanessa Munro and Anna Carline argue that the recent international legal perspective, or the domestic law informed by it, remain problematic in that a sex worker is constructed already as a victim and vulnerability remains a controversial legal element to be taken into account.[4]

Law and its legal subject of resistance seem to be repeating and appropriating the patriarchal and essentialized sexual difference division. This latter presupposes the existence of a dominant masculine subjectivity and a feminine subjectivity that is positioned as the object, or less-than-a-subject, within the self-same economy. The feminine, conceptualized on the basis of masculine parameters, is further cut into two: as either the asexual Madonna or the over-sexual whore.

Feminist scholars have underlined in different ways how the traditional and persistent objectification of sex workers in law is grounded in the patriarchal and essentialized understanding of sexual difference and in the fact that women have been alienated from their own sexuality, perceived as something to be exchanged.[5] For Anne Cahill, the notion of objectification, or derivatization, is based precisely on traditional constructions of sexual difference.[6] These constructions of femininity show that sex work is not the only place where sexuality is bartered; rather, women are brought up to think that through sexuality they can achieve success or prestige.[7]

Alison Young has also explained how criminology has historically reproduced a discourse on women as being determined by biology, rendering them as convenient: over-emotional, hideous, childish, devious, to be feared, out of control or unreliable, and thus inferior to men.[8] On the contrary, assumptions about masculine biology have produced the whole system of criminal law, such as for instance, the concept of *mens rea*.[9] However, for Young, the conception of woman, produced by legal representation, is a *mis-conception* that results in an image of criminology where women are already exchanged in the text of law prior to the exchange that happens in reality. Previous research also confirms that more

4 Vanessa Munro, "A Tale of Two Servitudes: Defining and Implementing a Domestic Response to Trafficking of men for Prostitution in the UK and Australia," *Social and Legal Studies*, 14 (2005): 91–114; Anna Carline, "Criminalisation or Protection? Tensions in the Construction of Prevention Strategies Concerning Trafficking for the Purposes of Sexual Exploitation," in *Gender, Sexualities and Law*, eds Jones, J. and Grear, A. (Oxon: Routledge, 2011), 175–187.

5 Jo Bridgeman and Susan Millns, *Feminist Perspectives on Law. Law's Engagement with the Female Body* (London: Sweet & Maxwell, 1998); Cahill, *Overcoming Objectification*; Alison Young, *Imagining Crime* (London: Sage, 1996), 1–50.

6 Cahill, *Overcoming Objectification*, 122.

7 Cahill, *Overcoming Objectification*, 122.

8 Young, *Imagining Crime*, 1–50.

9 Young, *Imagining Crime*, 1–50.

women were imprisoned as a punishment for the type of woman they were than for committing crimes.[10] Harsh sentences were given not only to prostitutes but also to single and poor women.[11]

The 1895 book by Lombroso and Ferrero, *The Female Offender*, is remarkable in this sense.[12] The book assumes that prostitution represents the female corollary to criminality in men; it also exemplifies deep prejudices against female criminals and prostitutes, the belief in the innate predisposition toward criminality or prostitution and the idea that prostitution is shameful and pathological, and explains the necessity of reforming prostitutes and controlling them which, in turn, made prostitutes objectified and vulnerable. As a consequence, law has appropriated this masculine thinking of essentialized sexual difference cuts and separations, reproducing the objectification of sex workers, offering moralizing solutions and treating sex workers as less than subjects.

Adriana Cavarero has pointed to the fact that sexual difference has been used as a tool of discrimination by the dominant sex.[13] For Cavarero, Western history appears to have been patriarchal since its origins, assuming sexual difference in terms of opposition between masculine and feminine, where the two poles are not posited on the same level but in a hierarchical scale of subordination and exclusion.[14] For Cavarero, the ontological operation that has occurred is a simple one: the masculine gender has become the paradigm for the whole of humankind and, as a consequence, the feminine gender comes to be perceived as not fully human, or as human at an inferior level.[15] The objectification of the sex worker marks these cuts and divisions of the essentialized perspective of sexual difference.

In opposition to the objectification of such a cut and divided thinking, I will embrace Cavarero's understanding of one's voice as a way to resist processes of ontological separation. One's voice can disobey objectification because it moves beyond the limits of essentialized sexual difference and the cuts and splits that sexual difference produces in subjectivity. Speaking in one's voice discloses one's unique corporeality and selfhood, touches the vulnerability of each unique human being, whether male or female, and supersedes stereotypical thinking about masculinity and femininity. In particular, through speaking in one's voice one can suspend the grid of linguistic and social identity and the categorical understanding of the individual. Thus one's voice can disrupt sex workers' humiliation and marginalization by the law, with its essentialized moralistic discourses on their vulnerability, and it can be a useful tool of awareness.

10 Pat Carlen, *Women's Imprisonment: A Study in Social Control* (London: Routledge and Kegan Paul, 1983).

11 Carlen, *Women's Imprisonment.*

12 Cesare Lombroso and William Ferrero, *The Female Offender* (London: Fisher, 1895).

13 Adriana Cavarero and Franco Restaino, *Le Filosofie Femministe* (Milan: Bruno Mondadori, 2002), 113.

14 Cavarero and Restaino, *Le Filosofie Femministe*, 115.

15 Cavarero and Restaino, *Le Filosofie Femministe*, 116.

Speaking in one's voice does not only help with understanding the essentialized mechanisms behind the legal subject. One's voice also implies finding one's own way of becoming aware and understanding one's vulnerability rather than thinking of vulnerability as constructed within a given identity or embracing a strong and empowered identity that is not one's own. Finally, one's voice is also a means for experiencing new modalities of interaction and thinking about sexuality in relation to one's body and other bodies. In fact, the ontological horizon of the voice excludes objectification by reframing precisely the kind of thinking that covets everything around women and sex. One's voice signifies a sharing of air, life in a polyphonic community of other voices, and this evokes the double principium of natality explained by Peg Birmingham that consists of initiation and givenness.[16] The principle of initiation calls objectification into question because it always happens in reciprocity and plurality; the principle of givenness escapes objectification because it is that which stands outside any identity, division and cut stereotype. By speaking in one's voice we have no viable solution but exposing and sharing the vulnerability of our life and our precarious and temporal human condition with others who are vulnerable.

Thus, in this chapter, I will try to show how one's voice disrupts the male's symbolic representation of himself and that of women (produced by the Man) – I explore the example of law. This means that for a sex worker there is also the possibility of resisting from herself and her vulnerability rather than by repeating a stronger but given identity. Finally, I see how one's voice rethinks sexual interactions. Sexual interaction becomes simply encountering another with one's body without reducing one to an other, overcoming the asymmetrical and unbalanced manner of turning another being into a reflection or projection of one's own identity and desire.[17] The chapter will begin by analyzing law's construction of sex workers in relation to objectification and will specifically focus on the case law of *R v Gary Lee Cole and Stephen Kevin Barik* in 1993.[18] It will then reflect on objectification and human interactions through the scholars discussed in the literary review of this study, such as Martha Nussbaum, Judith Butler and Adriana Cavarero herself.

3.1 Law, objectification and women in the sex industry

Law has since its beginning appropriated the discourse of the patriarchal and essentialized sexual difference division of subjectivity, and as a consequence its approach to sex work has been historically characterized by objectification.[19] Legal interventions have often aimed at withdrawing sex workers' legal rights,

16 Peg Birmingham, "On Action: The Appearance of Law," in *Action and Appearance: Ethics and the Politics of Writing in Hannah Arendt*, eds Yeatman, A. et al. (London: Continuum, 2011), 103–116.

17 For Cahill, derivatizing means to turn into a derivative, to render or approach another as reflection of one's being's identity, desires and fear. See Cahill, *Overcoming Objectification*, 32.

18 *R v Gary Lee Cole and Stephen Kevin Barik* (1993) 14 Cr. App. R.(S.) 764.

19 See: Lombroso and Ferrero, *The Female Offender*.

making it impossible for them to trade legally and thus, instead of supporting them, they have objectified them openly.[20] Some scholars have underlined how law's intervention in the objectification of sex workers' identities and bodies has

20 A historical approach to sex work can be found for instance in Laite, *Common Prostitutes and Ordinary Citizens* and Self, *Prostitution, Women and the Misuse of the Law*.

In the nineteenth century's UK legislation, prostitution was linked to vagrancy and associated with unemployment, poverty and crimes. In 1824, the Vagrants Act was passed and it dealt with situations of social instability. The Act criminalized idle and disorderly persons, rogues and vagabonds. Under the Act, people wandering or begging in public places, together with "common prostitutes" wandering in the public streets and behaving in a riotous or indecent manner, were deemed to be idle and disorderly individuals. By naming sex workers under the term of "common prostitutes," in the sense of common and available to all, the Act clearly objectified them.

A number of solicitation laws were subsequently passed. The Metropolitan Police Act 1839 and the Town Police Clauses Act 1847 provided for the arrest of prostitutes soliciting the streets and creating annoyance of the public. Those Acts gave power to the police to arrest women considered prostitutes and showed little concern about women's vulnerability in commercial sex. Law was directed against prostitutes criminalizing them. Those solicitation laws were complemented by a series of Disorderly Houses Acts, allowing legal authorities to prosecute brothels if peace was disturbed. On the one hand criminalization was a constraint, but on the other hand it also stimulated new ways of doing sexual business and expanding it, while women who sold sex were chased and objectified by police and exploited by criminals.

By the mid-nineteenth century the expansion of British military and naval activity and the development of medicine constructed prostitution into a medical problem. The resulting Contagious Diseases Acts of the 1860s are indicative of the level of societal objectification of women working in commercial sex and of the complete disregard for their vulnerability as opposed to the vulnerability of the men who made use of commercial sex and who were seen as the victims of the contagious women. In this way the Acts tolerated and legitimated the sexual exploitation and abuse of women by attempting to make buying sex safe for men. The Contagious Acts 1864, 1866 and 1869 provided for the surgical examination of women suspected of being common prostitutes and for their detention in locked hospitals if found infected with venereal diseases. The prostitute would remain on a register of "common prostitutes" and would have to submit to regular inspections. The arbitrary powers of classification and arrest given to the police constituted a menace for all women. Overall, the Acts encouraged increased repression and criminalization of the women involved in the sale of sex.

Toward the turn of the century, more attention to the subjectivity and vulnerability of women can be registered thanks to feminist campaigns. The Criminal Law Amendment Act 1885 increased the age of consent to sexual intercourse from 13 to 16 with the intent to protect girls from abduction for the purpose of prostitution in brothels. While the Act was intended largely to protect women and girls from sexual exploitation, it also provided for the prosecution of landlords, tenants and occupiers, if liable, for allowing a property to be used for the purpose of prostitution. A likely outcome of this was that prostitutes were chased by the police and were left more at the mercy of their landlords, who would charge increased rents for the risk run. Hence, vulnerability was increased rather than reduced.

Attention to the problematic of trafficking also began. A number of international conventions on the trafficking of women and children were adopted during the first decades of the twentieth century. On the national level, the international conventions were followed by the Punishment of Incest Act 1908 and The Criminal Law Amendment (White Slave Traffic) Acts 1912 and 1922.

After the two wars, the approach to prostitution became more one of public nuisance, confining the discussion to the soliciting of women – as revealed by the Wolfenden Committee 1954. The approach began to be the one of legal liberalism, which is based on the public/private distinction

ended up dealing with sex workers as if they were a sort of controllable substandard of the already excluded female body.[21]

If one looks, for instance, at the recent UK legislation of the 1980s and 1990s, it becomes apparent that the law has adopted a discourse of the protection of the public from prostitution, since prostitution had been seen as injurious and harmful and in need of being controlled.[22] Such an approach continues today in UK law along with a focus on the vulnerability of the sex worker, which derives from an international perspective that converges on trafficking for sexual exploitation.[23] By law, sex workers are consequently viewed as either a public nuisance or as victims, hence either objectified or denied a full subjectivity, or the attributed vulnerability is associated with stigmatization and used for constructing a moral discourse.

Since the late 1990s, the debate about prostitution has taken the shape of trafficking for the purpose of sexual exploitation. This form of understanding the debate on the sex industry focuses on innocent victims of abuse and exploitation. The issue of trafficking is currently dealt with by the United Nations Protocol to Prevent, Suppress and Punish Trafficking in Persons, especially Women and Children 2000 – which supplements the United Nations Convention Against

and on the belief in the autonomous choices of adult women. Prostitution began to be seen as a private choice of some women who choose an immoral life. The main aim seemed to be that of "cleaning up the streets" and stopping the visibility of the phenomenon. The Wolfenden Committee was followed by the Sexual Offences Act 1956 and the Street Offences Act 1959.

The 1956 Act criminalized brothel-keeping as well as letting or permitting premises to be used for brothels and prostitution and imposed heavy sentences upon men, making it an offense for a man knowingly to live wholly or in part on the earnings of prostitution or to be habitually in the company of a prostitute or exercise control over her. However, the enforcement of such law appeared problematic as in many instances the man living with a sex worker could have been her father, son, brother, husband, partner or people who were the only stable influence in a woman's life. Consequently, while the law showed the willingness to prosecute the man who exploited a woman, the prostitute was at the same time isolated in that the provision denied her, in some ways, the right of a lawful private family life.

The 1959 Act criminalized instead soliciting for prostitution. Such criminalization of sex workers can be argued to have rendered sex workers more vulnerable without the protection of the law. In the current approach of the UK law there is a discourse on nuisance together with one on morality that is derived from the international approach. In the 1980s and 1990s kerb-crawling was the focus of the law. The Sexual Offence Act 1985 is generally referred to as the Kerb Crawling Act. In its Section 1, the 1985 Act made it an offense for a man to solicit a woman for the purpose of prostitution so as to cause annoyance to the person being solicited or nuisance to the neighbourhood. Section 2 of the Act also created the offense of persistent soliciting in a street or public place for the purpose of prostitution. This approach also had the effect of increasing the speed of transactions and thus the vulnerability of the sex worker.

21 Judy Purdom, "Judging Women: Rethinking Shame Through Corporeality," in *Feminist Perspectives on Law and Theory*, eds Richardson, J. and Sandland, R (London: Cavendish, 2000), 209–228.

22 Laite, *Common Prostitutes and Ordinary Citizens*; Self, *Prostitution, Women and the Misuse of the law.*

23 Johanna Kantola and Judith Squires, "Discourses Surrounding Prostitution Policies in the UK," *European Journal of Women's Studies*, 11 (2004): 77–101.

Transnational Organized Crime 2000. The Council of Europe Convention on Action against Trafficking 2005 reflects the UN documents.

Vanessa Munro explains how the UN Protocol contains the two main competing positions in relation to commercial sex: the position that views prostitution as work and the one that sees it as violence against women.[24] Munro stresses how the Protocol recognizes trafficked persons as victims of a crime rather than criminals and calls for cooperation between the authorities involved. She notes how Article 3(b) of the Protocol states that a person's consent will be irrelevant if consent is obtained as a consequence of threat, coercion, fraud, deception, abuse of power or abuse of vulnerability.

Thus Article 3(b) puts an emphasis on vulnerability and this indicates that current international law tends to see the sex worker as a human being unlike the traditional legal objectification of women in commercial sex. However, according to Munro, the position of vulnerability is left undefined and is thus difficult to use.[25] In addition, saying that exploitation will make consent irrelevant makes consent a problematic concept, while at the same time it constitutes the only possibility of having a voice.

These international documents have had a major impact on UK domestic law, for instance in The Sexual Offences Act 2003 and in The Policing and Crime Act 2009. In particular, The Policing and Crime Act 2009, in its Section 14, criminalizes the act of paying a sex worker subjected to exploitation for sexual services and Section 21 introduces closure orders for premises used for prostitution.[26] As for Section 14, it deals with the demand for prostitution by introducing for the first time an offense which focuses on paying an adult for sexual services. The offense is strict liability and unless sex buyers are absolutely sure about the status of the sex worker, sex buyers are not supposed to buy. In relation to S. 21, police have the power to close premises when they have reasonable grounds to believe that they are going to be used for offenses related to prostitution, such as causing, inciting or controlling prostitution for gain under Articles 52 and 53 of the 2003 Act. Yet those measures can increase the vulnerability of the sex worker by pushing her to the street, where prostitution is more dangerous.

Anna Carline has noted how both Sections 14 and 21 of The Policing and Crime Act 2009 show a narrow and utilitarian approach to vulnerability, where vulnerability is used as a means to justify criminalization and objectification, and a moralistic view of sex workers.[27] For Carline, the criminalization of the sex buyer tends to lead to increased vulnerability of the sex worker, as transactions are

24 Munro, "A Tale of Two Servitudes," 91.

25 Munro, "A Tale of Two Servitudes."

26 The offenses concerned with criminalizing traffickers are contained also in S. 57 and 59 of The Sexual Offences Act 2003.

27 Carline, "Criminalisation or Protection?"

then conducted in secluded areas and the provision is not accompanied by the necessary decriminalization of the sex worker.[28]

Carline views the discourse on vulnerability as re-positing the immorality of prostitution and thus as a moral agenda that continues to objectify sex work and require its eradication.[29] However, as Carline notes, those offenses do not require any form of threat, deception or coercion on the part of traffickers and neither is the lack of consent of the victim a relevant factor.[30] Rather, in those sections, a woman is constructed as already a victim and without agency and sex work is thought of as amounting to an abuse of vulnerability. The notion of vulnerability is placed within a trafficking discourse that mainly aims to criminalize those who exploit, rather than protect those who are exploited.

As a consequence, we could argue that there still remains a specific ontological approach behind the way in which vulnerability is constructed and the criminalization of the sex work/worker is produced in law. According to Munro and Carline, the voice of sex workers in both the UN Protocol and The Policing and Crime Act 2009 is silenced and replaced with the voice of law. In particular, the vulnerability acknowledged by the law does not seem to reflect one's unique vulnerability as it is experienced in the objectification of the sex industry.

Several scholars have concurred that prostituting oneself puts one into an extremely vulnerable situation. Giving one's body in exchange for money, in fact, also implies the destruction of the prostituting self.[31] Although one sells sex, one may often try to avoid the commercialization of one's unique self and body by finding strategies to protect oneself, maintaining clear boundaries, protecting oneself from being completely invaded and destroyed or preserving one's ability to feel by reserving some parts of the body for uses other than sex work. One might then be facing the dilemma of avoiding prostituting oneself while prostituting oneself, thus avoiding splitting oneself while splitting.

Vulnerability is thus experienced not just physically at work when dealing with violent clients but every day and moment while enacting difficult strategies of

28 Anna Carline, "Critical Perspectives on the Policing and Crime Act 2009: An Unethical Approach to the Regulation of Prostitution," *Contemporary Issues in Law,* 10 (2010): 77–100, 92.

29 Anna Carline, "Critical Perspectives on the Policing and Crime Act 2009."

30 Anna Carline, "Perspectives on Trafficking and the Policing and Crime Act 2009: Challenging Notions of Vulnerability Through a Butlerian Lens," in *Regulating the International Movement of Women. From Protection to Control,* eds Sharron, A. and FitzGerald, A. (Oxon: Routledge, 2011), 135–140.

31 Katherine Gregory, *The Everyday Lives of Sex Workers in the Netherlands* (New York: Routledge, 2005); Vicki Brown, *Listening to the Streets: A Study of Young People Involved in Prostitution* (Thesis submitted to the University of Manchester, 2005); Cecile Hoigard and Liv Finstad, *Prostitution, Money and Love* (Philadelphia: Pennsylvania University Press, 1986); Teela Sanders, *Sex Work: A Risky Business* (London: Willan Publishing, 2005); Sophie Day, "What Counts as Rape? Physical Assault and Broken Contracts: Contrasting Views of Rape among London Sex Workers" in *Sex and Violence,* eds Harvey, P. and Gow, P. (London: Routledge, 1994), 172–189; Maggie O'Neill, *Prostitution and Feminism: Towards a Politics of Feeling* (Cambridge: Polity Press, 2001).

separation of oneself during work. Selling sex may have emotional and psychological effects, may cause symptoms of post-traumatic stress disorder, depression, distress and negative feelings such as guilt and disgust. The strategies one adopts do not provide satisfactory protection for the trading of one's sexuality. After a while, it may not be easy to distinguish fantasy from reality. The injuries and wounds may have already been swallowed up in the memories of countless customers passing before oneself. And yet, law remains incapable of understanding these levels of vulnerability that one may experience in sex work.

Changes in law have also been accompanied by changes in the possibility of consent for sex workers within law. As Barbara Sullivan underlines, traditionally women sex workers – or simply promiscuous women who lacked credibility within law – were also seen as available to men and thus as always consenting to sexual activities.[32] Men accused of sexual assault were able to use evidence of prostitution to defend themselves. In court, women who claimed rape were at risk of being extensively cross-examined about their sexual reputation and experience, and any evidence of prostitution was seen to compromise their credibility, thus denying any possibility of consent.[33]

There was no possibility of having agency to oppose the objectification in which they were positioned and to which they were subjected. It was reported that sex workers were arrested for not having paid fines when reporting sexual abuses, such as assault or rape, and thus often they avoided reporting those events to the police. Case law confirms the state of consent-less objectification of sex workers.[34]

32 Barbara Sullivan, "Rape, Prostitution and Consent," *Australian and New Zealand Journal of Criminology*, 40 (2007): 127–142.

33 Sullivan, "Rape, Prostitution and Consent."

34 Sullivan reports a few law cases. In the case of *R v Baker* (1829), evidence of prostitution was admitted as relevant in rape trials. In particular, the following questions to contradict the prosecutrix were admitted: "were you not on, since the time of the alleged offence, walking in the High St at Oxford, to look for men? Were you not on, since the time of the alleged offence, walking in the High St, with a woman reputed to be a common prostitute?" It was allowed also to show evidence of the general light character of the prosecutrix and of her being a street worker. The case was followed by *R v Clay* (1851), where evidence of the general character of the prosecutrix in relation to being a prostitute was admissible. In this case, a police officer was also permitted to provide evidence that the woman complainant was seen soliciting in the street 20 years earlier.

In the twentieth century such an approach continued to be applied. In *R v Greatbanks* (1959), evidence of behavior similar to prostitution, such as poor sexual reputation, was allowed to be presented and the woman complainant was held to have consented to sexual intercourse. In *R v Bashir and Manzur* (1969), the defense of two men accused of raping the woman complainant consisted of affirming that sexual intercourse was consensual. During defense cross-examination of the victim, she was presented as being a prostitute. She was accused of having invited another man to have sexual intercourse with her for money and of having made statements to other men that made it possible to infer that she was a common prostitute. Since the victim denied all the allegations, witnesses were called to corroborate the allegations that she was a prostitute. Under *R v Greatbanks*, the judge ruled the evidence admissible. It was said that despite the fact that generally evidence of sexual intercourse with men other than the accused is not admissible, evidence of prostitution is admissible because a prostitute who regularly sells her body is a different situation

The situation began to change in the late 1980s and 1990s. The admissibility of evidence relating to sexual reputation and past history began to be limited and sex workers' increased risk of rape started to be acknowledged, with sex workers being constructed as individuals capable of consenting or withholding consent.[35] The case law suggests that significant changes in social attitudes have taken place over the last few decades.[36] Today, it is possible in theory to succeed in rape prosecutions when the victim is a sex worker. Sex workers are in principle entitled to the same protection of the criminal law as any other person and to

than a woman who has sexual intercourse with men. In *R v Krausz*, a 22-year-old woman complainant claimed she had been assaulted and raped by a man met in a pub. She danced and drank with the accused man called Krausz; then she left and Krausz followed her and shared a taxi with her. Krausz persuaded her to come to his flat. She claimed that Krausz forced himself upon her and struck her on the face when she pushed him. As a result, she allowed him to have sexual intercourse with her because she was afraid. She was hit again in the face when she tried to run away through the lavatory. Krausz defended himself by saying that she consented to sex, demanded money for it and refused to leave. So consequently, he slapped her face and when she went to the lavatory, she fell down the stairs. The Court of Appeal upheld his conviction for assault occasioning bodily harm and quashed the one for rape. The judge, in the first instance, had considered inadmissible certain evidence about the claimant being a prostitute. It was generally accepted that a woman could not be cross-examined about sexual acts with other men at other times, unless the woman engaged in prostitution. Prostitution included both sex work and non-monogamous sex. Thus the evidence of prostitution was crucial for overturning a sentence. Despite the fact that the claimant was not found to be a prostitute in the strict sense, she was found to be a woman that submitted her body to different men with or without payment and therefore was to be considered as a prostitute and her claim of non-consent was invalid.

35 Sullivan, "Rape, Prostitution and Consent."

36 *R v White* (2004) involved a rape case of a former sex worker who claimed that she no longer was involved in prostitution. The complainant and the defendant had consumed alcohol and smoked cannabis. The defendant subsequently forced the complainant into the bedroom, placed his hands around her throat and removed her clothing and tampon and forced sexual intercourse despite her struggles. He also attempted to force her to have oral sex. The complainant ran out. The police took photo of her injuries. The defendant alleged that she instigated him to have sex with her and demanded money and that because he refused to pay, she had tried to take money from his wallet. The judge initially refused to admit a cross-examination about her history as a sex worker but allowed limited questioning about her expectation for payment from the accused. This paradoxically was equivalent to questioning about prostitution. The Court of Appeal upheld the defendant's conviction. The alleged contact with the defendant's wallet was bound with the issue of consent. The reasoning was that a prostitute was as entitled to say no as any other woman and that being or having been a prostitute did not make the complainant more likely to consent.

R v Thomas Brolly (1998) is a case of a street sex worker who had consensual intercourse with her client but who was subsequently raped by the client. The client was sentenced to four years' imprisonment. In *R v Byrne* [2003], a sex worker entered into a sexual contract with the defendant client, agreeing that intercourse was to take place with the use of a condom. The intercourse took place as agreed but was not to the client's satisfaction; he then removed the condom and forced the complainant to perform oral sex. The defendant was convicted of indecent assault.

Similar decisions were taken in such other cases as *R v Charles Grenville Shaw* [1997], *R v Arjumand Hussein* [1996], *R v Ian Bridgeman* [1996], *R v Kevin Davies* [1997], *R v Asif Masood* [1996], *R v Trevor Wells* [1998] and *Spencer James Mellor v R* [1999].

enjoy the same status as other women in their capacity to make and sustain complaints of sexual assault in the criminal justice system; they have consensual capacity and must be entitled to stipulate what they will and will not do. Sexual assault and rape are crimes, regardless of whether the victim is a sex worker or not.

However, despite the recognized consensual capacity, consent remains problematic and limited in the case of sex workers because of the involvement of payment and the objectification and degradation that continue to persist. The place and role of consent can become more understandable through the landmark decision in the case law of *R v Linekar*, where the defendant had intercourse with a prostitute but afterwards made off without payment.[37] While the complainant affirmed that she would not have agreed to sexual intercourse unless she was paid in advance and a condom was used, the court held that the consent of the victim cannot be withdrawn because of fraud. This means that it is the non-consent to sexual interaction, rather than the fraud, that makes an offense rape. Therefore, the only type of fraud that so far vitiates consent refers to the nature of the act itself or the identity of the person who performs the act.

A similar case is *R v Gary Lee Cole and Stephen Kevin Barik*, where the two appellants were convicted of raping a prostitute and of robbing two other prostitutes.[38] In this latter case, consent is treated in the same way as in *Linekar*, that is as non-vitiated by fraud. However, my analysis of this case will move beyond the problem of consent to the issue of the objectification of sex workers that takes place inside law.[39] The court's main focus regarding the case of *R v Gary Lee Cole and Stephen Kevin Barik* was paradoxically whether the trauma of rape is the same for prostitutes as for other women.[40] In the case, the sex worker, after an agreed intercourse with one client, was then kidnapped by the client and another accomplice to a deserted car park and raped by both.

The court held that a prostitute was entitled to refuse to have sex and that law upholds her right, while taking into account the factor that a prostitute is prepared to have sex with any man for payment. As a result, according to the court, the hurt a sex worker suffers from rape is inferior to that suffered by other non-prostitute women and often the hurt is related to the lack of payment rather than to the act of rape itself:

> *It is of course true that a prostitute is entitled to refuse to have sexual intercourse. She can always say "no" and the law will uphold that right. But, it is submitted – and*

37 *R v Linekar* (1994) *The Times*, 26 October. Queen's Bench Division.

38 *R v Gary Lee Cole and Stephen Kevin Barik* (1993).

39 *R v Gary Lee Cole and Stephen Kevin Barik* (1993).

40 *R v Gary Lee Cole and Stephen Kevin Barik* (1993). The two men assailants were driving in a van and picked up a woman who had sexual intercourse with one of the two for GBP 20. The other was hiding in the van and appeared afterwards to search her handbag. Then the two men drove the woman to a deserted car park and both men raped her threatening her with violence. While initially the two men were both sentenced for rape to nine years' imprisonment by the court, their appeal succeeded and their sentences were reduced to seven years on each count.

> *with some effect, as we think, that a factor which the Court can take into account is that the prostitute is, in the nature of her trade, prepared to have intercourse with any man who pays for it and that her situation and the hurt that she may suffer as a result of the rape is to some extent different from that of another woman who would only be prepared to have sexual intercourse with a man whom she knows and respects. To some extent the hurt in cases such as this is not simply the act of intercourse but the fact that no payment has been made for it. That being said, it is repeated that a prostitute is fully entitled to the protection of the law and if she says "no" and means it then the law will protect her by sentencing those who take advantage of her.*[41]

The court's ruling appears to be contradictory. While the court allows equality of consent, at the same time sex workers are treated as having a different subjectivity than other women; the rape of a sex worker is somehow considered as less serious. In the end, law may not offer the same protection that is provided to other victims of rape, merely because of one's status as a sex worker. The sex worker's vulnerability as a victim might be not fully taken into account. The assumption that there is less hurt in rape cases reflects in some ways the idea that women who have sexual contact with men and are sex workers are damaged, polluted, degraded, objectified. Sex workers are considered and perceived by means of their degraded job and not as human beings.

Although sex workers are now finally allowed to consent to sexual interaction, they are nevertheless viewed as always *prepared to have sexual intercourse with any man who pays for it*, that is to say, to accept with less suffering forced sexual interaction and violence. Thus, although sex workers are now consenting subjects, they are still not full subjects. In this sense, the sentence reiterates – behind the acceptance of their right to consent – the law's positing of sex workers as objectified subjects, treated as objects for sex, who exist only to provide sexual services to men. In some ways, to be a sex worker is to hold less value, to be in a position of sex object and to be already dehumanized. Sex workers are constructed as the opposite to the standard subject: as passive matter, that is, objectified bodies that lack minds and are characterized by a submissive stance with regard to clients. To be a sex worker implies being seen always as a sexualized object to be exchanged for money and the possibility of transaction implies that one is available and prepared at any time and under any circumstances to receive sexual intercourse, rather than getting involved in it with consent in an adequate context of autonomy.

The moral status of the sex worker, in the case, is lessened not only by the behavior of the two men who fail to recognize her full subjectivity, but also by the law itself that fails to recognize the non-sexual aspects of the sex worker and thus to see her as a unique self. For the law, it does not matter *who she is* but only *what she is*; it is only her identity as sex worker that defines her legally, only as a she

41 *R v Gary Lee Cole and Stephen Kevin Barik* (1993).

cut off from herself. And, in turn, the two assailant men, who have raped the sex worker, get a reduced sentence by the law; a decision that reinforces precisely the assailants' belief that raping a sex worker is a crime against a less-than-a-person, only because a sex worker performs a job where she is supposed to be available for sexual intercourse in exchange for payment. Yet experiencing rape is not intercourse. Rape involves the use of violence, an unbalance of power and forcing sexual intercourse against the consent of the person involved. This circularity of objectification indicates that to be associated with sex work or identified by one's sexual body parts and sexual function is still today to risk one's own subjectivity.

In the end, it appears that the court continues to approach rape events through a restricted jurisprudence, failing to see the case within a critical and general jurisprudence. In particular, the court fails to see rape within the context of wider sexual violence against women and objectification of their bodies. The court focuses narrowly on distinguishing the level of hurt between types of women, missing the fact that it is one's uniqueness that is offended beyond any categorizing and identity thinking.

From this point of view, it is not surprising then that sex workers become an easy target for violence and harm. Reducing sentences for rape on the basis that the sex worker is prepared to have sex is flawed, in that no one can ever be prepared to be abused, raped and to suffer harm. A sex worker is a full human person who suffers harm as other women do and sex work should never be intended in terms of abusive sexual interactions. To reduce the sentences on the basis of a claim of *being prepared to have sexual intercourse* means confusing sexual interaction with violence, condoning violence against women, and not according a sex worker the moral status of a unique selfhood.

In other words, it sends the message to the rapists that raping a sex worker is less than a crime, that it is not necessary to have a regard for her well-being, safety and subjectivity, because sentences are reduced in the case of a woman working in the sex industry. Rape denies relationality, separates power from sexuality, produces victims as object and becomes the hallmark of an inherently unequal sexual system. The two men in this case law imposed their will, body and sexuality upon a unique being, negating her ability to speak and have a voice; they projected their own desires upon her and she had to become what they wanted: an object.

3.2 Speculating on objectification

According to Anne Cahill, treating someone as a body does not necessarily involve objectification; what is objectifying is to reduce a subject to a mere reflection of another's needs and desires.[42] In commercial sex, one is precisely used as an object for the mere sexual satisfaction of another and one's body is

42 Cahill, *Overcoming Objectification*, 117.

reduced to the genitals. In this section I will reflect on theoretical approaches that resist processes of objectification in sexual interaction. More specifically, I will explore the perspectives of Martha Nussbaum and Judith Butler. While Nussbaum's perspective is located within the liberal economy, Butler explores the radical possibility of reconsidering vulnerability as one of the conditions of the very possibility of resistance and focuses on resisting objectification within the normative linguistic and political frame.

In general, the liberal perspective on sex work argues that it is necessary to see sex workers as respectable women doing dignified work, who freely choose to sell their bodies for money through consent and free choice. Coming from such a liberal position, in her essay "'Whether from Reason or Prejudice': Taking Money for Bodily Services" Nussbaum argues that it is useful for the debate to compare sex work with other jobs and she comes to underline constraints and advantages in many different jobs.[43] Nussbaum's aim is to show that it is not in itself the use of the body that objectifies the sex worker, since the body is used in exchange for money in all these jobs, even in the job of a professor:

> *The two figures have a very interesting similarity: Both provide bodily services in areas that are generally thought to be especially intimate and definitive of self-hood. Just as the prostitute takes money for sex, which is commonly thought to be an area of intimate self-expression, so the professor takes money for thinking and writing about what she thinks – about morality, emotion, the nature of knowledge, whatever – all parts of a human being's intimate search for understanding of the world and oneself.*[44]

In the chapter, Nussbaum does not seem to associate sex work with objectification and she rather advocates its decriminalization. Regarding consent, Nussbaum argues that it is important to expand choices and autonomy, as well as to improve working conditions and make sure that women are treated with dignity.[45] She distinguishes between different contexts of choices and autonomy:

> *First is the case in which a woman's entry into prostitution is caused by some type of conduct that would otherwise be criminal: kidnapping, assault, drugging, rape, statutory rape, blackmail, a fraudulent offer. Here we may certainly judge that the woman's choice is not a real choice, and that the law should take a hand in punishing the coercer [. . .] Different is the case of an adult woman who enters prostitution because of bad economic options: because it seems a better alternative than the chicken factory, because there is no other employment*

43 Martha Nussbaum, "'Whether from Reason or Prejudice': Taking Money for Bodily Services," in *Sex and Social Justice*, ed. Nussbaum, M. (Oxford: Oxford University Press, 1999), 276–298.

44 Nussbaum, "'Whether from Reason or Prejudice,'" 283.

45 Nussbaum, "'Whether from Reason or Prejudice,'" 298.

available to her, and so on. This too, we should insist, is a case in which autonomy has been infringed but in a different way.[46]

In her essay "Objectification," Nussbaum presents a more interesting position regarding objectification in sexual relationships.[47] Nussbaum suggests that objectification can involve different features, such as, for instance, instrumentality, denial of autonomy, inertness, fungibility, violability, ownership and denial of subjectivity.[48] Not all of these features are involved at the same time. According to Nussbaum, it is not objectification per se that is harmful; what counts in evaluating the moral character of a sexual interaction is the intimate context of the relationship. Reflecting on Cass Sunstein's thinking, Nussbaum suggests that in an intimate context of equality, respect and consent, objectification might not cause trouble.[49]

Nussbaum seems to defend a kind of objectification in sexuality as offered by D.H. Lawrence in his novel *Lady Chatterley's Lover*, in which, despite the fact that there is reduction of the persons to their bodily parts, the objectification appears to be benign because it is symmetrical and undertaken in a context of mutual respect.[50] Objectification is justified, then, if it takes place in a context of respect, equality and intimacy.

In such a context of respect, mutuality and intimacy, partners reduce one another to body parts and they surrender their autonomy, agency and subjectivity, letting themselves be overcome with sexual passion; and yet, such an objectification is not harmful. For instance, when a person rests her head on her lover's stomach, treating him as an object, she does this in a benign way because the two of them are in an intimate relationship and relate to one another with respect and equality.

For Nussbaum, in intimate contexts where there is mutual respect, objectification is morally benign because to be objectified in such a way means to be sexually awakened, or even to express new forms of autonomy, and this can become part of a pleasant sexual life. On the contrary, "under some specifications" such as

46 Nussbaum, "Whether from Reason or Prejudices," 295, 296.

47 Martha Nussbaum, "Objectification," in *Sex and Social Justice*, ed. Nussbaum, M. (Oxford: Oxford University Press, 1999), 213–239.

48 Instrumentality is a feature according to which the objectifier treats the objects as a tool of his or her purposes; denial of autonomy happens when the objectifier treats the object as lacking autonomy and self-determination; inertness implies that the objectifier treats the object as if it had no agency; fungibility happens when the objectifier treats the object as interchangeable with another object; violability consists of the object being treated by the objectifier as lacking bodily integrity; ownership is when the objectifier treats the object as something owned; and denial of subjectivity is when the objectifier treats the object without taking account of experience and feelings.

49 Cass Sunstein, "A Review of Nadine Strossen," *New Republic* (9 January 1995): 42–46.

50 *Lady Chatterley's Lover* is a novel, first published in 1928, that became notorious for the story of the physical relationship between a working-class man and an upper-class woman and its explicit descriptions of sex. D.H. Lawrence, *Lady Chatterley's Lover* (London: Penguin Books, 2006).

commercial sex, Nussbaum argues, sexual gratification is one-sided, or anonymous, and a person is used merely as an instrument. In this context, objectification appears to be morally troubling.[51]

Consequently, for Nussbaum what is problematic is not objectification in itself, but rather the context that renders the person a means. If there is respect and symmetry, objectification can lead to gratification and even joy in sexual life. What makes the difference in this latter case is the context and the intention, since vulnerability and risks are mutually assumed and there is no malign intent.

> *Under some specifications, objectification, I shall argue, is always morally problematic. Under other specifications, objectification has features that may be either good or bad, depending on the overall context [. . .] Some features of objectification, furthermore, I shall argue, may in fact in some circumstances, as Sunstein suggests, be either necessary or even wonderful features of sexual life. Seeing this requires, among other things, seeing how the allegedly impossible combination between (a form of) objectification and "equality, respect, and consent" might after all be possible.*[52]

However, this reasoning somehow contradicts Nussbaum's liberal view on consent and sex work. In her text on objectification, Nussbaum admits that in sex work a form of non-benign objectification happens because the selling of sex is done in a context of non-intimacy and non-equality and there is instrumentality in the treatment of another person. Unlike the general liberal position, according to which it is consent that determines the viability of sex work, Nussbaum appears to approach objectification in sex work as a morally troubling activity. It is rather only in a context of intimacy, equality and mutual respect that an objectifying sexual interaction can become viable and benign.

Patricia Marino has criticized Nussbaum's position on objectification.[53] For Marino, objectifying someone, even in a context of intimacy, remains problematic. Contrary to Nussbaum, Marino thinks that it is precisely in intimacy that it is not possible to provide genuine consent. In contexts of intimacy, consent becomes more difficult to be understood than when dealing with strangers. In intimate relationships, one is involved in interwoven requests and favors and can be easily treated instrumentally. Consequently, one's feelings, wishes and ends can get easily dismissed.[54] A wife, for instance, can feel coerced by intimacy and consent may not be genuine, or she can find herself in a web of exchanges that force her to do things without consent.

51 Nussbaum, "Objectification."
52 Nussbaum, "Objectification," 214–215.
53 Patricia Marino, "The Ethics of Sexual Objectification: Autonomy and Consent," *Inquiry* 15(4) (2008), 345–364.
54 Marino, "The Ethics of Sexual Objectification."

For Marino, then, it is not the context that matters but the mode of interaction, and good modes of interaction can also happen between strangers. As a consequence, Marino concludes that choice and autonomy, as qualities of interaction, are especially significant, whereas objectification becomes morally benign when there is autonomy:

> *The crux of the matter with respect to the ethics of objectification, I claim, has to do with respect for a person's autonomy, and not with other qualities of a relationship or a particular interaction. Therefore, proper context is indeed crucial, but it is the background social and political context that matters most, because background equality is necessary for genuine consent. The qualities of the relationship matter only insofar as they, too, render meaningful consent possible.*[55]

According to Marino, if instrumental use is not morally acceptable in one-sided and anonymous sex, neither can it be acceptable in mutual and intimate contexts. If the context/conditions are acceptable, there should not be anything wrong with one-sided, anonymous sex and nor, therefore, should there be with sex work.[56] This is because, according to Marino, it is ambiguous to say that while objectification is permissible as part of intimate relationships, it is morally wrong in one-sided contexts such as sex work. Thus, for Marino, consensual prostitution and one-sided sex can be considered to be morally benign and involve only weak instrumental use of another if one is involved in those exchanges within a context that allows autonomy. Unlike Nussbaum, what matters for Marino is not the intimate nature of the relationship but, rather, whether a social and political background context permits genuine consent and autonomy.

Marino's rebuttal of Nussbaum's perspective indicates that the concepts of objectification and consent are complex and that consent offers an ambiguous way to have voice within law. Nussbaum's view on intimacy and mutuality as the good context, where objectification is benign, can be seen as reflecting some of the problems of the liberal legal approach, where the private (intimacy) has often been idealized in the form of a protective context of equality outside the possibility of legal intervention.

However, as Marino points out, intimacy, mutuality and symmetry do not lead necessarily to a morally benign sexual objectification and may not be necessary for it. In addition, in her article Marino seems to suggest that when one consents to be used instrumentally, it may be the case that one is not choosing genuinely; the situation may rather indicate an adaptive preference that reflects distorted and unfree desires and choices, made in response to the pressures of the context, rather than a choice reflecting oneself.[57] Finally, we can say that mutuality, equality

55 Marino, "The Ethics of Sexual Objectification," 347.
56 Marino, "The Ethics of Sexual Objectification," 347.
57 Marino, "The Ethics of Sexual Objectification."

and symmetry only constitute standards. Nussbaum argued that these standards qualify private and intimate spheres of interactions and make objectification benign. However, they do not often reflect one's voice; the voice cannot be reduced to these standards. It is rather through one's voice that one is able to express one's own desires and needs.

Taking a different path from Nussbaum, Butler questions essentially how we are named and made intelligible by the political and legal frame in which we are necessarily situated.[58] There are often biases, fixed identities that are ingrained in those identities and frames of intelligibility and thus we are produced within different degrees of intelligibility. The sex worker gets objectified and stigmatized precisely by the way the sociopolitical, normative and legal frame constructs her identity. Most of Butler's work has focused on demonstrating how gender is a construction within the framework of hetero-normativity and how the subject outside this normative framework is considered deviant and, therefore, gets stigmatized, oppressed, rejected, becomes abject.[59] This is the case, for instance, for queer identities, but we could easily include sex workers, since in some ways they are considered to be outside the standard sexual normativity. The disciplinary and stabilizing naming and construction of gender is disrupted by the disorganization of body and sexuality. In *Gender Trouble*, Butler underlines precisely the regulatory fiction of hetero-normativity.[60]

In Butler's theory, an objectified identity can be explained by the fact that the universal and normative linguistic structure refutes the other and produces abjection in terms of fixed truths. Identities force sex workers to remain in an ecstatic condition of externalization, as "others," blocked from the possibility of returning to themselves. Yet precisely this condition allows for the possibility of an open journey of subversion and rebellion. For Butler, the process of objectification cannot, therefore, be either negated or resolved but it is unfolded and questioned in the process. As Elena Loizidou argues, it is important that Butler attempts to rethink the identity of the subject out of the existing linguistic construction, while the limitation of such a construction is open to questioning.[61]

It is through the naming of an identity that it is possible to question the objectification of persons, since objectification is a process that involves the linguistic and symbolic dimensions, as well as the bodily and personal elements, of the person. Butler proposes the possibility of thinking gender in terms of performativity. As such, the fictitious construction of gender can be repeated and

58 Judith Butler, *Gender Trouble: Feminism and the Subversion of Identity* (London: Routledge, 1990); Judith Butler, *Frames of War: When Is Life Grievable?* (London: Verso, 2010).

59 Butler, *Gender Trouble.*

60 Butler, *Gender Trouble*, 185.

61 Elena Loizidou, "The Trouble with Rape: Gender Matters and Legal Transformation," *Feminist Legal Studies*, 7 (1999): 275–279, 276.

possibly modified.[62] In *Frames of War*, Butler suggests that not only identities, but also the whole normative framework that traps us in forms of fictitious judgments, are open to the possibility of change:

> *Earlier we noted that one sense of "to be framed" means to be subject to a con, to a tactic by which evidence is orchestrated so to make a false accusation appear true. Some power manipulates the terms of appearance and one cannot break out of the frame; one is framed, which means one is accused, but also judged in advance, without valid evidence and without any obvious means of redress. But if the frame is understood as a certain "breaking out," or "breaking from", then it would seem to be more analogous to a prison break. This suggests a certain release, a loosening of the mechanism of control, and with it, a new trajectory of affect. The frame, in this sense, permits – even requires – this breaking out.*[63]

Therefore, for Butler the possibility for the sex worker to speak remains within and through the mechanisms of utterance and identity naming as well as within the intelligibility of the frame. It is in particular in *Frames of War* that Butler underlines the significance of investigating the conditions that make some lives more or less livable than others, of recognizing the ethical responsibility to protect life from abjection, and thus objectification, and to fight for equality within (and against) the schemes of intelligibility.[64] Law, for instance, distributes vulnerability unequally and this can be seen in the way law has contributed to the objectification of sex workers. Consequently, law needs to be rethought and critically examined in its forms of intelligibility, so that there is a more equal distribution of vulnerability for sex workers and non-participation in their objectification.

Applying the Butlerian reading, Anna Carline underlines how although The Policing and Crime Act 2009, which reflects the current international legal approach to trafficking, has introduced radical reforms related to the regulation of sex work, it has nonetheless reiterated the same old mechanisms of intelligibility in relation to sex workers, maintaining and perpetuating identities of victimhood and a moralistic conception of normal sexuality.[65] The law as it stands is then not capable of accounting and speaking for the complexity of the lives of people. Anna Carline employs Butler's perspective to read critically the 2009 Act and expose the way law frames the sex worker and her vulnerability, reiterating even today her exclusion through a moralistic perspective. However, Butler has shown that identities and schemes of intelligibility, through which sex workers are

62 Butler, *Gender Trouble.*
63 Butler, *Frames of War*, 11.
64 Butler, *Frames of War*, 159.
65 Carline, "Perspectives on Trafficking and the Policing and Crime Act 2009."

constructed, can be modified precisely through the subversion of the very scheme of intelligibility that constructs them as object and less livable.

For Butler, objectification consists precisely of conditions of inequality shared within the linguistic structures that frame us as subjects; we need to become critical of these processes of objectification, in an open journey of deconstruction of such naming, identity and schemes of intelligibility as are forced upon us. Nevertheless, we are immersed in such an intelligible framework, which renders life possible for us and thus we can only get out of those normative structures by performing those mechanisms of objectification in which we are trapped and by finding moments of rupture that expose the fictitious character of construction of those schemes. Such performances allow a more inclusive rethinking of the system of intelligibility that renders us subjects.

In *Vulnerability in Resistance*, Butler recontextualizes the discussion of vulnerability in new strategies of resistance against forms of paternalism, victimization and neoliberalism, moving beyond the conventional binarism that governs the relationship between vulnerability and resistance.[66] She sustains new modes of collective and grass-roots agency and wants to develop a different conception of the social body in resistance, showing that vulnerability is part of resistance itself. Her body ends up being a collective form of resistance, always politically produced, unequally distributed by differential operations of authority, and always exposed to power.[67]

Monia Andreani underlines how the body in Butler experiences both an individual, physical vulnerability and a social vulnerability.[68] The more the subject desires and goes outside itself, the more the subject experiences vulnerability, so that there is no possibility of the subject getting away from objectification.[69] A body that gets exposed becomes the target of individual and social objectification. As a result, Butler introduces the necessity of the social dimension of normativity; the latter is necessary in that it makes vulnerability a sharable characteristic of identity. Cavarero's ontology of relationality and exposure in relation to the voice demarcates from this position.[70] Butler's brilliant and intense argument regarding resistance remains entangled with the sovereign structure that constructs us. One can only speak against one's own objectification by using the social norms and frame of intelligibility that trapped one there in the first place; no voice of oneself outside the frame is possible.

66 Judith Butler, "Rethinking Vulnerability and Resistance," in *Vulnerability in Resistance*, eds Butler, J., Gambetti, Z. and Sabsay, L. (Durham: Duke University Press, 2016), 12–27.

67 Butler, "Rethinking Vulnerability and Resistance."

68 Monia Andreani, "Anatomia Politica dell'Orrore. La Questione della Vulnerabilità e la Figura dell'Inerme in Judith Butler e Adriana Cavarero" in *Differenza e Relazione: L'Ontologia dell' Umano nel Pensiero di Judith Butler e Adriana Cavarero*, eds Bernini, L. and Guaraldo, O. (Verona: Ombre Corte, 2009), 39–65.

69 Andreani, "Anatomia Politica dell'Orrore."

70 Andreani, "Anatomia Politica dell'Orrore."

3.3 The focus on the voice in relation to objectification

My assumption is that the current legal and political subjectivity reflects a sovereign and dominant subjectivity, divided and cut, grounded on the splits of mind and body and on the stereotypes of the masculine and feminine traits of sexual difference. It has been argued so far that precisely such an ontological approach produces processes of objectification of those subjectivities associated, for instance, with body and sex, and that those processes of marginalization and exclusion have also been appropriated by law. Objectification can be the effect of the interaction between texts and people, when texts focus only on one locus of subjectivity while other aspects of subjectivity are excluded or made superfluous and are constructed as an object, or as less-than-a-subject.

This book offers a form of resistance to sociolinguistic and discursive subjectivity through one's unique and corporeal voice (instead of a resistance based on the repetition or affirmation of strong forms of identity for sex workers, the very linguistic structures that create cut subjectivity). If embracing strong forms of identity can empower sex workers and provide them with legal rights, paradoxically it cannot address one's corporeal and inner vulnerability.

On the contrary, the focus on one's voice provides a threefold method of resistance against objectification in sex work. Firstly, the voice upholds one's unique singularity that breaks away from the construction of subjectivity in terms of masculine and feminine aspects, superseding the essentialized sexual difference divide and thus freeing sex workers from an understanding of themselves as subcategories of an already declassed feminine subjectivity. Secondly, speaking in one's voice involves connecting to one's body; this provides the tools to speak one's own vulnerability. It also allows an escape from discursive moralistic positions on the vulnerability of sex workers as victims degraded by misogynist culture that alienates not only sex workers but also women. Thirdly, one's voice is also connected to an ontology of reciprocity and love that excludes objectification in human interaction. Such an ontological perspective reorients current sexual interaction in commercial sex.

In relation to the first point of resistance provided by the voice, in *Le Filosofie Femministe* Cavarero writes precisely against the binary economy of the law of the Father or the phallocentric system.[71] The phallocentric system is grounded in a logic according to which the Man is the subject and the Woman is the object or the other-of-the-subject/man. Representation, for Cavarero, is only a representation of man himself. Man then represents woman according to his own desires. The masculine way of representation is of course complex and women are represented differently in the masculine symbolic order since men have different desires; so women can be represented as mothers, wives or prostitutes. These latter representations need also to become objects of the transgressive sexuality of men.

71 Cavarero and Restaino, *Le Filosofie Femministe*, 119.

Cavarero is critical of both the masculine and feminine identities, because both play the game of the phallocentric symbolic order, which is the game of sovereignty and speaking for others. One has to adapt either to the masculine identity to make a career or adjust to a supposed "natural" feminine model and often women need to be both subjectivities.[72] On the contrary, what Cavarero suggests we should do is precisely to speak in one's voice, which springs from the vibration produced by the passage of air in one's throat. The voice escapes the linguistic construction of the essentialized feminine subject – spoken by men – and necessarily reveals one's uniqueness.

In this sense, the focus on the voice resists the unethical exchange of essentialized and cut subjectivities, where one is the subject that speaks for all, whereas the other is less-than-a-subject or, even worse, treated like a thing and an objectified voiceless entity. One's voice precisely gives back a voice to everyone. The voice allows one to have awareness of oneself, to speak in one's own voice and to participate in the community of voices.

For Cavarero, one has to speak in one's voice, from one's singularity and vulnerable body beyond the *what* and the stereotypical traits of the subjectivity forced upon us. Her position does not counter-oppose the identity of women to that of men, but unfolds the whole language of the symbolic order through one's corporeal voice. The other is not a general category to be known and subsumed but another as uniqueness, in flesh and blood, here and now. In the ontological horizon of one's voice, sexual difference is understood as difference of exposed singularities rather than in terms of cuts between masculinity and femininity. The self is no longer thought of in relation to sexual difference but sexual difference is unraveled to show that both men and women are corporeal, vulnerable and can speak in their own singular voices.

The second point of resistance also consists of speaking in one's voice, since this leads to an awareness of one's vulnerability. In relation to sex workers, this means being able to speak one's own vulnerability, refuting the moralizing discourses on vulnerability by law. One's voice provides one with an awareness of oneself, which can confront the vulnerability of split and division that one may experience during sex work as one reconnects to oneself. In this respect, Cahill argues that a sex worker – for the sake of her own health – cannot be herself because there is no reciprocity and desire in the sexual interaction she engages in.[73] What Cahill may suggest is that a sex worker has to speak and act not having an awareness of herself, as if she finds herself in a position of a *what*, of a subject forced to act in ways that do not express herself.

Focusing on one's voice, body and vulnerability can provide a means of dealing with such split situations. In commercial sex, everything is in fact reversed. While sexuality is generally thought of as something that cannot be separated from

72 Cavarero and Restaino, *Le Filosofie Femministe*, 17.
73 Cahill, *Overcoming Objectification*, 111.

affective relations and sexual relationships and implies relationality to the other, in commercial sex, by offering money for sex, those implications of affectivity and relationality disappear. It is as if customers may buy the right to use bodies without faces and thus women without vulnerability, singularity and uniqueness. By paying, customers cannot be judged, do not run the risk of involvement and one does not need to take account of the other as a subject. In this symbolic and material dimension of exchange, the lack of relationality and level of separation are confirmed in commercial sex by women themselves, who may enact strategies of separation.

In fact, it could be the case that in engaging in commercial sex one may be defending oneself in all possible ways; for instance, by behaving as a body without a face and thus as a cut and a separated self, by separating the exchangeable parts of one's body from the non-exchangeable ones, by distinguishing what can be sold from what cannot be sold and by using body boundaries and splits as strategies.[74] The ontology of one's voice allows one instead to break with such a level of separation and cuts from one's vulnerability because the focus on the voice is a focus on one's uniqueness as detached from the normative and symbolic constructions, capable rather of reconnecting the disjunctions of identity thinking. Speaking in one's voice and one's vulnerability become fundamental to resisting the trap of objectification and the cuts between subjectivity, the self and the body.

Providing new identities for sex workers even beyond paternalism and victimization or reframing the linguistic structure to address their vulnerability equally to that of other political subjects must surely provide a sex worker with new tools of resistance, and one can be part of radical grass-roots groups with strong identities, thus addressing the social and political vulnerability of one's body. Yet there is another level of one's body and self that remain unaddressed. One may enact strategies of separation of one's body and self while still prostituting oneself. One's voice allows such a singular awareness of vulnerability.

Finally, the third point of resistance provided by one's voice reflects the plurality of the voice: speaking in one's voice always happens in a context of plurality and relationality, which is essentially a community.[75] In her article "Birth, Love, Politics," Cavarero explains that being within a community does not mean being an *aggregate* of individuals or being together next to others, but refers primarily to exposing one's internal uniqueness. Exposure is constitutive of relationality and *being with* and *with others*. There are, for Cavarero, two fundamental settings where such internal and constitutive uniqueness is revealed in a community: in birth and in the relation between two lovers:

> *The first setting in which uniqueness and community meet each other is that of birth. Here the existent is found in its incarnate concreteness: this boy, this*

74 Gregory, *The Everyday Lives of Sex Workers in the Netherlands*; Hoigard and Finstad, *Prostitution, Money and Love*; Sanders, *Sex Work: A Risky Business*; Day, "What Counts as Rape?" O' Neill, *Prostitution and Feminism*.

75 Adriana Cavarero, "Birth, Love, Politics," *Radical Philosophy*, 86 (1997): 19–23.

> *girl [. . .] The newborn, as Hannah Arendt would say, appears as singular and unrepeatable, different from all those who have lived before or will live after it.*[76]

> *The second setting in which the existent and the community intersect is the community of lovers [. . .] In this second setting of appearance, the lovers love one another, love who they are. As Hannah Arendt would say, they love their who. One does not love the what of the beloved, one loves instead who he is. Moreover, one often loves him in spite of what he is.*[77]

For Cavarero, a lover – similarly to a mother – loves *who you are* even when disapproving of *what you are.*[78] Both the lover and the mother speak the *same language of the in-spite of language.*[79] Both show the nakedness of an existent that simply exists in being with and exposed. There are *two unrepeatable singularities who distinguish themselves by appearing together.*[80] Cavarero is interested in loving interactions, in those interactions that precisely express a community and reveal the meaning of one's uniqueness, unlike the objectification process that indicates a loss of meaning and reflects the categories of the what; of a subject that is cut and divested from the who one is.

> *The map of erogenous zones of the body are therefore ridiculous technical supports (a product of the scientific community of sex) for those who ignore that they are touching an existent in the wholeness of its exposure.*[81]

If we act according to an ontology of one's uniqueness, then treating a person as mere body parts cannot happen. Commercial sex and the objectification that results from it express an ontology of divisions and cuts, an ontology grounded on a subject as separated from one's uniqueness, an ontology that is not consonant to one's voice.

In addition to the community of birth and of lovers, Cavarero refers to another community setting, that of politics, where politics is to be intended in the way Arendt intended it, a plural space of reciprocal appearing. In such a space of appearing, any type of interaction can only be reciprocal and thus love and politics belong together. In both love and politics, what is constitutive is precisely the relation of the self with oneself and others. In the space of appearance, in politics or love, there is existence without the qualities of the subject. Thus one is not able to objectify or be objectified because one is not cut from oneself. On the contrary, the patriarchal division of

76 Cavarero, "Birth, Love, Politics," 19–20.
77 Cavarero, "Birth, Love, Politics," 20.
78 Cavarero, "Birth, Love, Politics," 21.
79 Cavarero, "Birth, Love, Politics," 21.
80 Cavarero, "Birth, Love, Politics," 21.
81 Cavarero, "Birth, Love, Politics," 21.

sexual difference forces women not to appear but to rest within the cut and divided qualities of the subject:

> *Due to their well- known patriarchal character, the forms of domination produce a prohibition of political appearance which applies above all to women. Stifled by socially defined qualities (like maternal caring or bodily seductiveness), a woman is thus by and large forced to exhibit what she is, while the drive towards the self-exhibition of who she is becomes perceptible to her as a sort of secret resistance to the prohibition against expression.*[82]

Cavarero focuses on the interactions in the community of unique selves beyond the levels of standards such as equality and autonomy. Consequently, and in contrast to Nussbaum's perspective, sexual interaction does not need to happen in a context of equality, intimacy or symmetry; it needs simply to be experienced at the level of the singularity of difference, of one's uniqueness, for it not to be objectifying. When speaking in one's voice, there is a sort of dialog between people as each is unique and with a specific voice and body. The existent, Cavarero says in "Birth, Love, Politics," is one's uniqueness in her unrepeatable difference that simply appears for *who one is*, beyond the essentialized sexed identities, in her inescapable finitude and vulnerability.

In order to explain her understanding of human interaction, Cavarero engages with the thought of Georges Bataille. It is by means of transgression that the self in Bataille can crack open the forced jacket of separations imposed by the limits of subjectivity. In Bataille's book *Eroticism*,[83] sexual interaction is seen in contrast to the logic of exchange in commercial sex. For Bataille, in sexual interaction there is the possibility of a sort of nakedness, which allows precisely for the possibility of being stripped naked of the discontinuous existence of our constructed subjectivities by forging the sexual moment with death. Death precisely interrupts discontinuity and rather conduces continuity by dispossessing the subject.

At this point, sexual interaction in Bataille becomes mingled with fascination, violence and violation and those in turn show the excess. Sexual interaction becomes sacrificial and transgressive of the limits, and the sex workers the sacrificial object that paradoxically could move outside the utilitarian logic of exchange. The insubordinate feminine identity is seen as disconnected from money and capable of breaking from morality and possession. In general, sexual interaction becomes an occasion for destroying the self-contained character of normality and for overcoming the limits of the symbolic order. Yet it is difficult to imagine any political application of the thought of Bataille on to sex work. In fact, Cavarero is critical of the transgressive myth of dissolution and continuity in sexual interaction proposed by Bataille.

82 Cavarero, "Birth, Love, Politics," 22–23.

83 Georges Bataille, *Eroticism*, trans. Mary Dalwood (London: Pearson, 1957).

Unlike Bataille, in Cavarero's perspective there is no fusion of lovers into unity, and no turning of sexual interaction into a death drive, or pleasure that coincides with annihilation and the sacrifice of the other in the impersonal flesh. For Cavarero, it is a myth to think that love and death merge into dissolution and continuity. On the contrary, Cavarero affirms that sexual interaction repeats the exposure of uniqueness. She focuses on love rather than death and sacrifice, because love is capable of escaping the appearance of indifference and thus of objectification.[84] In love, there is the renewal of birth and coincidence of life and existence, the disclosure of who someone is; whereas, in death and sacrifice, there is just an attempt to forget the *what* that constitutes us. Unlike Bataille, there is no need for transgression or fascination with sex and death for continuity to be achieved. Rather, in one's voice there is the possibility of a unique inner experience that moves toward the continuity of our radical human condition. Cavarero notes that in Bataille there is a passion for suffering and a community as an abyss of nothingness. The corporeal aspect of us is more flesh than body, a general flesh that is directed toward negation, death and destruction and that is in opposition to birth, love and beginning.

The focus on the voice is able to reframe the ethical and political phenomena associated with objectification in different ways by grounding a positive model of ethical sexual behavior and suspending the hegemonic sexuality of violence, fascination and death. Under the perspective of one's voice, objectification can be understood as the failure to be aware of and recognize the radical ontological uniqueness of others. Thus the ontology of one's voice allows for an avoidance of objectification in human interaction.

In *Horrorism*, while discussing the torture in Abu Ghraib, Cavarero shows that what creates horror is precisely the interaction between people without reciprocity and awareness of uniqueness and vulnerability.[85]

> *In torture the asymmetry of power emerges as absolute: the victim is in a position of complete vulnerability and exposure, the torturer in one of perfect control and inscrutability. In this sense, torture is an intensely malign form of human relationship, its most radical perversion. [. . .] The other, the torturer, wounds him and is there only to wound him. There is no alternative or reciprocity. There is no way out, only the infinite and prolonged repetition of unilateral suffering.*[86]

Going back to sex work, sexual interaction in Cavarero can be interpreted as something no longer outside the selfhood, that can be treated as possession and stolen from another selfhood, transformed into sameness and understood as an

84 Cavarero, "Birth, Love, Politics," 21–22.
85 Adriana Cavarero, *Horrorism: Naming Contemporary Violence*, trans. William McCuaig (New York: Columbia University Press, 2009). See also: Timothy J. Huzar, "Horrorism in the Scene of Torture: Reading Scarry with Cavarero," *Journal of Interdisciplinary Voice Studies*, 2 (2017): 25–43.
86 Cavarero, *Horrorism*, 114.

equal exchange. Sexuality is rather part of one's unique corporeality, distinctiveness and reciprocity because it is constitutive of one's uniqueness.

Unlike Nussbaum, for whom the politics of interaction is regulated by standards of equality and mutuality and with conditions of intimacy between subjects, in Cavarero's perspective those parameters are precisely constitutive of processes of objectification and exclusion because one can only fit into them as a linguistic subject already divested of one's voice and uniqueness; one can only exist as a *what* and an identity already decided by the rational law of the Father. Cahill also notes that Nussbaum's account of sexual objectification is dependent upon a Kantian model of subjectivity; that is, a model where the body is excluded and marginalized and where corporeal and sexual experience is not sufficiently accounted for.[87] On the contrary, for Cavarero, one's corporeal body is intertwined with the uniqueness of the existent.

According to Butler, objectification can be avoided by questioning the constructed subjectivity, as well as the fictitious mechanisms of intelligibility within the normative frame. Thus objectification is resolved by means of repetition of those fictitious constructions and in the possibility of reworking linguistically such formations and redirecting them toward more just formulations and a better understanding of the vulnerable body exposed to power. However, there is no account of one's voice as suspension and rupture from those very objectifying mechanisms; objectification in sexual interaction is resolved by reframing the same symbolic order that produces exclusion and objectification even if the body is reached and touched through the reframing.

The focus on one's voice and uniqueness instead opposes the notion of sexuality as being harmful with a sexuality that safeguards uniqueness and reciprocity. For Cavarero, one's uniqueness and corporeality consists of a fundamental ethical and ontological bodily openness to the other's vulnerability and a corresponding responsibility to the other. The decision to wound or to care for the other rests on one's unique selfhood. Because one's uniqueness is a *who-ness* without cuts and separation, an awareness of oneself, there is the necessity to take care of and attend to the other.

The exposure of one's unique voice is also rooted in natality, regeneration and birth. Eros and sexuality are embraced by such natality, which means seeing sexuality as reciprocity and with a sense of the vulnerability of the other. Ricoeur has defined reciprocity as giving and receiving in a circuit of generosity. This will be discussed further in the next chapter. There is indeed implicit in the voice and in the awareness of one's uniqueness an idea of corporeal generosity. To force such a gift by coercion would not be an upholding of corporeal generosity and one's voice but a violation of it. Thus, according to Cavarero's ontology, in the case of *R v Gary Lee Cole and Stephen Kevin Barik* the injustice lies in removing from the corporeal selfhood of the sex worker her most salient capacity to give

87 Cahill, *Overcoming Objectification*, 14.

voice to such a gift. Regardless of whether she works in the sex industry, forcing a woman to give corporeality through sex is unjust. Sexual interaction needs to be seen instead as contributing to the enrichment of uniqueness and relationality. An ethical sexual interaction requires that one enters the interaction with unique desires and an awareness of one's voice and vulnerable body.

There is vulnerability, wonder, singularity and difference, and all are deeply intertwined in the interaction and open to change and transformation by means of such interaction with one another. And the other cannot be known, subsumed, dominated but there is, rather, a sort of unknowability at stake; the other is just there in her vulnerability, exposed to me, and I am ethically called upon to respond to such exposure with responsibility. Sexual objectification does not find a place in the ontology of one's voice because what counts is one's relationality with the other. Speaking in one's voice implies being aware of one's vulnerability and the vulnerability of others, acting ethically, being aware of the uniqueness of others as an ethical guide for our action.

Natality remains central to the account of the voice offered by Cavarero. One begins one's existence as a vulnerable infant, and hence there is the need to take responsibility and care for the vulnerable one. Lisa Guenther explains how we are born before another one who gave birth to us.[88] Thus birth suggests that one's time is already connected to the time of others. Birth becomes awareness of the vulnerability of others; vulnerability is intrinsic to sex work and needs to be taken into account in processes of resistance.

One could argue that love and the reciprocity of the ontology of the voice are of no help to sex workers. But one can rebut this by saying that conceiving of an ontology that resists objectification is the first step toward changing commercial sex, as it is today, with its ethical dilemmas. To overcome the deep and sustained inequality that often runs in the exchange between a sex worker and a client, it is of paramount importance not to associate sexual interaction with objectification. What Cavarero intends to do is precisely to consider relationality and reciprocity as the constitutive dimension of human interaction.

The ontology of one's voice can therefore also trouble the discursive objectification appropriated and repeated by law, which reinforces the material objectification of women. In commenting on Arendt's relation to law, Birmingham mentions that for Arendt, law was initially constituted as a wall or a border, whereas in her later works, as Loizidou also notes, Arendt embraced law as an ally because, for Arendt, to turn against the law amounted to becoming an enemy of the city itself.[89] For Birmingham, the alliance with law is inspired by the miraculous principles of givenness and initium that are constituted through

88 Lisa Guenther, *The Gift of the Other: Levinas and the Politics of Reproduction* (Albany: State University of New York Press, 2006).

89 Birmingham, "On Action: The Appearance of the Law," 112; Elena Loizidou, "Disobedience Subjectively Speaking," in *Disobedience: Concept and Practice*, ed. Loizidou, E. (Oxon: Routledge, 2013), 108–124.

praxis. This means similarly that the ontology of one's voice, despite suspending law, needs to engage with law as well, although it cannot remain within the sole limits of law. Thus the voice can contribute to the transformation of the violent and sovereign constituted power of law into the Arendtian *shared political praxis of the living space of the law*.

Conclusion

This chapter has aimed to rethink resistance to the objectification in sex work through the voice. It has tried to consider the place of one's voice in commercial sex and how one's voice can resist otherwise. Objectification signifies more than treating someone as a body; it means, as Cahill suggests, reducing someone to a reflection of one's own desires and needs, disregarding the other self.[90] It is easy to objectify in a situation in which subjectivity is predicated on belonging to one sex, whereas the other sex is cut out and excluded from it. It has been argued that sex work marks the division of women from masculine subjectivity in radical ways. Law's perspective has appropriated such a division, showing itself to have incorporated a historical approach grounded on objectification, shame and the victimization of the sex worker. Recent changes in law do not necessarily lead to providing a voice to sex workers. Scholars such as Munro and Carline suggest that women in sex work are still constructed already as victims, without agency, and that criminalization increases around sex work. The case law of *R v Gary Lee Cole and Stephen Kevin Barik* confirms that sex workers are still regarded as less than full subjects.

Nussbaum thinks that objectification in sexual interactions is not morally malign, if enacted in intimate contexts of equality and respect; sex work is thus excluded from such a consideration, even if it is reputed to be a free and autonomous choice within liberal terms. Butler focuses on the normative processes of objectification, which are enacted by fictitious identity formation and by frames of linguistic intelligibility. Butler wants to make those linguistic structures – including vulnerability – diversely intelligible and capable of protecting all vulnerability by finding cracks that allow for some sort of change in the intelligible vulnerability of sex workers.

On the contrary, I propose a threefold way of resistance through one's voice. Firstly, the ontology of one's voice, as theorized by Cavarero, implies a different conception of existent beyond the linguistic symbolic order. In the symbolic order, we are represented in terms of cut and separations, through a masculine representation of the subject that pretends to be a neutral subjectivity, where the body is associated with feminine traits devalued, excluded or even objectified, as in the case of sex workers. It has been argued that the historical objectification of sex workers in law marks radically the cracks of a patriarchal and essentialized sexual difference division of the subject. The estrangement of women in

90 Cahill, *Objectification*, 32.

commercial sex shows precisely the violence of identification of a cut subjectivity and of the separation produced by discursive practices.

In opposition to this, it has been suggested one needs to begin with one's voice that reveals one's uniqueness. One's uniqueness does not possess the appropriating power of the subject and does not speak the language of proper identity, but offers an ontological approach to resistance that avoids those separations. The alienating effect of the current subjectivity that objectifies some people originates precisely from the feeling that *who one is* is not being addressed and has no place in the symbolic order. The *who* of selfhood and one's voice are totally disregarded. With the ontology of one's voice, we can overcome the divisions and cuts because the voice reveals selfhood as unique.

Secondly, awareness of one's vulnerability through one's voice can help one address the vulnerability experienced in commercial sex. One can resist both moralizing and discursive legal approaches and the actual experience of vulnerability and splits that sex work may produce. One who is engaged in commercial sex might face several splits and cuts, such as, for instance, the separation of personal and intimate experiences and body parts from those used and experienced at work. One's voice, by providing an account of oneself, allows one to suspend separations, viewing things via one's uniqueness and a reconnection to vulnerability. For the subject, and specifically a sex worker, to be heard could involve the abandonment of the way one is framed, defamed or made vulnerable within the various symbolic discourses and institutions, such as law and feminism, and to speak in one's voice and listen to one's own vulnerability. In court, this could mean that one could deal with one's own vulnerability and refuse to be addressed by discourses that act and speak on one's behalf.

Thirdly, the focus on the voice brings to life an ontological space of reciprocity that moves away from objectification in all human interactions, suspends any defined sovereign subjectivity and allows positive reorientation of thinking and action. The ontology of the voice is centered on natality, newness, in the sense of acting anew toward vulnerability and reciprocity. Birth signifies precisely the reunion of lovers.[91] Natality becomes then the condition of relationality and reciprocity in a community of lovers.[92] As Birmingham suggests, in Arendt's late works the ontology of givenness of uniqueness and initium of plurality also becomes the answer for forging alliances with law, thus allowing the voice not only to resist law by suspending it but also to approach and engage with law for transformation.[93] In the next chapter, the voice is explored in relation to justice beyond resentment. Arendt's forgiveness becomes central to this. The action of forgiveness becomes possible if one speaks in one's voice and connects to the body and vulnerability of oneself and others.

91 Patricia Bowen-Moore, *Hannah Arendt's Philosophy of Natality* (London: Macmillan Press, 1989).
92 Bowen-Moore, *Hannah Arendt's Philosophy of Natality*.
93 Birmingham, "On Action: The Appearance of the Law," 114.

Part III

The ethical justice of the voice

Chapter 4

Moving away from justice as resentment[1]

This chapter will consider the action of forgiveness as an ethical development of the focus on the voice. In fact, one's voice implies a different awareness of the kind of selves we are. Speaking in one's voice leads to an awareness of corporeality, uniqueness, relationality and vulnerability; our selves are no longer given and autonomous monads, already narrated, but rather "narratable selves" that tell their stories while in relationality, revealing unique aspects of themselves and becoming aware of themselves and others.[2] The point this chapter aims to make is that this different understanding of the self makes it possible to think of an ethics that exceeds the forms of resentment reflected in the liberal legal and political logic.

Scholars such as Jennifer Culbert and Austin Sarat have reflected on ways in which the state, in the liberal political and legal tradition, authorizes violence as a response to injury, on how state violence is connected with ideas of sovereignty, and on the need to change the state's relationship to violence by seeing the violent state as a state of mind that is not just a social or psychological condition but an ethical and ontological position.[3] Contrary to the logic of resentment adopted by the state and its legal apparatus, one's voice allows a response with awareness, thus contributing to a reframing of the current conversation on justice. One's voice can also transform the understanding of actions such as forgiveness. Spoken from one's voice, forgiveness is intended as an unexpected action from within.

1 Versions of this chapter can be found in the following papers: Elisabetta Bertolino, "Predictable Medea," *Studies in the Maternal*, 2(1) (2010): 1–10. DOI: http://doi.org/10.16995/sim.96; Elisabetta Bertolino, "Forgiveness, One's Voice and the Law," in *The Philosophy of Forgiveness. New Dimensions of Forgiveness*, ed. Lewis, C.D. II (Wilmington: Vernon Press, 2016), 187–214; Elisabetta Bertolino, "The Injustice of Justice. Feminist Ethical Reflections on Subjectivity," *WAGADU Special Issue on Epistemic Justice in Practice*, 15 (2016): 72–121.

2 Adriana Cavarero, *Relating Narratives. Storytelling and Selfhood*, trans. Paul Kottman (London: Routledge, 2000).

3 Jennifer Culbert and Austin Sarat, "Interpreting the Violent State" in *States of Violence. War, Capital Punishment and Letting Die*, eds Culbert, J. and Sarat, A. (Cambridge: Cambridge University Press, 2009), 1–24. See also Jennifer Culbert, *Dead Certainty. The Death Penalty and the Problem of Judgment* (Stanford: Stanford University Press, 2008).

This understanding of forgiveness indicates that the intent of this chapter is not to moralize the argument of one's voice, but rather to emphasize the ethical and unique potentiality of the voice. Speaking in one's voice exposes one's uniqueness and allows awareness of our human condition of frailty, breaking with forgiveness understood as a story told by others or an institutional choice. One's voice has to do with a singular, vulnerable and binding selfhood, not with any sovereign command or construed subjectivity. One's voice transforms one's thinking from within, making one refuse resentment or forgiveness if they are told by sovereign scripts. On the contrary, one's voice allows a recovery from hurt in community.

In relation to this, Jill Stauffer defines *ethical loneliness* as the isolation one feels if one is abandoned by society after violation.[4] This happens precisely because selves and worlds are built by human interaction. Within her perspective, recovery from hurt is central in thinking about justice. Simply finding someone to blame or achieving revenge does not help a victim of violence; rather it is necessary to voice what one has suffered to an audience and confirm the violence as something that should have never happened. Both Stauffer and I think that such an open and accepting speaking context would then allow the inner move toward forgetting and forgiveness.

For Stauffer, it is necessary to restore safety and create forms of revisionary practice in which everyone involved in violence – victims, perpetrators and bystanders – can speak and listen to allow recovery and resist conditions of *ethical loneliness*.[5] What matters is not achieving forgiveness per se. Only when present conditions restore the safety and trust on which humanity relies can forgiveness become a possible option for justice and pacify the protest of resentment, making it unnecessary. In this way the need for resentment might be relieved as the threat is diminished. Recovery is then grounded in the re-establishment of the ordinary conditions of everyday life, which requires a community, thus showing that responsibility rests in a much broader field. Revision can be created only by a plurality of persons, and law is not the only possibility for Stauffer.[6]

The forgiveness that springs from one's voice is precisely not an institutionalized form of forgiveness, nor is it the expression of a general voice or command. On the contrary, it happens in relationality with others, during exposure to others, and it involves becoming aware of the uniqueness and vulnerability of this exposure. There is in fact a strong connection between speaking in one's voice and enacting forgiveness. I think that enacting forgiveness to end violence in place of punishment requires an ontological awareness of life as connection and dependence, a life in community rather than a life of separation and independence

4 Jill Stauffer, *Ethical Loneliness. The Injustice of Not Being Heard* (New York: Columbia University Press, 2015).

5 Stauffer, *Ethical Loneliness*, 81.

6 Stauffer, *Ethical Loneliness*, 140.

such as that of the liberal autonomous individual. Through speaking in one's voice one speaks one's vulnerability as well as becoming aware of the vulnerability of others and this awareness connects rather than separates.

It is precisely this awareness and connection that opens the self to the possibility of radical actions such as forgiveness. Forgiveness – in this perspective – is an action of reconnection, first of all to oneself and then to the community of vulnerable selves, an action where the self is bound to others, where one understands oneself as dependent and so one inclines, to help others. On the contrary, the ontological subject of resentment is understood as a subject that is separated, cut, independent and disconnected from life. Through resentment, the subject is imagined as capable of separating from her wronged subjectivity and that of the perpetrator and achieving autonomy and independence. Law makes use of such a subject of resentment to resist intolerable conditions and achieve justice.

Intolerable and repressive conditions do provoke acts of resistance, since the subject wants to break free from them. Yet resistance can assume various forms, some of them reactive, like vengeance. Vengeance is precisely the most common form of resistance. Howard Caygill explains how the logic of resentment builds upon the Hegelian thought that resistance is dependent upon what it opposes.[7] The Hegelian resistance results in an endless and irreversible polarity of opposition and antithesis. Caygill argues instead for a type of resistance that does not just react to an intolerable situation but transforms itself and the original conditions.[8]

New ways of thinking about the subjectivity of resistance and the capacity to resist become, then, necessary elements of a resistance that breaks from the past and opens to the future.[9] The voice also resists a subject of resentment, disclosing a unique existent, and offers the capacity to avoid the terrain of the enemy, affirming instead an ontology of natality, reciprocity, inclination and forgiveness, opening in turn new possibilities for justice and supplementing some of the reflections of current critical legal theory on the theme.

In *Critical Jurisprudence*, critical legal scholars including Costas Douzinas and Adam Gearey resist the legal approach to justice.[10] Drawing on Levinas, Douzinas and Gearey embrace the infinite openness of ethical alterity. Against the law's tendency to calculate equally and to make things symmetrical, Emmanuel, Douzinas and Gearey disturb this totalizing tendency by opening it to ethical alterity.

Similarly, the focus on the voice brings together the justice offered by law and the openness of disclosure of one's uniqueness. This effectively opposes the indifference of the equal exchange that operates in law through resentment and

7 Howard Caygill, *On Resistance. A Philosophy of Defiance* (London: Bloomsbury, 2013), 97, 135.
8 Caygill, *On Resistance,* 97, 135.
9 Caygill, *On Resistance,* 97, 135.
10 Costas Douzinas and Adam Gearey, *Critical Jurisprudence: The Political Philosophy of Justice* (Oxford: Hart Publishing, 2005), 173.

punishment. The voice suspends such a judgmental operation of law and resists it by standing outside the legal ontology.

This chapter deals first with the violent reaction of Medea[11] and connects it to the theme of "the subject of resentment" through the insights of Wendy Brown and Gilles Deleuze. It then compares forgiveness with the position of feminist theory, arguing that feminism has tried to make visible the female subject fighting gender violence by focusing on the same emotion of resentment. The character of Chiara of Assisi, as described by Dacia Maraini, will be compared to Medea. Forgiveness is then analyzed in the thinking of feminist philosophers such as Adriana Cavarero, Hannah Arendt and Christine Battersby. And, finally, forgiveness is speculated upon through the theoretical positions of Jacques Derrida, George Bataille, Paul Ricoeur and Arendt.

Overall, the chapter underlines how one's voice is connected to unpredictable actions such as forgiveness and this latter is understood as coming from within, after one has been able to speak what one has suffered. Through one's voice, the chapter attempts to go beyond masculine or feminine forms of resistance and embrace actions that spring from one's uniqueness.

4.1 Predictable Medea and resentment

In *Antigone's Law*, Costas Douzinas and Ronnie Warrington trace the question of law's origins, value and ethics by offering the spectre of Antigone.[12] Douzinas and Warrington draw on Antigone because Antigone laid down, in some ways, the philosophical foundation of law.[13] Antigone wants to bury the corpse of her brother, Polynices, whereas her uncle, King Creon, prohibits the burial of Polynices for being a traitor. While Creon proclaims the vision of law based on calculation, and utilitarian and normative general rules, Antigone shows that another ontological level to law is possible as opposed to law's general, indifferent and vindictive perspective. I like to think that Antigone's different way is due to the fact that she chooses to speak in her own voice rather than the voice of law. Her voice reveals her uniqueness and vulnerability within a community of singular and vulnerable beings and makes her respond accordingly: thus Antigone decides to bury her brother.

However, in this chapter I will not refer to Antigone but to another character, Medea.[14] Medea's analysis is interesting in that it offers a view of resistance that

11 Medea is a female character in an ancient Greek tragedy by Euripides that has attracted renewed interest in feminist theory because in the tragedy she struggles to take charge of her own life in a male-dominated society and reacts violently by killing her own children after her husband has left her for another woman.

12 Costas Douzinas and Ronnie Warrington, "Antigone's Law: A Genealogy of Jurisprudence," in *Politics, Postmodernity and Critical Legal Studies*, eds Douzinas, C., Goodrich, P. and Hachamovitch, Y. (London: Routledge, 1994), 187–225.

13 Douzinas and Warrington, "Antigone's Law," 195.

14 Euripides, *Medea*, ed. Page, Denys, L.P. (Oxford: Clarendon Press, 1971).

leads to forgiveness through one's voice. In the Greek tragedy, Medea's character becomes unexpectedly one of resentment, vengeance and infanticide, breaking away from the stereotypes of women seen as traditionally passive and victims under patriarchy. Rather, Medea follows the path of masculine aggression and resentment.[15]

Medea and Jason lived together for years and had two legitimate children. Medea loved Jason faithfully, risked her life for him, sacrificed home and family and even committed crimes to help him. Later, Jason decides to marry another woman, Creon's young daughter, to secure himself a social position; Jason's act follows the script of patriarchy. At this point Medea's world is on the verge of collapse and she finds herself in an unbearable condition. In ancient Greece, women were perceived as childbearers and wives and valued in relation to this. Consequently, losing her family signified the falling apart of Medea's world and status.

By the end of the tragedy, Medea chooses to be victorious, powerful, to possess the lives of her children, to remove from Jason all sources of security and to enact vengeance, finding a way to wound him. She thinks that the killing of her own children is the only way she can restore balance and make things equal. Medea is full of resentment and sees in the murderous act the appropriate reaction to her loss. By killing her children, she asserts herself as a subject of resentment but also as a subject that shows herself to be powerful, independent and capable of making justice.

Her infanticide is generally seen as an unpredictable action that does not repeat the stereotypes of the feminine as passive, docile and forgiving. This thinking is rather reversed in this chapter. I argue that Medea's action resists Jason by enacting the same subject of resentment as that of the legal subject and by moving within the same terrain of the enemy. Thus Medea's reaction can be considered predictable and common among all human beings who find themselves in intolerable conditions.[16]

Medea's retributive emotion contains a demand for justice and is not foreign to the symbolic legal order. The very emotions of resentment, vengeance and retaliation that Medea experiences are cognitive states and states of belief that become rationalized and institutionalized in law and rights alike. Law and rights communicate the message that the anger we feel toward those who commit wrong is entirely appropriate and that it is just not to give up those emotions. Thus it is possible to say that Medea's story is a story of vengeance and violence, the story of all of us, of the righteous subject who needs retaliation and retribution against wrongs committed. Medea's reaction is also an example of inappropriate and immoderate human resistance, a reaction to violence through violence; it shows how the oppressed can react in ways that perpetrate the same abuse suffered as a victim.

Medea's gesture of violence has been considered unpredictable, moving away from the stereotypes of the feminine subject because she does not comply with

15 Euripides, *Medea*.
16 Bertolino, "Predictable Medea."

the essentialized feminine traits of a mother that is supposed to be caring, weak, able to accept injustice in her passivity. On the contrary, Medea appears as a woman who acts as the other; she is the murderous mother that undermines one of the basic assumptions upon which all societies are constructed: that mothers protect and care for their children. In challenging the men's symbolic order Medea represents the rage of women betrayed by men, and from a victim of Jason's betrayal she turns into a victimizer. As she is brutally oppressed by Jason, she fights back using the same tools of violence. I think, therefore, that Medea is a mother that by refusing and resisting the essentialized predictability of motherhood does not do anything unpredictable; rather, she follows the predictable identity of the subject of violence who is willing to master others, re-appropriating the subject of patriarchy, liberalism and feminism.

Medea's reaction is then an example of inappropriate resistance, a resistance to violence through violence, of a world that destroys itself. She shows precisely that the oppressed can react in ways to perpetrate new abuses and even increase violence. In particular, Medea's reaction to patriarchal violence indicates how often women seek political and public solutions for their sufferings that reflect the same masculine symbolic order that they seek to run away from. By doing this, women leave the place of singularity, vulnerability and relationality and inevitably disconnect from themselves. I see a feminist incongruence and dilemma in a resentful reaction to violence, a simultaneous wish to be different from the masculine order but also to remain equal to it and within it. On the other hand, I would like to connect feminism to one's voice and look for the possibilities of ways of being and acting that escape masculine and feminine binarism, revealing instead one's uniqueness.

Cavarero has been critical of the stereotypes around women.[17] For Cavarero both the good maternal figure and the destructive Medea reflect a sovereign and masculine power that perceives women through binary opposition.[18]

> *If we work only with the stereotype of spiritual maternity (la Madonna, Our Lady) or with that of destructive maternity (Medea), we risk tracing two different versions of patriarchal discourse rather than disclosing the radical dilemma that is at the basis of an ethics of relation.*[19]

Cavarero works instead with the voice and through the voice she finds human categories that help her rethink ontologically the selfhood of women and men in a non-binary schema. The focus on the voice reveals one's uniqueness,

17 Adriana Cavarero, *In Spite of Plato: A Feminist Rewriting of Ancient Philosophy*, trans. Serena Anderlini-D'Onofrio and Aine O'Heady (Cambridge: Polity Press, 1995).

18 Adriana Cavarero with Elisabetta Bertolino, "Beyond Ontology and Sexual Difference: An Interview with the Italian Feminist Philosopher Adriana Cavarero," *differences: A Journal of Feminist Cultural Studies*, 19(1) (2008): 128–167.

19 Cavarero with Bertolino, "Beyond Ontology and Sexual Difference," 148.

corporeality and vulnerability. Those traits belong both to men and women and cannot be reduced to predictable stereotypes associated with women only. Rather the traits of the voice escape binarism and make people's actions unpredictable and responsible for the ethical dilemma of wounding or caring. Consequently, what is at stake with one's voice is the potentiality to resist violence without engaging with it because of the awareness of the vulnerable condition exposed by the voice in the polyphonic community.

For Arendt both action and speech (the voice) are deeply related, as both reveal someone's uniqueness and thus both reveal the actor, the one who acts revealing her uniqueness.[20] And for Arendt, precisely this disclosure of the actor – who someone is – leads to a resistance that, instead of repeating violence, affirms unpredictable actions. Forgiveness can be one of such actions. Forgiveness is an action that lets go of the past and invests in the future, and can thus energize the ability to resist in the present.[21] The voice contains precisely the potentiality for an unpredictable response to violence because it implies a selfhood that reconnects to the vulnerabilities of others and takes into account the possibility of forgiveness. In this framework, forgiveness cannot be refused simply because it has traditionally been associated with the stereotype of the feminine (women have been taught, for instance, to forgive and accept injustice). Neither should one resent and fight back in an attempt to re-appropriate the law of the father.

In Chapter III, for instance, I dealt with the process of objectification and sex work, where women are construed within the stereotype of the sexually promiscuous woman, the prostitute, both as a social reality and a male fantasy figure. Such a cut and split construction of women contrasts with the opposite stereotype of woman, that of the virgin and the good mother. Chapter III underlined precisely how historically law has placed women sex workers within that stereotype, considering sexually available women as criminals and thus as less than full subjects.

In this chapter, I reflect critically on a forgiving selfhood that corresponds neither to the feminine stereotype nor to the neutral (in reality, masculine) subject, but to a type of resistance, grounded in one's voice; that is, in singularity and vulnerability. In addition, the forgiveness of one's voice is neither institutionalized nor already thought for the subject. The forgiveness that arises from one's voice differs from forgiveness in transitional justice and in political reconciliation, and from political forgiveness. Those approaches to justice are not neutral and do not come from oneself. They are rather interventions that have been chosen, decided for one by others.

Differently, the forgiveness that comes from one's voice heals, restores the wholeness of oneself, allowing being with oneself. In addition, one's voice gives

20 Hannah Arendt, *The Human Condition* (Chicago: The University of Chicago Press, 1958).
21 Arendt, *The Human Condition*.

the possibility of speaking and denouncing the violence suffered. The experience of speaking openly facilitates the healing process for victims.[22] Contrary to an act of forgiveness that springs from one's voice, those who harm others stand in an unsustainable and illusory position of separation, cutting off from relationality. Legal justice is used to transform suffering into something more livable. Yet peace in the community is broken by their harmful actions.

It is important to take into consideration that Medea's actions did not bring her any happiness but only desolation and suffering as she destroyed her own community. If, in the short term, by killing her children Medea asserts herself as independent from her husband and patriarchy and as a subject of resentment and hatred, in the long term she is the one who suffers mostly for the loss of her children. By acting in such a way, Medea has not followed her vulnerability, *who she is*, but only an abstract and separated subject of vengeance, an identity, a *what* that is cut, divided from her unique selfhood. Conversely, one's voice discloses one's uniqueness and the truth that one is, not a subject already conceived in isolation but a unique selfhood in relationality. A being is always a being *with*, always relational, always exposed to others[23] whereas, in responding to violence through violence, Medea severs the relationality with her family and community, showing disconnection and separation.

Even if institutions for legal justice respond reparatively to past harms, scholars such as Stauffer are in doubt whether they benefit people who have been harmed, as legal proceedings neutralize the needs and wishes of victims of violence.[24] A forgiveness that springs from one's voice is instead an act of newness that allows the possibility of restoring a community. One's forgiveness does not involve complicity, acquiescence in wrongdoing or forgetting. Rather, it involves an awareness of the unique vulnerability of each of us coming from one's voice.

This new kind of response would require Medea to act creatively, anew, not as an essentialized female figure/mother, but rather as a calm and centered self. She would not have shown weakness but the strength of a forgiving self that comes from awareness, a being who ends suffering and does not reproduce it. Harming other people, especially those who are vulnerable, is not an act of freedom but an act of despair and does not bring peace or happiness. In the end, Medea shows clearly that the other or enemy lies within us, in our wrong perception of human vulnerability and uniqueness. In opposition to such an understanding of reality, awareness of uniqueness and vulnerability might have important implications for feminism.

22 Stauffer, *Ethical Loneliness*, 57.

23 See: Adriana Cavarero, *For More Than One Voice: Toward a Philosophy of Vocal Expression*, trans. Paul Kottman (Stanford: Stanford University Press, 2005); Jean Luc Nancy, *Being Singular Plural*, trans. Robert D. Richardson and Anne E. O'Byrne (Stanford: Stanford University Press, 2000).

24 Stauffer, *Ethical Loneliness*, 53.

4.2 The subject of resentment

This book has argued that the current legal subjectivity is grounded on the fiction of the autonomous individual; a subject thought of as general and abstract and, moreover, in isolation. Consequently, as legal subject, one is disconnected from oneself and the community of others. Such a disconnection is particularly visible in issues of violence and survival. There is a discrepancy between surviving the wound of violence on a singular level and as a general legal subject. Surviving violence for oneself means essentially getting on with one's own life, overcoming an identity as a victim, reconnecting to oneself, speaking the injury and especially releasing suffering and letting go. While for the legal subject surviving violence means becoming aware of the offense of the injury, feeling resentment, pursuing retribution and then appreciating that justice has been accomplished when punishment is inflicted on the one who has caused suffering.

The point that needs to be emphasized here is that retribution does not improve the conditions of the victim of violence, of the singular person, but only of the general subject. In fact, achieving retribution can be understood as the effect of a cut subject, separated from oneself and the community of others. This is because trapping oneself in resentment, in the compulsion of victimhood, revenge and desire for punishment does not allow movement, a letting go, but endlessly proceeds from wrong to wrong. On the contrary, surviving violence on a singular and vulnerable level means speaking in one's voice, from an awareness of oneself, and reconnecting to oneself and the community.

At this point, I would like to reflect a bit more on the mechanism of resentment that can develop after an injury. Surviving violence is a difficult process. If one is a victim of someone else's violence, this can have immobilizing effects, in the sense that one can be damaged so deeply that life can stop at the moment of the injury because the injury can continue to deliver pain throughout one's life. A victim of violence can be acted upon by the experience of pain because pain becomes internalized and as a victim one reacts by blaming the object of suffering, getting trapped in resentment. The point to stress here is that unfortunately the legal justice system can become a way through which one acts upon one's resentment by pursuing the punishment of the perpetrator. Consequently, justice becomes a manifestation of a subject of resentment, disconnected from the self.

We can therefore say that with respect to injuries, there are two different levels to conceiving ourselves ontologically. There is the possibility of speaking in one's voice that discloses an ontology of oneself as singular, corporeal and vulnerable and this is the unrepeatable *who-ness,* capable of unexpected actions such as forgiveness. There is then the ontology of the righteous subject who often chooses resentment and needs to restore a balance by punishing the other who has committed the injury. This latter position entails a subject who is cut and separated from uniqueness and corporeal vulnerability.

This is not to say that the ontology of law and justice can be replaced *tout court* by the ontology of one's voice. Law and its institutions are necessary places where one can speak in public the injury suffered. Through law, one can denounce one's injury and let others know about one's suffering and this is an important condition for justice to happen.

However, as Stauffer notes, the legal moment focuses narrowly on legal culpability and fails to address justice in terms of repair.[25] Beyond the legal moment one's voice shows the constitutive ontology of our human condition of being in the world with others. Such an ontology makes one critical of the fictitious subject of resentment that lies behind the legal justice system, precisely because the voice allows one to become aware of oneself in relationality and reconnects the subject's disjunctions.

But what is a subject of resentment? A subject of resentment is essentially a person that does not seem to be able to stop the pain of injury. This individual is paralyzed by injuries and reacts to wrongdoing with resentment; it is a sovereign and righteous subject that needs to retaliate through mechanisms of retributive justice and has the rights to speak and decide for others. It is a subject searching for retribution that looks outside itself for someone to blame and sees the other only for what the other has done and not for who the other is. The emotion of resentment gets directed against the other, for it is the other that is the object of hatred.

A subject of resentment can only repeat the logic of separation from the community, one that is familiar to the subjectivity of violence. I think that violence is committed precisely because one is separated from one's vulnerability and voice and from the vulnerability and voice of others in the community. A resentful action is a violent action, indicative of splits and cuts from life and is deemed to fail because the relationality with the community and oneself becomes destroyed and the position of separation is shown to be unsustainable.

Drawing on Nietzsche, some scholars have theorized critically on the subject of resentment.[26] In her article "Wounded Attachments," Wendy Brown explains the subject of resentment in relation to liberalism's failure of inclusion.[27] Current liberal identities presume to be universal but in reality exclude many who do not reflect the standard of the liberal bourgeois middle class.[28] Such exclusion leaves an injury in the subject's identity and desire for recognition, causing resentment. For Brown, on the one hand, liberalism reiterates the terms of a unified and

25 Stauffer, *Ethical Loneliness*, 46.

26 Wendy Brown, "Wounded Attachments," *Political Theory*, 21(3) (1993): 340–410; Gilles Deleuze, "From Ressentiment to the Bad Conscience," in *Nietzsche and Philosophy*, ed. Deleuze, G., trans. Hugh Tomlinson (New York: Columbia University Press, 1983), 111–146; Adriana Cavarero, "Recritude: Reflections on Postural Ontology," *The Journal of Speculative Philosophy*, 27(3) (2013), 220–235; Adriana Cavarero, "Canetti: Dritto Davanti al Morto," in *Inclinazioni: Critica della Rettitudine* (Milan: Raffaello Cortina Editore), 118–130.

27 Brown, "Wounded Attachments."

28 Brown, "Wounded Attachments."

universal subject and its regulatory and normalizing mechanisms, and on the other hand, liberalism's unemancipatory language of unfreedom in relation to identity recognition results in the logic of the Nietzschean *ressentiment*.[29] The cause of resentment is the suffering that is a reaction to the failure of the desire for identity that cannot be met. The subject, who has been failed, pursues revenge by imposing suffering and revaluing a recognition that is grounded on injury.

Brown reflects on how much subjection and impotence is invested in this identity that seeks to alleviate suffering by repeating the exclusion and the suffering itself. The excluded subject resists the intolerable condition of exclusion by perpetuating the suffering caused by liberalism, continues to exclude others and seeks the punishment of those who commit wrongs. Instead, the subject could resist by being critical of the structure, reversing the negative terms of liberalism and affirming a positive resistance.

Likewise, Gilles Deleuze in his interpretation of Nietzsche offers a critical understanding of the emotion of resentment, introducing in some ways his own position on resentment.[30] In interpreting Nietzsche, Deleuze distinguishes between active and reactive forces. Active forces are creative, whereas reactive forces produce nothing and only lead to *ressentiment* and bad conscience. In his reading of Nietzsche, for Deleuze the problem seems to reside on the fact that the subject's reactive unconscious gets defined by mnemonic traces. The subject can never renew his consciousness and is incapable of forgetting the traces. A man of resentment is precisely a man whose consciousness is invaded by mnemonic traces and his reaction consists of blaming the object that has caused suffering and a continuous desire to take revenge against it.[31] For Deleuze, Nietzsche exposes the man of resentment as a fictitious subject that multiplies its pain, interiorizes it and produces what Nietzsche calls "bad conscience"; that is, a hard man.[32]

Cavarero also touches on the theme of the subject of resentment when she focuses on the vertical subject that egoistically becomes powerful precisely when the other is punished, dead and reduced to a horizontal position.[33] In particular, she reflects on Elias Canetti, for whom a survivor is a subject who stands upright, vertically, in front of his rival, a dead man who lies on the floor, horizontally.[34] According to Cavarero, this moment of revenge and victory for Canetti makes the subject feel he has grown taller in his verticality and also has become invulnerable as opposed to the horizontality and vulnerability of the dead enemy.[35]

29 Brown, "Wounded Attachments," 399.

30 Deleuze, "From Ressentiment to the Bad Conscience."

31 Deleuze, "From Ressentiment to the Bad Conscience," 119.

32 Deleuze, "From Ressentiment to the Bad Conscience," 119.

33 Cavareo, "Recritude," 228; Cavarero, "Canetti: Dritto Davanti al Morto," 118.

34 Elias Canetti was a modernist, playwright, memoirist and non-fiction writer. See: Elias Canetti, *Crowds and Power* (New York: Farrar, Straus and Giroux, 1984); Elias Canetti, *The Conscience of Words* (New York: Seabury, 1979).

35 Cavarero, "Recritude," 228.

The subject survives violence by killing through resentment, following a logic of repeated violence through a vertical posture, as opposed to the horizontal posture of the dead; and the dead man ends up becoming an opportunity for glory in the subject's egoistic verticality and invulnerability.[36] For Cavarero, what emerges from the subject is the *killability* rather than its *vulnerability,* that is the quality of being killable rather than vulnerable. What is missing for Cavarero in the vertical subject of egoistic autonomy and violence is precisely some inclination, some attention to the other.

In the next section, we are going to deal with ways of resisting such a subject of resentment through some streams of thought in feminist philosophy.

4.3 Resisting the subject of resentment in feminism

In this section I am going to explore a feminist way of "being" that can resist the ontology of resentment. I argue that speaking in one's voice can lead to an ethical justice of unpredictable actions such as a forgiveness from within and that this can constitute a sort of anarchic space of difference for feminism. Such a space is foreign to both the alleged neutrality of the legal frame and the essentialized binarism of sexual difference. Some feminist scholars frame resistance in terms of reforms within the same ontological mechanisms of resentment in law; other feminists seem to explore resistance by means of reframing identity thinking, while nevertheless not exhausting the open possibilities of resistance.

Nussbaum, for instance, justifies anger by arguing it is a reasonable emotion after an injury.[37] For Nussbaum, emotions are parts of our system of ethical reasoning – they contain some sort of cognition and are not seen as incontrollable forces, but rather as responses to what is of value to us. Emotions can be considered as judgments of values of reality that are important to people's flourishing. Consequently, for Nussbaum, anger as an appropriate response to injustice cannot be extirpated without also extirpating the necessary demand for social justice. Nevertheless, Nussbaum claims it is necessary to resist the anger that can lead to personal revenge. One has to control and channel the development of emotion to make it less ambivalent, integrating the emotion of anger with compassion.[38] Even though the theorization offered by Nussbaum seeks to control negative emotions within the current justice system, still it remains focused on reforms and policies within the institutional practice of resentment and punishment and does not resist violence.

For feminism, such a move of embracing the subject of law and rights and remaining within a reformative framework contains potential problems in relation

36 Cavarero, "Canetti: Dritto Davanti al Morto," 118.

37 Martha Nussbaum, *Upheavals of Thought* (Cambridge: Cambridge University Press, 2001), 396.

38 Nussbaum, *Upheavals of Thought*, 396.

to violence. Espousing the legal subject implies that one holds on to the same cut subjectivity that is currently adopted in law and rights, where violence is dealt through mechanisms of separation and women are requested to feel the emotion of resentment and the desire for retribution. Thinking through the subject of law and rights produces nothing new and only contributes to an ontological re-theorization of a more empowered feminine subjectivity.[39] Yet, in achieving a feminist legal subject, the ontological mechanism of violence and separation of the subject of resentment in law becomes re-appropriated by feminism.

Indeed, in order to resist the ordinary, routine and gendered violence against women in all societies (manifested in everyday community life, in the domestic sphere, in wartime and other contexts), feminism and women activists have sought to make the hidden violence against women visible, and achieved it by fighting for the inclusion of women within the law and the rights agenda.[40] We can say that feminism has constructively fought sexual and gendered violence. It has opposed an empowered feminine subjectivity to the standard masculine one through women's rights and legal reforms and has provided valid critiques of masculine subjectivity itself.[41]

Yet, we can also say that feminism has remained trapped in the old ambush of the public male symbolic order. The achieved visibility of violence against women has not disrupted the ontological way of approaching violence. Often this visibility of violence against women has not opened up the complex relationality and material dimension of violence.[42] Instead of rethinking the ontology of violence and unfolding the implied categories, the discourse on violence against women has just been integrated into the existing legal framework of rights. The categories upon which both law and rights sit have not been touched, remaining thus unchallenged.

Sally Engle Merry shows, for instance, how rights work differently with reference to men and women; a discourse of rights provides protection to the victim

39 Elisabetta Bertolino, "The Politics of Subjectivity in the Women, Law and Development Discourse," *Australian Feminist Law Journal*, 25 (2006): 119–142. See also: Maria Drakopoulou, "Feminism, Governmentality and the Politics of Legal Reforms," *Griffith Law Review*, 17 (2008): 330–356.

40 Mohamed Mattar, "Trafficking in Persons, Especially Women and Children in Countries of the Middle East: The Scope of the Problem and the Appropriate Legislative Response," *Fordham International Law Journal*, 26 (2002–2003): 721–743; Donna Hughes, "The Use of New Communications and Information Technologies for Sexual Exploitations of Women and Children," *Hastings Women's Law Journal*, 13 (2002): 127–146; Kathy Steinman, "Sex Tourism and the Child: Latin America's and the United States' Failure to Prosecute Sex Tourists," *Hastings Women's Law Journal*, 13 (2002): 53–76.

41 Rebecca G. Cook, ed., *Human Rights of Women. National and International Perspectives* (Philadelphia: University of Pennsylvania Press, 1995).

42 Doris Buss, "The Curious Visibility of Wartime Rape: Gender and Ethnicity in International Criminal Law," *Windsor Yearbook of Access to Justice*, 25 (2007): 3–22; Rebecca G. Cook, "International Human Rights Law Concerning Women: Case Notes and Comments," *Vanderbilt Journal of Transnational Law*, 23 (1990–1991): 779–796.

but requires necessarily the punishment of the perpetrator, whereas in some cases women would like to end violence without losing the connection.[43] She explains that in order to escape violence, a woman is requested to become member of a subjectivity that might not be able to deliver its promises. Within law and rights, escaping violence requires from a woman some specific, powerful and public traits of the masculine symbolic order, such as self-assertion, autonomy, toughness, the sacrifice of connection, relationality and negotiation.[44] Therefore, women are encouraged to separate from violent relations and those that threaten violence. Abusive behavior is constructed as crime and is subjected to legal punishment; nevertheless, violence often takes place in everyday life in relational and familiar contexts.

As a consequence, it becomes necessary to resist violence by approaching it not just as an individual problem independent of the context (as law and rights do). Rather, violence needs to be approached as a problem of the community and of relations between human beings. Therefore, it seems necessary to rethink resistance through new ontological ways.[45] Violence is a problem of the relations among singular human beings within their community. A violent action is an action that trespasses against others, their vulnerability, and dissolves the community, leading to a breach of peace. It derives that violence needs to be seen as a problem of the community and requires awareness of oneself in relation to the community.

I can now look at approaches other than those of law and rights, which draw on an ontology of singularity, corporeality and birth. Feminist philosophers such as Adriana Cavarero, Hannah Arendt and Christine Battersby, for instance, offer a way of resisting violence that escapes the logic of resentment and affirms positive ontological perspectives; such a way allows the conceptualization and practice of new forms of subjectivity and solidarity that avoid the terrain of the enemy. In "Archeologia dell'Omicidio," Adriana Cavarero appears critical of the current ontology of violence and resentment.[46] She looks at the Judeo-Christian tradition and notes how it is grounded on the ontology of violence. In particular, the new version of the sixth commandment reads: "Thou shall not murder" – where "murder" is used rather than "kill" because "murder" does not refer to killing in general but to malicious and unlawful killing. In addition, Cavarero underlines how, while in a different part of the Bible God forbids killing, at the same time God commands the killing of the one who kills: "Whoever sheds the blood of man, by man shall his blood be shed, for God made man in his own image." (Genesis 9:6)

43 Sally Engle Merry, "Wife Battering and the Ambiguities of Rights," in *Identities, Politics, and Rights*, eds Sarat, A. and Kearns, T.R. (Ann Arbor: University of Michigan Press, 1995), 271–306.

44 Engle Merry, "Wife Battering and the Ambiguities of Rights."

45 See, for instance: Lisa Baraitser, "Mothers Who Make Things Public," *Feminist Review*, 93 (2009): 8–26.

46 Adriana Cavarero, "Archeologia dell'Omicidio," in *I Comandamenti. Non Uccidere*, eds Cavarero, A. and Scola, A. (Bologna: Il Mulino, 2013), 68–139.

For Cavarero, the sixth commandment is a weak commandment, not because men continue to kill one another regardless of it, but because its conceptual grid is discrepant. Killing or, better, murdering, for Cavarero, has become an ordinary gesture in our culture that springs from the archetype of a murderous, sanguinary and vindictive male subject and that has developed a juridical perspective on homicide and punishment. It is as if killing has become part of our nature and as if our essence has become violence. There is then, for Cavarero, the triumph of a destructive conception of the human, of an aggressive subjectivity. War is no longer necessary to justify killing because killing has become natural, legitimate, ordinary. And women kill too. The example of Medea testifies that women, too, appropriate the subject of violence and resentment. The whole context makes it difficult to think of a peaceful and non-violent subject.

And yet, Cavarero's philosophy offers the ontology of a unique and relational selfhood beyond the normativity of the neutral (in reality masculine) subject.[47] When one speaks in one's voice, many traits of the self are revealed: one's uniqueness, vulnerability, corporeality, relationality. The voice opens up the categories of the private and shows that those traits belong to all of us, men and women, and they accompany us in the public as well as in the private sphere of life. In addition, one's voice always speaks to and with others in a plurality of voices implying a communal and relational context. One's voice resists both the masculine and feminine language, moving away from patriarchal binary logic and touching upon one's uniqueness.

We cannot fight violence as separation from the community through an emotion of disconnection such as resentment. It becomes important to not follow the script of a fictitious, public and divided legal subjectivity; a subject that is cut, divided by the essentialized sexual difference split from itself and the community and is moreover posited on a fictitious community of reasonable and independent individuals who have the rights to pursue resentment in the face of injuries. Through the vulnerability angle that springs from the voice, a violent act can be seen to be the result of one misjudging reality and acting in isolation and apart from the community. One's voice leads rather to actions that reconnect to oneself and the community, such as a forgiveness from within, because one's voice is dependent on other voices and reveals one's vulnerability and one's need for connection.

The voice indicates that violence can be seen to be a sort of delusion because it does not proceed from a healthy singularity, acting according to one's vulnerability and relational exposure. A violent act consists rather in trespassing, missing, failing, going astray from the community. And, as Sally Engle Merry analyzes, to choose violence creates control and power only in the short term and does not ensure connection.[48]

47 Cavarero, *For More Than One Voice.*

48 Engle Merry, "Wife Battering and the Ambiguities of Rights," 299.

If one is a victim of violence, it is important to talk about what has happened and what one has endured. The current liberal subject of law and rights allows such public speech, where injuries can be denounced. But then, as Judith Butler has underlined in a talk, we need to be patient with the unbearable rage and grief that follows injuries.[49] We often repeat the injury and embrace resentment, revenge and violence, forgetting that we are bound by and to others. Butler suggests that we can instead learn from grief, slow down such a driving away, be patient with the unbearable, so that this slowness and the condition of staying with the unbearable can show to us what we value in a life of community.[50]

Consequently, I believe that the legal way of speaking must give way to another ontological perspective that is critical of the ontology of blaming and resentment that characterizes the current legal subject, and that has the potentiality to transform the legal subject itself. To speak in one's voice means responding and being responsible for *who one is* and one's uniqueness and implies an awareness that allows one to stay with the unbearable and to approach life through an ontology of reconnection to oneself and the community. The focus on the voice in terms of one's unique voice, as theorized by Cavarero, is precisely grounded on a diverse ontology that begins from oneself and moves beyond stereotypes, an essentialized gender divide and subjectivity.[51]

The ontology of the voice begins with the experience of a singular body in flesh and blood in relationality. One's uniqueness is exposed to oneself and others. Such an exposure and awareness of dependence and vulnerability can resist the subject of resentment. If, as Cavarero says, we are confronted with the option either to care for or to harm the other, speaking through the voice leads to an awareness of corporeality, an opening to oneself and others and an ethical responsibility for the vulnerability of others and, as a result, the voice pushes us toward care and connection.[52]

The awareness of vulnerability that springs from speaking with one's voice confronts us with the ethical responsibility of enacting either caring or wounding. Because of the awareness that speaking in one's voice brings, there is a response, not a reaction, a response as response-ability, as the ability to respond ethically toward vulnerability. Although Cavarero has not focused directly on forgiveness in her work, I think that her vocal ontology necessarily emphasizes ethical actions such as forgiveness which relates to her thinking about the subject as someone who is capable of inclination and who opposes the egoistic, autonomous and vertical legal subject.

When one speaks in one's voice, one notices the vibration and the sound of one's own body; one experiences one's vulnerability and the vulnerability of other speakers with whom one is communicating. In such an ontological context, the

49 Judith Butler's talk on "Speaking of Rage and Grief," Talk at *10th Annual PEN: World Voices Festival of International Literature*, New York: 28 April–4 May 2014.

50 Butler's talk on "Speaking of Rage and Grief."

51 Cavarero with Bertolino, "Beyond Ontology and Sexual Difference," 147.

52 Adriana Cavarero, *Horrorism: Naming Contemporary Violence*, trans. William McCuaig (New York: Columbia University Press, 2009).

content of communication is not as important as the uniqueness of the one who speaks, beyond any wrong committed. The voice is then linked to vulnerability, inclination, the community, and consequently to actions of reconnection and thus forgiveness. The relation between the voice and forgiveness shows how Arendt's thought has most inspired the philosophy of Cavarero.

Like Cavarero, Arendt spoke of uniqueness and *who-ness* and theorized a resistance to the current ontology and subjectivity that breaks from vengeance and resentment. Arendt linked uniqueness to natality, action, promise and forgiveness.[53] For Arendt, it is because of our uniqueness that we can act anew, bringing natality into the community. Arendt sees forgiveness as the opposite of vengeance because forgiveness brings newness and unpredictability, whereas vengeance is a repetition of violence and remains predictable.[54]

Forgiveness is unpredictable because it frees the person from the consequence of an act. Enacting forgiveness implies resisting the separations and divisions of the subject, inclining toward others rather than being upright and vertical, becoming aware of one's vulnerability and the vulnerability of others. Thus forgiveness links a person to one's voice and that of others, because when one speaks in one's voice, one becomes aware that the other is more like oneself than one might think. The other is vulnerable and in search of connection. Both one's voice and the action of forgiveness reveal our uniqueness. Forgiving also implies giving away the cut mask of the current legal subjectivity, removing such a mask, which is not organically a part of the injured and vulnerable singularity. Forgiveness allows movement toward a new relationality and community between the two singularities of the offender and the injured one.

Surely, forgiveness requires a time of withdrawal, slowness, reflection, awareness and gradual release; but only forgiveness, as linked to our condition of vulnerability, can allow the experience of change and newness. Forgiveness changes the influence of the past over the present and the future. In this sense, for Hannah Arendt, forgiving and promising are related categories of the political that can bring unpredictability and newness.[55]

The attention to vulnerability, forgiveness, the community and natality move us to the thought of another feminist philosopher, Christine Battersby, who has theorized the radical traits of the female body as an ontology of newness and natality. In *Le Filosofie Femministe*, Cavarero discusses the *metafisica carnale* theorized by Battersby, a fleshy ontology that commences from the act of being born and giving birth and that has been disregarded by the philosophical tradition.[56] As Cavarero argues, the philosophical tradition generally considers human beings

53 Hannah Arendt, *The Human Condition* (Chicago: The University of Chicago Press, 1958).

54 Arendt, *The Human Condition*, 240–241.

55 Arendt, *The Human Condition*.

56 Adriana Cavarero and Franco Restaino, *Le Filosofie Femministe* (Milan: Bruno Mondadori, 2002), 100.

to be already independent adults, failing to see and take into account the act of coming to life and being born that is visible in the female body. A woman giving life, giving birth, becomes central in Battersby's ontology of the flesh.

Therefore, as Cavarero notes, drawing on Battersby, one is born of and is dependent on a woman and is not thrown into the world as a generic individual, as the philosophical tradition implies. This dependence on a woman signs the beginning of an itinerary of inclination toward the other for the self that opposes the vertical and righteous legal liberal subjectivity. Cavarero's reading of Battersby shows that the self is a continuous becoming; it is never a unity but rather a multiplicity. There is, therefore, in Battersby's subjectivity something fluid that begins from the body of a woman, moves and changes.[57]

For Battersby, the female body unsettles the notion of identity as fixed, because it gives birth, or is born out of other bodies; the female body is an example of dependence of one upon another; pregnancy menaces any division between self and others, upsetting the cuts and divisions of the liberal subject.[58] We can see how the idea of dependence in Battersby offers an opportunity for a cognitive disengagement from resentment and violence, opening up to actions that connect to others and escaping the logic of violence in resistance.

If in Battersby's work one can trace a discourse on women that echoes metaphysics and essence, the same cannot be said of the voice that de-essentializes the feminine traits and uses those traits strategically to unfold them into the uniqueness of each one of us, beyond divisions and cuts. When speaking in one's voice, one reveals individual traits that are traditionally associated with the feminine stereotypes but that, in reality, belong to both men and women. Indeed, as Cavarero argues, the traits of vulnerability and exposure to others are thought to be stereotypes of the feminine,[59] yet they contain radical non-violent forms of resistance against the dominant symbolic order.

The underlying argument of this book consists of a feminist theory of difference that needs to explore ways to unlearn and break away from the violence of the symbolic order and subsequent violent reactions to injuries. Feminism must escape ontologically the violent thinking of both patriarchy and law, where women can only get killed or kill, be dominated or dominate, and think of ways to resist violence without repeating violence, avoiding the appropriation and repetition of the ontological mechanisms of patriarchal domination. Choosing to be righteous and to dominate brings women to a level of equality and a position of good defense, if not of good attack. Yet it reproduces the ontology of violence of a subject of resentment.

57 Christine Battersby, *The Phenomenal Woman: Feminist Metaphysics and the Patterns of Identity* (New York: Routledge, 1998).

58 In relation to this, see also: Lisa Baraitser, *Maternal Encounters: The Ethics of Interruption* (Oxon: Routledge, 2009).

59 Cavarero, *In Spite of Plato*; Cavarero with Bertolino, "Beyond Ontology and Sexual Difference."

According to Howard Caygill, the logic of opposing sovereignty with another form of sovereignty is "dependent upon what opposes and in some sense is also complicit with it," proposing a type of resistance that can be considered reactive and within the logic of *ressentiment*.[60] Caygill rather suggests a resistance constituted of all that is left after the capacity to resist; that is, opposing the sovereign patriarchal symbolic order with what has been considered superfluous and can be taken up and enhanced.

The focus on one's voice reflects what has been cut and left out from the construction of subjectivity and language and needs to be enhanced as a means of resistance. The voice reveals the singularity and corporeality of each person, pays attention to the practice of interrelating and discloses an ontology of the self as unique that goes beyond the indifference and the violence of the righteous and autonomous subject and stays in line instead with *who someone is* and the possibility of unpredictable actions, such as forgiveness.

I suggest, along with Cavarero and Arendt, that feminism as a theory of difference can focus on one's voice and one's forgiveness, as an action that resists violence and its continuation by reaction. In order to do this, feminism needs to center around a selfhood that is singular, capable of awareness and relationality, thus capable also of suspending the juridical frame. Such a selfhood would not resist violence by running away or fighting back, but would stay clear, centered, connected to herself and the community of selves. This is a selfhood that begins precisely from her voice as the passing of air, breathing and producing a unique sound cut out from language and subjectivity.

By speaking in one's voice, selfhood does not resist violence by reacting through resentment but is able to act in terms of forgiving and promising, to move forward from the past and embrace the future.[61] I would like to underline that a forgiving selfhood does not imply a weak feminine subjectivity but a strong one, one that is able to withdraw after the injury, become aware of the experience of the injury, delimit the experience of the injury, face, speak the injury, discern, decide, but also let go, tolerate and accept. However, if feminism embraces the subject of resentment as it appears in legal justice, the feminist subject will continue to blame the external system for her pain and injuries, and thus will remain trapped in the pain of the past.

Contrary to legal justice, in the action of forgiveness there is the Arendtian "miracle of natality," which reflects in some ways the speaking of one's voice in Cavarero. The birth of a baby gives a glimpse of hope and shows the power of natality in the human condition. As Cavarero says, the newly born is a new life completely exposed to others and vulnerable because it is totally dependent on others for its safety.[62] When one speaks in one's corporeal voice, one's unique

60 Caygill, *On Resistance*, 174.
61 Arendt, *The Human Condition*.
62 Cavarero, *Horrorism*.

vulnerability is necessarily exposed and calls for the necessity of breaking from the cycles of violence among human beings.

Indeed, when one speaks in one's voice, one posits oneself on a different ontological level, where one breathes and shares air with others and, in doing so, one does not need to struggle with others. Speaking in one's voice is also speaking together with other voices in a polyphonic community. Such a sharing of life allows us to become aware and share our human condition of vulnerability. When we speak we expose ourselves to others in our vulnerability. Forgiveness becomes a necessary singular action within a community of sharing of air, voices and vulnerability. Both one's voice and a forgiveness from within provide a counter-gift to feminism and women and reveal one's uniqueness.

Forgiveness also disturbs the distance between selves operated by essentialized sexual difference, where the masculine or the feminine are experienced as other, unknowable, foreign, dissimilar and discontinuous. A female or male self is perceived, rather, as another singular self that reveals her or his uniqueness and vulnerability through speaking and actions. Consequently, in embracing a selfhood that speaks in one's voice, feminism can also empathize with what is foreign, fearsome, even repugnant, and engage with, rather than disengage from, the other. This could lead to a feminism of singular selves that would not morally judge the offender; it could be rather a feminism that transforms relationships and offers compassion for the other's confusion, distortion and failure, a feminism that views action within the ontology of one's vulnerability and that responds rather than reacts. As such, feminist action could become an ever-present reminder that people will die but that, as Hannah Arendt says, they are not born to die but to begin; that is, to speak and act something new.

I think Cavarero, Arendt and Battersby are all suggesting that feminism, as a theory of difference, can use the master's tools strategically, the same strategies of the patriarchal, sovereign subject but in a strategic way, to resist cycles of violence and vengeance. Action becomes reconnection to one's voice, oneself and others and a form of newness and natality. Forgiveness is understood here as deriving from awareness of oneself and others, and therefore is viewed as radically connecting to one's voice.

The call for strong and centered selves has been seconded by the Italian writer Dacia Maraini in her work on the character of Chiara of Assisi and her disobedience to the unjust, gendered and social conditions of the time.[63] Beyond the fact that Chiara became a religious person, Maraini focuses on Chiara's voice and on her affirmation of a resistance that refuses to react with further violence and, rather, affirms a different type of ontology. Chiara of Assisi disobeys the gendered rules by inventing new forms of "being" and "being in community." She embraces the convent, sacrifice and poverty as an ontological approach that starts from one's uniqueness and vulnerability in relationality to others. Chiara refuses to marry a

63 Dacia Maraini, *Chiara di Assisi: Elogio della Disubbidienza* (Milan: Rizzoli, 2013).

rich man, chosen by her family, and thus refuses to repeat the life of injustice and violence suffered by other women. Maraini sees in Chiara's gesture the dislike of and resistance against any crystallization of power and the corruption of the clergy.

Maraini's work constitutes a critical reflection on the impact that the male symbolic system (and law) have on the singular lives of women. In this respect, Patrick Hanafin underlines how Maraini seeks to restore agency to women by refusing the disembodied universal male subject.[64] According to Hanafin, Maraini allows for the reconstruction of the past through an ethics of the voice and looks *for something more* than what patriarchal society offers to women.[65] Hanafin shows how the work of Maraini has similarities with that of Cavarero since in Maraini's work the female characters assume a face and a voice that transform them into *who-ness* and unique beings.[66]

In the next section I will speculate on forgiveness in law and how this differs from a forgiveness that springs from one's voice. In relation to law, I shall consider the example of restorative justice and then explore the work of Jacques Derrida, Georges Bataille, Paul Ricoeur and Hannah Arendt.

4.4 Forgiveness: conditionality, unconditionality and circulation

Restorative justice shifts the focus of criminal justice from incarcerating offenders to holding them accountable in meaningful ways, showing a concern for the needs of victims and communities.[67] Restorative justice makes use of tools such as victim–offender conferencing, or dialog, that allows victims to understand an event, assess it and be open to the possibility of forgiving.[68] There are several positive points in restorative justice. The parties can benefit from a process of *humanization* of legal justice, where the focus is precisely justice rather than vengeance or punishment; there is also a broader meaning of justice because the needs of both victims and offenders in the community are taken more seriously into account. Nevertheless, there are limits in the application of forgiveness within this framework. Treating forgiveness as something that can be facilitated, induced within the institution of law and exchanged conflicts with a forgiveness that springs from one's voice and vulnerability.

In fact, the forgiveness of the victim within the restorative justice system requires some conditions, such as the apology, and some forms of restitution, reparation or recompense by the offender. Offenders are asked to repent and take

64 Patrick Hanafin, "An Ethics for Dead Voices: Law and the Politics of Sexual Difference in Dacia Maraini's Isolina," *Law and Humanities*, 4 (2010): 195–209, 198.

65 Hanafin, "An Ethics for Dead Voices," 208.

66 Hanafin, "An Ethics for Dead Voices," 198.

67 David M. Lerman, "Forgiveness in the Criminal Justice System: If it Belongs, then Why Is it So Hard to Find?" *Fordham Urban Law Journal*, 27 (1999–2000): 1663–1675.

68 Lerman, "Forgiveness in the Criminal Justice System," 1663–1675.

responsibility for their actions and to repair the harm they have caused through apologizing, community service or returning stolen money. In restorative justice, punishment is also not excluded. Nevertheless, restorative justice is not used for all crimes; rather it is used mainly in cases of less violent or of juvenile crimes.[69] Some scholars view restorative justice as not being about forgiveness but primarily about reconciliation over retribution.[70]

Consequently, even though forgiveness has begun to find its place within the legal justice system, there are limits to its application, mainly because of the requirement for repentance and also because forgiveness cannot be extended to serious crimes. Overall, law implies the existence of reasonable conditions for forgiveness to be met and requires people to agree to an inner change from an outside and a general and given voice. Yet as Stauffer underlines, no institution's power of enforcement can compel people to let the past go and embrace forgiveness.[71] Law's conditions contrast with the idea of the inner forgiveness that springs from one's voice. This latter occurs through the awareness of one's vulnerability and that of others in community. Speaking in one's voice indicates openness to a desire to get on with one's own life and contrasts with the closure of wanting repentance, punishment and revenge.[72]

There are many questions that emerge around forgiveness and law. For instance, to what extent is mainstreaming forgiveness within law possible; how does seeking revenge and applying forgiveness within the limits of law differ from a forgiveness that springs from one's voice; how much can the law translate singular and unique feelings within general, narrow and technical legal ends? I shall disentangle those questions by understanding what forgiveness consists of. I am therefore employing the perspectives offered by Jacques Derrida, Georges Bataille, Paul Ricoeur and Hannah Arendt.

Jacques Derrida has worked on a range of key concepts, one of which has been forgiveness.[73] The logic theorized by Derrida on forgiveness takes the shape of a contradiction between unconditional and conditional forgiveness; that is, between the pure idea of forgiveness and its practical application.[74] The result, for Derrida, is that the action of forgiveness presents limitations and necessarily demands compromises. He thus argues for a type of forgiveness in terms of ethical direction. For forgiveness to be pure, according to Derrida, it must not succumb to the

69 Julie Juola Exline et al., "Forgiveness and Justice: A Research Agenda for Social and Personality Psychology," *Personality and Social Psychology Review*, 7 (2003): 337–348, 338.

70 Everett L. Worthington, "Is There a Place for Forgiveness in the Justice System?" *Fordham Urban Law Journal*, 27 (1999–2000): 1721–1732, 1729.

71 Stauffer, "*Ethical Loneliness*," 119.

72 Susan Bandes, "When Victims Seek Closure: Forgiveness, Vengeance and the Role of Government," *Fordham Urban Law Journal*, 27 (1999–2000): 1599–1606.

73 Jacques Derrida, *On Cosmopolitanism and Forgiveness*, trans. Michael Hughes (London: Routledge, 2001).

74 Derrida, *On Cosmopolitanism and Forgiveness.*

logic of exchange. Unfortunately, in law and politics, Derrida says, forgiveness is often confused with and replaced by calculated actions and often repentance becomes the proviso of a forgiveness that can only be conditional.[75]

For Derrida, actions of forgiveness within law, such as excuses and regrets, remain manifestations of forgiveness as acts of comparison, conditional and subject to exchange. Yet, even though such a proliferation of repentance is surely an expression of something good, it also lacks sincerity and may participate in political hypocrisy, calculation and the logic of exchange. Often, then, the language of forgiveness serves various finalities and cannot be said to be pure or disinterested. In addition, in law there are still violent actions which cannot be forgiven, such as crimes against humanity. Precisely the concept of crimes against humanity shows the conditionality of forgiveness, when it has entered law and politics. In law and politics, then, forgiveness re-establishes what is considered normal.[76]

For Derrida, when forgiveness serves a finality, or attempts to re-establish a normality, then forgiveness is not pure and noble. Derrida thinks that true and pure forgiveness consists of forgiving the unforgivable. If forgiveness forgave only what is forgivable, then it would not be forgiveness. Forgiveness needs to forgive the unforgivable and it is therefore an *impossibility itself*.[77]

A similar approach to forgiveness, even though within a different structure and with different outcomes, is provided by the position of Georges Bataille. In his book, *The Accursed Share*, Bataille explains how the movement of classic economy is only a sub-category of the more general economy of energy that extends as far as the energy of the sun.[78] What is important in his account is that such an energy produces excess. That is, the general economy described by Bataille is explained from the point of view of excess rather than scarcity and such an excess needs to be expended. On a singular level, one can choose to expend the excess energy by way of resentment and aggression, reproducing the cycle of violence, or by forgiving, or other options. Therefore, for Bataille, both revenge and forgiveness would only be modalities of the expenditure of such energy.

For Bataille, the rite of sacrifice represents an expenditure of the excess removed from the game of utility. In the case of sacrifice, people are not dominated by the utility of the restricted economic system; the victim of sacrifice is removed from the utility of the system and consumed profitlessly. Thus the sacrifice can be understood in terms of a gift, completely beyond the utility system of the restricted economy. And, in turn, the gift also resembles forgiveness as a form of gift that involves a conscious decision to let go or forego bitterness and vengeance, escaping the regime of utility. Therefore, by giving or by for-giving, one engages

75 Derrida, *On Cosmopolitanism and Forgiveness*, 27.

76 Derrida, *On Cosmopolitanism and Forgiveness*, 32.

77 Derrida, *On Cosmopolitanism and Forgiveness*, 32.

78 Georges Bataille, *The Accursed Share, An Essay on General Economy, Vol. I: Consumption*, trans. Robert Hurtley (New York: Zone Books, 1989).

with the expenditure of the excess outside the logic of utility.[79] Bataille's theory of the gift escapes the logic of return, which is part of the logic of exchange behind the gift. Yet Bataille's approach leads to moments of fascination with eroticism, sacrifice and death.

From Marcel Mauss's point of view, a gift always expects another gift in return and its circularity can amount to a form of self-interest, not too different from retribution.[80] At the same time, Mauss underlines how there must be an elapse of time between the gift and the counter-gift and how the gift is excessive, in the sense that it moves beyond the logic of exchange. If the gift is always returned and thus annihilated by the subsequent gift, what remains is the interval of time between the gift and the counter-gift. Such an interval, when the gift is not yet repaid, is precisely what binds one to the others, in a relation either of resentment or cooperation. Going back to Bataille, giving or for-giving consists essentially in an elapse of time that escapes the rational discourse of economic utility, a way to avoid determinism and allow freedom to the subject through the paradox of giving away and expending the excess. Yet such a conception of forgiveness, in terms of gift sacrifice and freedom from restrictions, cannot find application in law, since the latter functions within the logic of utility and exchange.

Paul Ricoeur has also commented on forgiveness. In his book, *Memory, History, Forgetting*, Ricoeur underlines how forgiveness is necessarily linked to the experience of fault and guilt, as fault constitutes the occasion for forgiveness. There can be a forgiveness only when we can accuse someone of something. Therefore, forgiveness relates in some ways to the experience of punishment. However, Ricoeur's position on forgiveness is linked to memory and the just allotment of it in relation to the past.[81] Forgetting, in Ricoeur, becomes central to achieving forgiveness. Forgetting opens an aporia in the representation of the past and breaks with the dialectic of presence and absence which is essential for the representation of the past. Both forgetting and forgiveness aim at the same horizon of appeasement of the memory. In other words, for forgiveness to happen, we need to forget the traces of our memory.

For Ricoeur, forgiveness is difficult not only to give but also to conceive of. Like Derrida, Ricoeur is critical of the forgiveness that has been used in the legal justice system. Exceptions such as the imprescriptibility of some crimes testify to the difficulty of both giving and conceiving of forgiveness. The imprescriptibility of crimes against humanity constitutes the first major test for forgiveness because it shows that forgiveness is difficult to institutionalize as it underlines how the extreme gravity of the crimes justifies the tracking down of criminals without any time limit. For Ricoeur, such an exception of the law authorizing the indefinite

79 Bataille, *The Accursed Share, Vol. I*, 58.

80 Marcel Mauss, *The Gift. Forms and Functions of Exchange in Archaic Societies* (Glencoe: The Free Press, 1954), 71.

81 Paul Ricoeur, *Memory, History, Forgetting* (Chicago: The University of Chicago Press, 2004).

pursuit of the authors of crimes shows a deep hatred of the other and indicates how in law unforgivability persists.[82]

Imprescriptibility shows precisely the condition through which the gift of forgiveness is understood in law. If we intend forgiveness as a gift, which as Mauss noted contains the seeds of a logic of return, forgiveness would operate by balancing people in a sort of horizontal relation of exchange. A gift otherwise, for Ricoeur, would be giving without expecting anything in return, thus requiring the extraordinary. However, even offering love and forgiveness might contain the expectation of transforming the enemy into a friend and therefore some form of exchange and circularity of the gift.

In order to escape the exchange and the conditionality, Ricoeur proposes a recovery of the asymmetry in the process of for-giving. He suggests a rethinking of forgiving in terms of giving and receiving rather than giving, receiving and giving in return. When we are giving and receiving, we focus on the communal dimension of forgiveness and avoid the logic of exchange. On the contrary, for Ricoeur, when forgiveness is institutionalized in the legal discourse, the process of giving and receiving is interrupted and gets channeled through the logic of giving, receiving and giving in return; that is, through conditionality and the logic of exchange.[83]

Going back to the necessity of forgetting, Ricoeur argues that in some ways for forgiveness to be possible it is also necessary to allow the memory to forget; that is, to stop one being angry with oneself and others. There is a need to forget the unforgettable and silence the non-forgetting of memory so that forgiving also becomes an act of renouncing memory against the will not to forget. By remembering and focusing on past memories, we hold ourselves open to the past, we remain concerned about the past, and this might lead us toward concerns for retribution. In this sense, retention of memory means enduring and remaining the same, and sameness, predictability of thinking and action. Thus Ricoeur invites us to develop an *ars oblivionis* together with the *ars memoriae* that has been so much celebrated; to return to the present one must in some ways suspend the links with the past.

Finally, forgiveness has also been an important concern for Hannah Arendt. In *The Human Condition*, Arendt stresses the importance of revealing who one is in speech and actions.[84] Forgiveness is precisely a special type of action that springs from one's uniqueness and *who-ness* and reveals who one is. That is, forgiveness does not come from above in Arendt; it is not a general principle but an action that arises from unique human beings, from knowing who we are and what we are doing; and equally for Cavarero, forgiveness arises from one's unique voice.

82 Ricoeur, *Memory, History, Forgetting*, 473.

83 Ricoeur, *Memory, History, Forgetting*, 481–482.

84 Arendt, *The Human Condition*; Hannah Arendt, *The Life of the Mind* (New York: Harcourt & Co, 1981); Bat-Ami Bar On, *The Subject of Violence* (Lanham: Rowman & Littlefield, 2002).

Forgiveness is, indeed, a new action, one that breaks from the past, from what is normal and requires unexpected thinking and acting. For Arendt, the plurality of our uniqueness inevitably entails weaknesses and wrongdoings. Through acting anew, and thus through forgiveness, it is possible to disrupt the normalizing philosophical and political settlements of violence and trouble the identities of resentment.[85]

For Hannah Arendt, one is not responsible for *what* one is, or what one has been made by history or circumstances. But one might always be responsible for *who* one is. For Arendt *who one is* gets revealed through words and deeds. When one behaves predictably one is irresponsible, one lets history act for oneself. A woman or a man who enacts violence reacts predictably and only repeats the identity which she or he is supposed to be. Responding in a different way is being unpredictable, being *who someone is* and thus speaking in one's voice.

In *Eichmann in Jerusalem*, Arendt shows the banality of evil, in the case of Eichmann, and how easy it is to repeat violence by acting within the constructed identity imposed on us. In the trial, Eichmann appeared thoughtless, not fully aware of what he had done, and replied by saying that he had only obeyed orders, thus demonstrating the banality of evil. Arendt suggests that one should resist such a banality of evil, one needs to know who one is, what one is doing and respond through new actions. For Arendt, one needs to counterpose the need for awareness against Eichmann's lack of thinking and reflexivity about what he was doing. Evil is, for Arendt, this thoughtlessness, the fact that one is not aware of what one is doing:

> *The deeds were monstrous, but the doer – at least the very effective one now on trial – was quite ordinary, commonplace, and neither demonic nor monstrous. There was no sign in him of firm ideological convictions or of specific evil motives, and the only notable characteristic one could detect [. . .] was something entirely negative: it was not stupidity but thoughtlessness.*[86]

The Arendtian forgiveness is an action that fights against thoughtlessness and that requires, on the contrary, awareness. Forgiveness is always of the *who* beyond the *what* and beyond identities; it reflects a self whose *who-ness* is always revealed, despite any injury suffered and any wrong committed. Forgiveness requires a unique self that is able to separate the guilty person from their act, forgive the guilty person while condemning their wrong actions. The *who-ness* of a person goes beyond any what-ness, any action determined by circumstances. Our *who-ness* embraces speaking in one's voice and an awareness of vulnerability. And such awareness brings us to the Arendtian faculty of interrupting and beginning something new through action, and reminds us that although we will die it is

85 Arendt, *The Human Condition*, 237.
86 Arendt, *The Life of the Mind*, 3–4.

possible for us to begin anew during our lifetime. Birth and natality interrupt violence and resentment while they disengage from the past and generate renewal, thus allowing openness rather than closure.

To sum up, I think that the positions on forgiveness and on the gift proposed by Derrida, Bataille, Ricoeur and Arendt complement the focus on the voice. Those four philosophers talk of forgiveness as something that touches the dimension of the extraordinary and the unexpected and overcomes the normalizing and predictable reaction of violence, retribution and exchange.

Yet in theorizing forgiveness, those scholars do not focus on the dimension of uniqueness. They talk of how forgiveness should be in general. It is only with Arendt that forgiveness becomes a gift of who one is, which is the same unique experience of forgiving in one's voice. This is perhaps the main difference between forgiveness in law and within one's voice. The justice system employs forgiveness to deal with wrongs but only in a centrifugal way. With one's voice, on the contrary, one can only act forgiveness in a centripetal way, beginning from oneself and body, coming from awareness and producing awareness.

Even in the case of restorative justice, forgiveness does not spring from an inner awareness of relationality but maintains an institutionalized character decided upon from outside. Instead, one's voice's detachment and suspension from language and institutions and the inner awareness this involves make vocal resistance centered and effective, allowing the possibility of forms of radical openness in justice that are beyond conditionality.

Conclusion and progression in chapters

I have argued that within justice in law we are constructed as subjects of resentment. A subject of resentment seeks to end the pain of the injury by means of retribution, which is essentially a mechanism of exchange, of getting equal, and a means for self-interest. The ontological perspective on justice offered by the legal justice system assumes that one is disconnected from situations and thus does not feel one's uniqueness and is aware neither of one's own vulnerability nor of the vulnerability of others. Speaking in one's voice discloses one's uniqueness and the awareness of vulnerability and therefore the voice leads to potential and ethical possibilities of resisting violence and resentment. If one speaks in one's voice, one is brought to act otherwise, anew, unpredictably, creating a rupture with the cycles of violence. Forgiveness is one of these acts that spring from one's voice, from within.

As for feminism, it appears to have sought to fight violence mainly by achieving more inclusion within the legal subjectivity, embracing the righteous subject of law and rights. In law, when we perceive that an injustice has been done to us, we require that justice is restored through punishment, thus we seek reparation for the cost that we incurred and often by being righteous in our claims we return more violence than we incurred. However, this means staying with the same ontological categories of law and its mechanisms of justice.

On the contrary, speaking in one's voice teaches us that both voice and action happen in the context of a community and that one's uniqueness is necessarily disclosed. This implies that violence is to be understood as a problem of the community and from the ontological point of a unique selfhood in relationality. This perspective changes the mode of action. Philosophers such as Cavarero, Arendt and Battersby have theorized in terms of an ontology of uniqueness, newness, unpredictability, natality and the body.

The chapter has also dealt with forgiveness and its possibility within the institutions of law and politics and has analyzed forgiveness in terms of being a gift. The perspective on forgiveness by Derrida, Bataille, Ricoeur and Arendt suggests that there remains a problem with the institutionalization of forgiveness. One's voice could find space within a thought-provoking form of restorative justice requiring openness to develop forms of forgiveness beyond any conditionality.

The theoretical speculation throughout the chapters reveals that the subject of law and rights is founded on an ontological violence that paradoxically, in Benjamin's terms, becomes lawful or legitimate insofar as it works to posit and preserve the legal framework itself. In this book, one's voice opposes and resists the ontological position of separation and sovereign violence of the general voice of law as well as the philosophical sovereign imposition of liberalism. Other implications of speaking in one's voice have been explored in earlier chapters.

The second and third chapters indicated how the voice consists of the entanglement of our current legal subjectivity with the essentialized sexual difference perspective. The two chapters explore the voice through issues such as female genital cutting (FGC) and objectification in commercial sex. In relation to FGC, we can see that consent is paternalistically denied in the case of adult women consenting to it and allowed in cases of cosmetic surgeries that modify the body for non-therapeutic reasons. In addition, within law FGC is seen monolithically as an unreasonable practice that destroys the integrity of the body and mutilates it. Such an approach of law contrasts with the possibilities of one's voice to overcome divisions and cuts.

In the case of sex work, a historical look at the legal approach in the last two centuries shows objectification and exclusion of sex workers, denying them even the possibility of being accountable to the legal frame itself. For instance, sex workers were traditionally denied the very possibility of consensual capacity in relation to sexual assaults and rapes, leaving them in a position of individuals without agency, excluded from the subjectivity of the legal frame. More recently, law has begun to insert the concept of vulnerability to mitigate difficulties in the use of the notion of consent. Such an approach derives from an international and European legal intervention. However, the idea of vulnerability appears linked to stigmatized subjects, exploitation and victimhood and thus to moralist constructions of reality. The voice is able to resist the approaches of the body in FGC and sex work precisely by offering a resistance through an awareness of vulnerability and an ontology that radically escapes objectification and monothetic thinking and rethinks our constitutive relations.

In contrast, in the first chapter the possibility of speaking in one's voice and resisting law was explored within the perspective of scholars such as John Rawls, Martha Nussbaum, Judith Butler and Adriana Cavarero. John Rawls and Martha Nussbaum attempt to resist the voice of law by speaking using the same institutional voice, theorizing reforms that allow more equality inside the subjectivity of the individual and building social policies. Judith Butler and Adriana Cavarero share a number of concerns and offer insights into a voice that resists and breaks with the institutionalized normativity of law; they both revisit the question of the subject, although in different ways.

I see in Cavarero the possibility of awareness of oneself, an awareness of the *who one is* as opposed to the *what* of the subject or identity. The theorization of an awareness of oneself in relationality constitutes a moment of detachment and suspension from the frame and cannot be institutionalized within the current legal and political subjectivity. Precisely because of such a dimension of suspension and detachment, *who one is* has the potentiality to speak and act unpredictably. For Butler, only when one is a subject, speaking the language of identity, is one made intelligible. In other words, one can speak to the extent that one becomes a subject. The voice is the voice of the linguistic symbolic order, without which the subject remains voiceless, unintelligible and unsayable.

This is precisely the main difference between Butler and Cavarero. Cavarero tries to disengage from subjectivity and the symbolic order. For Cavarero, speaking as a subject is not the only way to speak. The passage of air in a singular throat and the sharing of air in a community of voices constitute another way of speaking. Indeed, according to Cavarero, meaning does not lie in the intelligible voice of a linguistically construed subject but rather in the unique voice of a self, made of flesh and blood. For Cavarero, there is another sort of intelligibility, one that is not born in language but in one's voice, precisely when the voice is not yet subjected by language and categorized in already chosen possibilities. One's uniqueness is revealed through the voice; a voice in which one speaks before it gets codified in the normative sphere of language and that constitutes an ontological and ethical openness to the polyphonic community of unique beings. A focus on one's voice – while one speaks – is in fact a space where one's uniqueness is exposed to others and where one can begin new things outside the codified bond of language.

> *Insofar as language is characterised by a rationality that is normative (or universal) for all those who are bound to it, language constitutes the bond between individuals as members of the ideal linguistic community [. . .] For Arendt, what makes speech political is not signification, expression, or the communication of something [. . .] The political sphere is generated precisely by this sharing of words and deeds that Arendt puts under the name of action. This sharing is*

> *the political form of a bond that is inscribed in the ontological condition that makes human beings a paradoxical plurality of human beings.*[87]

To return to the current chapter, the voice inspires unpredictable actions such as forgiveness precisely insofar as the vocal resistance remains detached and non-accountable to the linguistic frame or to the extent that one speaks from one's voice and it becomes aware of the sharing community of voices and the vulnerability involved. Voice and forgiveness, interrelated through uniqueness and vulnerability, can offer possibilities of resistance for law and feminism too. A woman can react in a vindictive and resentful manner to her injuries as Medea did, or through awareness she can become capable of overcoming the pain of an injury and move toward newness and unpredictability in the community.

87 Cavarero, *For More Than One Voice*, 189.

Concluding remarks

This book has focused on the voice and it has sought to interpret possible ways to resist law, its essentialized sexual difference division, its cut and divided liberal subject and the problems and violence derived from the cut, such as the subject of resentment and thus justice in terms of retribution. The voice has been considered as the means to such a resistance. The voice has been intended in the sense of a singular and relational sound, that by revealing one's uniqueness and corporeality, provides an awareness of oneself and a shared bond.

Understood in such a way, the voice breaks with the generality of established modes of speaking, language and law. Drawing on Adriana Cavarero's thought, it is precisely the voice, as sound and vibration of air passing in one's throat, that this book has attempted to recuperate, because such a dimension of the voice reveals one's body and who one is; all of these are aspects of us that are cut out from current legal and political subjectivity. The voice precisely links one's body to language and can reconnect the disjunctions and cuts of our construed subjectivity.

This book complements the resistance to law offered by the critical legal movement. I have proceeded through different lines of thinking. Firstly, I have attempted to see how a focus on the voice as a sound and vibration of a selfhood rather than a focus on the sign can resist law as an institutionalized, sovereign and already constituted system of power. This has implied taking into consideration the limits of liberalism in the construction of a subject as autonomous, independent, and in terms of standards.

Secondly, I have taken into consideration the fact that a cut subject produces violence. The cut to the subject is also the effect of an essentialized sexual difference perspective and I have confronted the voice with gendered situations such as female genital cutting (FGC) and objectification in sex work. I have also considered the violence of cut subjectivity in terms of justice.

Thirdly, I have argued that there are alternative ways of thinking of ontology; more specifically, in terms of an empty ontology that escapes the metaphysics of presence. The metaphysics of presence is precisely the philosophical and theoretical tendency to access reality through immediate meanings that become a presence and substance rather than absence and emptiness. Metaphysics often creates dualism, privileging one term over the other. For instance, in the case of essentialized sexual difference, the masculine subject is privileged and sovereign. While Derrida opted for an infinite deferral of meanings to resist the metaphysical approach, the ontology of the voice focuses on those aspects that are cut out from the dominant subjectivity, namely one's uniqueness, corporeal specificity, vulnerability, relationality. And one's voice does not constitute new forms of substance or presence, because it rather reflects a singular self in flesh and blood that will die and who is transient in this life; in other words we are confronted with an empty ontology. For Cavarero it is necessary to deal with ontology rather than running away from it, to treat ontology ironically, liberate it from the sacred truth of traditional philosophy and so transform it.[1]

A further point that I have underlined in this book concerns the ethical possibilities of a resistance that begins from one's voice and from the awareness of oneself that is capable of avoiding the repetition of resentment and violence. Violence can be avoided precisely because exposing one's voice results in awareness, suspending expectations or constructions.

Moreover, I have linked the voice to the subject capable of inclination which is described by Cavarero. A self who is capable of inclination is a self who speaks in one's voice, aware of vulnerability, and in my opinion such a selfhood is capable of acting anew, in an unpredictable way, following the ontology of birth and natality of one's voice. The latter also suggests new paths of resistance, for feminism too. Speaking in one's voice affirms precisely an ontology of one's uniqueness, which is translated into speaking beyond the essentialized sexual difference divide, overcoming the limitations and cuts of the liberal subject but also enacting processes of resistance that exclude sovereign and violent reactions.

One's voice is important to women because speaking in one's voice means being able to be oneself, breaking with essentialized constructions, listening from within and with others, exposing one's uniqueness and vulnerability, being strong and centered. Yet the focus on the voice can benefit everyone, especially groups of people that are marginalized, scapegoated or essentialized, for instance migrants or people in the LGTBQIA community. Speaking in one's voice can provide a way of being and acting outside identity thinking. The voice exposes the profound meaning of any signification, connecting it to vulnerability and thus it redirects actions accordingly.

It is important to underline that this book has been contextualized within the critical legal tradition, which offers a more general approach to jurisprudence – a perspective of law as law of the law – as opposed to a restricted and technical approach. Since the beginning, the critical legal tradition has focused on resisting the texts and structures of law and its metaphysical tendency. I have attempted to rethink resistance through a philosophical discourse that has adopted a sort of anti-metaphysical-visual metaphor.

1 Adriana Cavarero with Elisabetta Bertolino, "Beyond Ontology and Sexual Difference: An Interview with the Italian Feminist Philosopher Adriana Cavarero," *differences: A Journal of Feminist Cultural Studies*, 19(1) (2008): 128–167, 141.

An example of this anti-metaphysical-visual metaphor is Cavarero's work. Critical legal scholars such as Costas Douzinas and Peter Goodrich, drawing on Derrida's work, have theorized resistance in terms of the deferral of signs in the written text of law, which amounts to a form of visual resistance to the fixed truth of the legal texts.[2] For these critical legal scholars, deferral of the sign has been a central strategy to recuperate the lost meaning and voice of law that has been excluded from its texts.[3]

Cavarero, however, focuses on the voice, on something non-visual that speaks from a specific mouth, that can be listened to and is necessarily exposed. One's voice is both anti-metaphysical and anti-visual. In this she intersects with speech act, performative and deconstructive theorists such as Marianne Constable and especially Shoshana Felman and Judith Butler, but their focus is not on the vocal; they still treat the visual part of the spoken language even while criticizing and rearticulating it. What is more radical in Cavarero is this emphasis on a voice that has the sound of a singular and corporeal self, that comes from one's own mouth and is exposed necessarily when one speaks. Speaking in one's voice becomes a metaphor for breaking with ontology and essence and with the construction of visual ideas.

In her article "Politicizing Theory," Cavarero explains how the tendency to articulate a voice that does not have a sound is rooted in the Western philosophical and critical theory tradition.[4] Such a concept of theory in terms of seeing derives in turn from Plato's ideas.

For Cavarero, it is only with Jean Luc Nancy that the voice begins to resonate, because Nancy distinguishes what is audible from what is intelligible and focuses on listening, thus making a turn to the visual anti-metaphysical strategy of philosophy and critical theory.[5] With Nancy, the sound rather than the sign becomes the horizon of sense and meaning because Nancy is interested in the audible or acoustic sphere rather than the visual sphere. However, despite Nancy's shift to the acoustic sphere, Cavarero remains critical of Nancy's intentions.

For Cavarero, Nancy shows that in the sound and listening there is a deferral of one element to another, as the sound precisely vibrates, resonates, defers to itself.[6] Therefore, Cavarero sees in Nancy the same Derridean strategy of deferral. However, as Cavarero argues, in Nancy the act of deferring consists of resonance

2 Adriana Cavarero, "Dedicated to Derrida," in *For More Than One Voice: Toward a Philosophy of Vocal Expression*, trans. Paul Kottman (Stanford: Stanford University Press, 2005), 213–241.

3 Peter Goodrich, *Languages of Law: From Logics of Memory to Nomadic Mask* (London: Weidenfield and Nicolson, 1990); Costas Douzinas, Matthew Stone and Illan Wall, eds, *New Critical Legal Thinking. Law and the Political* (New York: Routledge, 2012); Costas Douzinas, Peter Goodrich and Yifat Hachamovitch, *Politics, Postmodernity and Critical Legal Studies: The Legality of the Contingent* (London: Routledge, 1994).

4 Adriana Cavarero, "Politicizing Theory," *Political Theory*, 30 (2002): 505–532, 507.

5 Adriana Cavarero, "L'Orecchio di Nancy," *Aut Aut*, 316–317 (2003): 68–76.

6 Cavarero, "L'Orecchio di Nancy."

rather than of a visual strategy as in Derrida.[7] In Nancy the subject that listens is the subject that resonates and, similarly to Derrida, it is a subject always to come, never already there and therefore never metaphysical. Cavarero argues that in Nancy sonority consists of essentially *différance*, while the theme of singularity is only dealt with marginally in his book *Listening*.[8]

Cavarero concludes that Nancy is not interested in the unique human voice but only in the generality of the acoustic sphere, in the audible. According to Cavarero listening, for Nancy, is a condition that belongs to the general phenomenon of sonority rather than the position of a unique subject who listens. Despite the turn from the visual sphere to sound and listening, for Cavarero, Nancy's voice still reflects a general voice of resonance.[9] This critique indicates the meaning given by Cavarero to the voice. The voice is intended as one's uniqueness, as a sound springing from the specificity and singularity of one's body.

My intention in this book has been to complement the work of critical legal scholars – such as Douzinas and Goodrich – in resisting the metaphysical tendency of law. Nevertheless, for me, choosing to focus on the voice offers a unique radical critical legal resistance that differs from the deferral of the sign or the general acoustic sphere of resonance. With one's voice there is an emphasis on the uniqueness of the one who speaks, her corporeality and relationality and a moment of suspension from the linguistic and legal frame.

In my introduction I have aimed to contextualize this work within the critical legal tradition and, in particular, I have shown how the focus on the voice for Cavarero signifies a turn from the visual approach of Derrida based on the deferral of the sign. For Derrida, the voice means presence and metaphysics, whereas the sign (as a visual strategy) can better resist the metaphysics of presence through deferral. On the contrary, Cavarero provides a re-valuation of the sound of the voice as a non-metaphysical strategy of resistance.

In the first part of the book I have provided a review of the literature of scholars such as John Rawls, Martha Nussbaum, Judith Butler and Adriana Cavarero – I will refer to those scholars again later in these concluding remarks. The book draws on Adriana Cavarero's work in its focus on the voice. The first chapter demonstrates the importance of the awareness of one's uniqueness and thus self-awareness that comes from speaking in one's own voice. In my opinion self-awareness through speaking in one's voice is a form of new subjectivity, one that is not construed through standards but rather springs from a singular and material selfhood and can provide a radical means of resistance. Such self-awareness allows one to act unpredictably because it is situated outside the normative frame. In such a way, resistance becomes posited in a space as detached from the frame,

7 Cavarero, "L'Orecchio di Nancy."
8 Cavarero, "L'Orecchio di Nancy"; Jean Luc Nancy, *Listening*, trans. Charlotte Mandell (New York: Fordham University Press, 2007).
9 Cavarero, "L'Orecchio di Nancy."

on the awareness of oneself as opposed to the traditional accountability to the frame. The focus on the voice discloses not only awareness of oneself but also an ontology that is different from the one currently used by law and rights; the voice reflects an ontology of one's uniqueness, a corporeal specificity, relationality and exposure, as opposed to the ontology of the general and unspecified individual of liberalism.

The second part of the book is comprised of the second and third chapters. In those chapters, I attempt to juxtapose the voice and the gendered situation of FGC with the voice of objectification in sex work and the legal approach. In those two chapters, I try to bring alive the theory on one's voice and to apply it to law and specific cases. Chapter II deals with FGC, taking into account the legal approach on consent and integrity of the body and exploring how the voice moves beyond identity discourses, requiring ambivalence in the reading of FGC. The case of *Re MB (Caesarean Section)* (1997) is explored, showing the essentialized bias against sexual difference in law and the potentiality of one's voice to resist such a position. Scholars such as Renata Salecl and Bruno Bettelheim contribute to understanding the importance of ambivalence and the potentiality inherent in speaking in one's voice.

Chapter III reflects on the historical approach the law has taken in relation to sex work and the ways the law has objectified women working in this field. Furthermore, the chapter points to law's essentialized views of sexual difference, where the masculine subject is sovereign and the feminine subject is seen as a passive body which becomes marginalized. I point out the possible splits and cuts that happen to the self because of objectification. The case of *R v Gary Lee Cole and Stephen Kevin Barik* (1993) is analyzed in terms of objectification. The chapter then attempts to see objectification through the work of the scholars discussed in the literature review in Chapter I, and underlines how the voice avoids objectification through a threefold way of resistance.

The third and last part of the book is comprised of Chapter IV and reflects on possible ways of responding to injuries and resisting violence, and thus on the ethical implications of the voice for justice. While the legal justice system constructs us as subjects of resentment who need to retaliate when injured by others – and thus again in terms of cut and separated subjects – speaking in one's voice, being connected to oneself, being corporeal and vulnerable rather than constructed as a cut subject can lead to unexpected kinds of resistance, such as forgiveness. Forgiveness can oppose the tendency to withdraw from others, as well as the emotions of resentment of the cut subject that prevail in the context of justice. Forgiveness is not intended as an institutionalized action, but as an ethical singular possibility from within when one speaks in one's voice with others.

Throughout the book, the theme of resistance in relation to the voice is central. A detailed critical reflection is attempted on the relationship between the voice and resistance through some streams of thought in the literature review. The perspectives of scholars such as John Rawls, Martha Nussbaum, Judith Butler and

Adriana Cavarero have constituted the backbone of this book, whereas Cavarero's thought has enabled a critical approach to their limitations. It has been argued that scholars such as Rawls and Nussbaum have undertaken to resist the unvoiced legal system from within the system and the perspective of *theoria*; that is, of a politics grounded on reflections, ideas, standards and thus on resistance as a visual metaphor.

According to Cavarero, Rawls has viewed justice as order, reflecting a *theoria* applied to politics.[10] But this application of *theoria* has stripped politics of its characteristics of plurality and action. It is especially the unpredictability of voices that is excluded from Rawls' theory. Similarly, Douzinas makes us note that even if Rawls is interested in distributing goods and thus voice, by focusing on those who are least advantaged in society Rawls' principle of difference comes after his first principle of individual freedom that safeguards the right to property.[11] This means that the frame of the political, legal and economic system speaks for the individual and that no voice is left to the subject. The unequal capitalistic system comes before distribution to the one who is least well off in society. In Rawls' view, the principles that regulate social justice reflect the voice of people, in that those principles are the ones that free and rational people would necessarily choose in a democratic society. Resistance is only possible within the limits of law and in case of dissent on fundamental questions.[12] Like Rawls, Nussbaum theorizes resistance within the constituted legal and political framework. Although Nussbaum puts more emphasis on the notion of difference and the needs of everyone, rights and legal principles remain constitutive of people's voice.[13]

I have pointed out that Judith Butler has approached resistance differently. For Butler, people need to be made visible through the grids of intelligibility, which allow them to be recognized and have a voice. The process of materialization of the voice proceeds through the linguistic intelligibility of the frame. The voice matters only if one gets recognized as a subject that matters. Thus what is important is that there is no obstruction to the voice's recognition. "The critique of violence" – says Butler – "must begin with the question of representability of life itself."[14] For Nick Couldry, who has applied Butler's thought to the voice, voice in politics depends then on "becoming visible, that is being relevant to the distribution of the speaking opportunities."[15]

Despite the fact that Nussbaum has been critical of Judith Butler,[16] arguing for instance that Butler offers no justification for her subversive politics and that she

10 Cavarero, "Politicizing Theory," 511–512.

11 Costas Douzinas, *Philosophy and Resistance in the Crisis* (London: Wiley and Sons, 2013), 181.

12 John Rawls, "The Justification of Civil Disobedience," in *Revolution and the Rule of Law*, ed. Kent, E. (Princeton: Princeton University Press, 1971), 30–45.

13 Martha Nussbaum, *Sex and Social Justice* (Oxford: Oxford University Press, 1999), 3.

14 Judith Butler, *Frames of War: When Is Life Grievable?* (London: Verso, 2010), 51.

15 Nick Couldry, *Why Voice Matters* (London: Sage, 2010), 107.

16 Martha Nussbaum, "The Professor of Parody," *New Republic* (22 February 1999): 37–45.

rejects moral values such as basic human needs, authority, equality and respect, or that Butler does not address practical questions and her mode of political action remains only symbolic and discursive,[17] one could argue that it is Nussbaum's resistance that remains enclosed within policy change and thus offers a limited perspective on resistance, and that she is unable to see change through language subversion and recognition as Butler does.

Likewise, Adriana Cavarero theorizes a form of resistance that cannot be limited within an institutionalized mode of policies and reforms but that touches other ontological and material levels through which resistance can be imagined. For Cavarero, it is important not to neglect the immediately audible, the uniqueness of one's voice. Unlike Butler, Cavarero focuses on a voice that is unique and corporeal beyond the mechanisms of recognition of the grids of intelligibility and language itself. Speaking through one's voice becomes a way to resist the mode of thinking that only proceeds through the *visual metaphor* of language and thought.

> *In other words, speaking is an interlocution with others and requires a reciprocity of speech and listening. Unlike thinking, speaking does not allow its protagonist to be an abstract subject; instead, it implies that the speakers are human beings in flesh and bone, with mouths and ears.*[18]

A unique voice is also, as Cavarero suggests, relational, always open to the ear of the other and it is precisely from this relational character that the political resistance of one's voice derives. It is because the voice exposes one's uniqueness to others that it offers a way of doing politics that differs from and resists forms of constituted power, logocentrism and the superiority of *theoria*. The exposure of the voice implies communication, listening and a sort of Arendtian possibility of resistance as opposed to contemplative thinking and action:

> *[T]he first entails a solitary thinker who withdraws from the world of human plurality to enjoy the noetic vision of desensitized and therefore abstract and universal objects. The second is a shared and relational space generated by the words and deeds of a plurality of human beings.*[19]

Indeed, in this study the voice constitutes a vocal challenge to conventional and traditional understandings of *being with* and, therefore, of politics and resistance. What the voice is doing is opening to another, generating awareness of oneself in relationality and interdependence within the community of speakers. The voice gives rise not just to reflective support of one's selfhood and awareness from

17 Nussbaum, "The Professor of Parody."

18 Adriana Cavarero, *For More Than One Voice: Toward a Philosophy of Vocal Expression*, trans. Paul Kottman (Stanford: Stanford University Press, 2005), 175.

19 Cavarero, "Politicizing Theory," 506.

within but also to processes of resistance against the constituted and sovereign structures. One's voice can resist in ways that are not possible through language. This is because one's voice springs from one's body in relationality and this contrasts with the violence of sovereign apparatuses of constituted language systems such as law; thus the voice breaks with the production of voiceless subjects that proceed through fixed categories of thinking.

The voice uses another Logos, one that vibrates in a unique throat of flesh, producing unique sounds in each of us, and as such expresses the singular body when in relationality to others. This radical and corporeal singularity that still participates in the production of words is usually made superfluous, cut out by constituted powers. By reversing this logic and by focusing on one's voice, I have tried to resist law and thus politics as *theoria*. Resisting through the voice complements the thought of critical legal scholars such as Costas Douzinas and also Illan Wall who have talked of resisting constituted systems of power precisely by emphasizing the radicality of those forms of power that are constituent and not yet constituted into a system.[20]

In *Philosophy and Resistance*, Douzinas talks of the Syntagma – which in Greek means square – as a constituent space, where in times of austerity non-institutionalized voices could speak and express their ideas, as opposed to the unitary power of institutions that speak for all.[21] Similarly, in *Human Rights and Constituent Power*, Wall explains how in modern democratic theory people are viewed as unitary actors capable of self-determination; the voice of people becomes one general voice connected to law and state institutions.[22] For Wall, the raw power and voice of people is to be seen in terms of constituent power; that is, the voice of the people in a more radical sense. One's voice resists – by means of unique sounds – the constituted power of language and law and reveals the constituent power of each unique body in relationality before being constituted into the general system. The voice links body and language and opens up the relation of one body to other bodies:

> *The voice not only announces this relation, but it announces it as corporeal, material, and rooted in the always embodied singularity of an existent that convokes the other with the rhythmic and sonorous breath of his or her mouth. Actively and reciprocally communicating their uniqueness, the speakers above all make heard a mutual dependence on a voice that is invocation, no longer autonomous or self-sufficient individuals in search of something that binds them, but already tied (to use Nancy's term) by an acoustic dialogue that takes its cadence from the very rhythm of breath.*[23]

20 Costas Douzinas, *Philosophy and Resistance in the Crisis: Greece and the Future of Europe* (London: Wiley and Sons, 2013); Illan Wall, *Human Rights and Constituent Power* (Oxon: Routledge, 2011).

21 Douzinas, *Philosophy and Resistance in the Crisis.*

22 Illan Wall, *Human Rights and Constituent Power.*

23 Cavarero, *For More Than One Voice*, 200.

This book attempts to deal with a few questions related to the theme of the voice, such as: how would resistance through the voice either engage with or disengage from forms of constituted power; how does the voice allow the reconnection of the cuts and divisions within subjectivity; what type of ontology subtends the voice; and what are the implications of the voice for sexual difference and for justice? I have argued that the voice calls for a process of resistance that does not always need to be thought of within the institutionalized limits of the legal and symbolic system. In the first part of the book, I have also argued that resistance can be located in moments of suspension of the system-frame, moments when one does not speak the language of the frame but of one's own voice. Those moments allow awareness and the possibility of a reflective selfhood.

Walter Benjamin has theorized such a possibility of suspension through the practice of a general strike against the state. His theory has influenced the methodological aspects of this book.[24] Benjamin envisioned how the general strike produces a release from legal accountability. For Benjamin, the general strike has the potential of a non-violent resistance, since it brings an entire legal system to its knees without the need of violence. The latter can be perceived as a moment of suspension of the legal frame, an anarchic space of detachment from it.

Critical legal scholars such as Douzinas, Goodrich and also Loizidou in different ways seem to agree that it is not possible to intend resistance in terms of complete disconnection from the legal system but that it is necessary to engage by disengaging.[25] This can be achieved by conceiving of ethical and ontological ways that both suspend and create new possibilities for reworking law and constituted systems of power. Therefore the voice has been considered as a suspension of the linguistic and legal construction of subjectivity, but also as engaging with it by considering different ontological possibilities for action. At the basis of the voice there is a selfhood that is no longer neutral, universal, disembodied, but that rather becomes aware of oneself through one's voice and by speaking to others.

The implications of such an ontological approach of being, as unique, corporeal and relational, have also been discussed in detail. Monia Andreani notes how, for Cavarero, one's name and surname do not alone suffice to reveal one's uniqueness; it is necessary instead to go back to one's voice as an unrepeatable and singular trait of each of us.[26] The voice links to one's unrepeatable, unique

24 Benjamin, Walter, "Critique of Violence," in *Reflections: Essays, Aphorisms, Autobiographical Writing*, ed. Peter Demetz, P., trans. Edmund Jephcott (New York: Harcourt Brace Jovanovich, 1978), 277–300.

25 Douzinas, Goodrich and Hachamovitch, *Politics, Postmodernity and Critical Legal Studies*. See also: Costas Douzinas and Adam Gearey, *Critical Jurisprudence: The Political Philosophy of Justice* (Oxford: Hart Publishing, 2005); Elena Loizidou, "Before the Law, Encounters at the Borderline," in *New Critical Legal Thinking. Law and the Political*, eds Douzinas, C., Stone, M. and Wall, I. (New York: Routledge, 2012), 181–197.

26 Monia Andreani, "Anatomia Politica dell'Orrore, La Questione della Vulnerabilità e la Figura dell'Inerme in Judith Butler e Adriana Cavarero," in *Differenza e Relazione: L'Ontologia dell' Umano nel Pensiero di Judith Butler e Adriana Cavarero*, eds Bernini, L. and Guaraldo, O. (Verona: Ombre Corte, 2009), 39–65.

body that was born and will die. Cavarero thus stresses an element of radical vulnerability connected to the voice. The human being coincides with the vulnerable uniqueness of each of us and this is not a metaphysical essence. We can say that the self who speaks in one's voice does not belong to the metaphysical sphere but rather to the scene of politics.

If Butler criticizes, as Andreani disputes, the centrality of singularity found in Cavarero, by showing that in a Hegelian way singularity is just another way of saying the universal, and argues instead for a necessary transferability and interchangeability in the subject,[27]Andreani rebuts this by saying that Butler does not center the meaning of singularity in Cavarero. Butler intends to show instead how vulnerability has a different meaning for her. When talking of singularity and vulnerability, Cavarero does not allude to the gnoseological field of perception but rather to a political field where unique selves meet one another.[28] Such a relation is dictated by accidentality and cannot be generalized.

To the contrary, Butler considers the social aspects of both voice and vulnerability, in which for her there is a social dimension. Even sexuality is an expression of a power that is rooted in the body but that appears to be determined by society. Therefore, for Butler, it is necessary to add the social dimension to the singular experience of voice, body and physical vulnerability. It follows that in Butler it is only with an ethical work grounded on the dimension of social normativity, centered on both singular and social vulnerability, that we can resist violence and sovereign impositions in a responsible way.

And yet, drawing on Cavarero, the focus on one's voice as unique and vulnerable contains for us already the responsibility to resist. There is self-exposition in the voice and traits of oneself that cannot be quantified or determined by language or social conditioning. The voice discloses the irreducibility of one's body, an irreducibility that reveals a *who*. This *who* does not know who is exposed but only that it is exposed, and in such vulnerable exposure lies the unpredictable resistance offered by the voice. The identity of *who is speaking* is given by the dimension of speaking: while one is speaking, when one is exposed to others. One's voice and vulnerability coincide with a way of resisting that is relational.

The self becomes a narratable self, neither an already narrated self nor narratability or exposure per se.[29] The narratability of the self or speakability of the voice cannot be taken away. Now resistance through one's voice needs precisely to fight any ambiguity and equivocation of such an ontological dimension of the voice. One's voice resists the possibility of becoming anyone and the violence of constituted power.

27 Andreani, "Anatomia Politica dell'Orrore," 54; here Andreani refers to: Judith Butler, *Giving an Account of Oneself* (New York: Fordham University Press, 2005).

28 Andreani, "Anatomia Politica dell'Orrore," 54.

29 Adriana Cavarero, *Relating Narratives. Storytelling and Selfhood*, trans. Paul Kottman (London: Routledge, 2000).

However, in a collective dimension of interchangeability, transferability and generalization, each can be anyone, all ambiguous beings, and thus violence and injustice can easily proliferate within constituted systems of power. The voice precisely resists the passage from one's uniqueness to anyone else's. I think that the political knot of violence and sovereignty requires a resistance that pushes toward dimensions of awareness of oneself and the others in the community. The voice not only suspends language but opens the space for unpredictable actions and a different sense of justice that interrupts the repetition of violence. The voice emphasizes suspension and the potential of a future, which can energize resistance in the now.

In his book *On Resistance*, Howard Caygill, commenting on the work of Raoul Vaneigem, underlines how until now the only possible way to resist violence and injustices has consisted of choosing either Mao or Gandhi; that is, either repressing and punishing or enacting the passive resistance of the Satyagraha.[30] However, Caygill makes us note how the Maoist strategy implies entering the terrain of the enemy and, consequently, implies a subject of resentment (discussed in Chapter IV), whereas the Gandhian strategy is only viable when the power to be resisted already contains some ethics.

In the contemporary horizon, it is perhaps necessary to resist by affirming an ontology that reverses the terms of the constituted sovereign ontology. Caygill mentions how Raoul Vaneigem, in his book *The Revolution of Everyday Life*, originally published in 1967, urges us to resist the ontology of sovereign power that is manifested in the exploitation of nature, in predatory relationships of exchange, in the separation from the self, the fetishism of money and the fear of women, and suggests a third possibility of resistance; that is, breaking with the impossibilities of sovereign power by means of affirmation.[31]

If sovereign power and violence reduce life to mere survival by excluding from it aspects of participation, communication and fulfillment or realization as being superfluous or impossible, then Vaneigem suggests that resistance should affirm rather than erase those aspects of life that are made superfluous. In other words, we should transform the impossibilities of life into possibilities by enacting precisely those aspects of life that are cut out and made superfluous (e.g. participation, communication, fulfillment or self-realization). For Caygill, the Zapatista movement is an example of actualization of the possibilities of life. Chiapas teaches us that everyone can participate and speak in one's voice, that resistance can be enacted through love and creativity and that there are other ways to live.

Using Vaneigem's and Caygill's insights, I attempt in this book to conceive of and imagine a way to resist the impossibilities of life by means of affirming the ontology of one's voice that has been cut out by language and law. In order to

30 Howard Caygill, *On Resistance: A Philosophy of Defiance* (London: Bloomsbury, 2013), 180.

31 Raoul Vaneigem, *The Revolution of Everyday Life* (London: Left Bank Book and Rebel Press, 1983).

resist, we must speak in one's voice, suspend the symbolic order, the law of the Father, the essentialized sexual difference divide that marks law; we must think about justice outside resentment; we must love, attempt to let go and forgive, circulate gifts, see things through their ambivalence, resist the indifference of the system, fight indifference, and affirm our singularity and uniqueness as ontological points of reference for unpredictable actions.

There are several refutations and arguments that could be made against the centrality of the voice in this book. Some may argue, for instance, that it is impossible to apply or use one's voice in law, that law necessarily proceeds through visual and written texts codified in abstract language, through general standards valid for all, of which equality is the main pillar. It could further be argued that *reasonableness* is a good standard criterion for consent, even if grounded on a cut subjectivity that excludes many other aspects and traits of the subject; that it is inevitable that justice must end in the retribution and punishment of those who commit wrong; that the ontology of singularity revealed in one's voice collides with the current legal ontological framework; and that all that has been said is problematic if not unapplicable.

Others might disagree with the idea of ontology itself and sustain that ontology has to be refuted a priori because it leads to metaphysics, essentialism and closure in thinking, and that rather a poststructuralist, deconstructive approach of openness and deferral is preferable and more productive. Some may argue against the many limitations in the book, for instance those regarding the small number of authors dealt with in the literature review, the analysis of the possibility of the voice or in the use of black letter laws.

However, if we think that the only way to deal with resistance to law and sovereign impositions is through a juridical model of analysis, a restricted legalist application of its already codified mechanisms within a certain ontological inscription, then very little space is left for the imagination of resistance. It would mean that it is impossible to reflect on new ontologies and thus on new actions to be undertaken, because the only way is the way of things as they are formed in the present. It would mean accepting the law of the father, the essentialized sexual difference paradigm, the sovereign state imposition of a legal voice, already constructed and chosen for us and on our behalf.

From such a perspective, we can only continue to fight the violence of the sovereign through mechanisms of violence; that is by denying who we are, our singularity and vulnerability. In this sense, it is as if we imagine ourselves as already ontologically scarred and determined by the cuts, splits and separations from life, we keep on surviving within the sovereign violence of the frame that makes of us "anyone" and we have no hope for a way of resisting in which one can speak in one's own voice and reveal one's uniqueness.

In relation to ontology, we can say that ontology is simply the thinking of our being in the world and there is always an ontological frame behind our thinking and actions. A poststructuralist and deconstructive approach also represents an ontology or a way of thinking even if it maintains the necessity of openness and deferral. Moreover, ontology in this study is not fixed and metaphysical and does not make use of essentialisms. It rather resists those categories of thinking. It is an ontology of one's uniqueness and of the exposure of one's uniqueness, relationality; it is rooted in the vulnerability of one's material body that is born, grows, becomes old and dies, thus it is an ontology that changes. Cavarero calls it an *empty ontology*.

Finally, ontologizing may be inevitable. Caygill and Vaneigem consider, for instance, resistance within a third possibility: a resistance that opposes by constructing new terrains rather than reproducing the terrain of violence or silent deconstruction. Commenting on the thought of Vaneigem, Caygill also argues for a new ontological approach to life, grounded on love and generosity, as in the example of the Zapatists.

Regarding the literature review, given that there are many frames to be considered when dealing with resistance, it became necessary to be selective but also inclusive. Each frame provides certain conditions of possibility for considering resistance. As for a sparing use of black letter laws, I would like to cite some thoughts from the critical legal tradition that provides the contextualization of this book. Critical legal scholars such as Douzinas and Gearey have shown that there is another way of approaching law, in terms of law of the law and via a general jurisprudence that escapes the restricted view in which the study of law usually takes place. Douzinas and Gearey have underlined the fact that few legal scholars "have escaped the dry taste in the mouth occasioned by the study of jurisprudence."[32]

For Douzinas and Gearey, there has been in law "a gradual diminution of scope and the replacement of thinking about the law of the law by a technical and professional approach"; that is, a restricted type of legal thinking.[33] What is necessary, for the two critical legal scholars, is an approach to jurisprudence as general jurisprudence that returns to philosophical concerns, capable of viewing law through wider concepts of legality, disengaged from the voice of state law.[34] In this book, the focus on one's voice is intended to continue such a critical legal tradition and a critical approach to law.

This work represents just a small step into the vast field of the possibilities of resistance provided by the voice. Adriana Cavarero, whose work and ideas inspired this book, has written *For More Than One Voice* and has underlined the aspect of uniqueness and relationality of the voice, while other scholars have discussed the voice from other perspectives. Mladen Dolar has, for instance, given attention to the voice in his book *A Voice and Nothing More*.[35] The voice Dolar is interested in is a different voice from Cavarero's; it is the voice as object voice, as surplus, excess of language and meaning, a voice as a vanishing mediator. It is a voice that

32 Douzinas and Gearey, *Critical Jurisprudence*, 3.
33 Douzinas and Gearey, *Critical Jurisprudence*, 4.
34 Douzinas and Gearey, *Critical Jurisprudence*, 10.
35 Mladen Dolar, *A Voice and Nothing More* (Cambridge: The MIT Press, 2006).

lies "beyond the voice with flesh and bones, it is a fleshless and boneless entity defined by its function – the silent sound, the soundless voice."[36] This object voice interrupts the full presence of metaphysics because it only refers to a void where the voice resonates. Like Cavarero, Dolar thinks that phonocentrism is not infected by logocentrism, as Derrida has thought, but that rather there is a dimension of the voice which runs counter to self-transparency and presence.

More recently, Nick Couldry has written a book titled *Why Voice Matters*, where he seems to draw from the work of Judith Butler and underlines the current crisis of the voice and the importance of making the voice matter.[37] He attempts to work on multiple levels of the voice that culminate in the voice as materialization. This latter level of voice allows only some types of voices to become visible, and he reflects on resisting those processes of materialization of the voice.

However, with this book, I wished to think of the voice as exposure of one's uniqueness in relationality, as Cavarero has theorized. I have also seen in one's voice a series of implications within and outside law with the aim of revitalizing debates within the critical legal tradition. The understanding of the voice goes beyond a voice as a metaphor. Cavarero's corporeal sense of voice, her insistence of voice as sonorous expression of one's breath, has animated the possibility of having an inner and reflective awareness of oneself while one is speaking. It is such a moment of corporeal and singular awareness that in my view resists and refuses the logics of law's structure by addressing the command of an abstract subject. And this also allows us to conceive of an ethics that exceeds the subject of resentment of liberal legal logic and open other ways to respond.

I would like to conclude the book with the tale commented on by Dolar himself at the beginning of his book on the voice.[38] In the middle of a battle and in the trenches, the Italian commander shouts in a clear voice, "Soldiers attack!" but nobody moves. The commander cries out even louder only to hear a soft comment: "Che bella voce!" (What a beautiful voice!). Beyond the stereotypes of Italian soldiers not being the most courageous soldiers in the world, Dolar makes us notice that the command fails because the Italian soldiers concentrate instead on the medium of voice. While there is first a failed interpellation of the command, on a second level there is an interpellation that works; the Italian soldiers, concentrating on the voice instead of on the message, appreciate the aesthetic of a beautiful voice. But also in this case, the Italian soldiers still act stereotypically as Italians who love opera and *bel canto*.

For Dolar, beyond the voice as the vehicle of meaning or as aesthetic admiration, there is a third type of voice, as object voice that only functions as a "disturbance of aesthetic appreciation."[39] The soldiers in this case, as Dolar comments, would not attack or go to the opera but would make use of psychoanalysis, because the

36 Dolar, *A Voice and Nothing More*, 17.
37 Couldry, *Why Voice Matters*.
38 Dolar, *A Voice and Nothing More*, 3.
39 Dolar, *A Voice and Nothing More*, 4.

voice can emancipate itself from its original function and start resisting by operating as a surplus and thus as a means of resistance.

However, in this study the voice can offer an ontological approach to resistance by revealing *who someone is*, by opposing the anonymity of anyone and a general notion of the individual. Going back to the soldiers, these are anonymous and impersonal subjects. It is perhaps only when the soldier is wounded and made vulnerable that he may acquire a position outside the impersonal subjectivity of the soldier, when he is taken care of because of the injury. But even in that situation his voice may remain anonymous; his life receives attention only when he is in danger.

Speaking through Cavarero's voice, I can rather say that it is only when a soldier speaks in his own voice and we listen to such a sound and vibration that his uniqueness and bodily specificity is exposed to us and he reveals the singularity and vulnerability of his life. And here lies the importance of the voice as one's uniqueness and as a means of resistance. A unique voice, and thus life, occupies a space outside any categorizing or hierarchy, enjoys a strong sense, not in relation to this or that subjectivity but in relation to the simple exposure of speaking and disclosing one's uniqueness. It is precisely this sense of the voice that can make a soldier resist and disobey any commanding imposition, injustice or the sovereign rule of law.

It could also be argued, along with Cavarero, that the focus on one's voice does not eliminate the sphere of sight because vision and imagination are necessary in considering resistance. What the voice does for me is rather to reconnect the cut and split subject to one's human condition of materiality and vulnerability, and this makes of the *theoria* of a vision of fictitious entities a politics of concrete and corporeal speaking voices.

Bibliography

Books and chapters in books

Aladjem, Terry, *The Culture of Vengeance and the Fate of American Justice* (Cambridge: Cambridge University Press, 2008).

Andreani, Monia, "Anatomia Politica dell'Orrore. La Questione della Vulnerabilità e la Figura dell'Inerme in Judith Butler e Adriana Cavarero," in *Differenza e Relazione: L'Ontologia dell'Umano nel Pensiero di Judith Butler e Adriana Cavarero*, eds Bernini, L. and Guaraldo, O. (Verona: Ombre Corte, 2009), 39–65.

Arendt, Hannah, *The Human Condition* (Chicago: The University of Chicago Press, 1958).

Arendt, Hannah, "Civil Disobedience," in *Crisis of the Republic: Lying in Politics*, ed. Arendt, H. (Harmondsworth: Penguin Books, 1973), 49–102.

Arendt, Hannah, *On Revolution* (Harmondsworth: Penguin Books, 1973).

Arendt, Hannah, *The Life of the Mind* (New York: Harcourt & Co, 1981).

Arendt, Hannah, *Eichmann in Jerusalem: A Report on the Banality of Evil* (New York: Penguin Books, 1994).

Aristodemou, Maria, *Law and Literature: Journeys from Her to Eternity* (Oxford: Oxford University Press, 2000).

Austin, John Langshaw, *How to Do Things with Words* (Cambridge: Harvard University Press, 1975).

Bantas, Hercules, *Understanding John Rawls* (Melbourne: Reluctant Geek, 2010).

Bar On, Bat-Ami, *The Subject of Violence* (Lanham: Rowman & Littlefield, 2002).

Baraitser, Lisa, *Maternal Encounters: The Ethics of Interruption* (Oxon: Routledge, 2009).

Bataille, Georges, *Eroticism*, trans. Mary Dalwood (London: Pearson, 1957).

Bataille, Georges, *The Accursed Share, An Essay On General Economy, Vol. I: Consumption*, trans. Robert Hurtley (New York: Zone Books, 1989).

Battersby, Christine, *The Phenomenal Woman: Feminist Metaphysics and the Patterns of Identity* (New York: Routledge, 1998).

Bell, Vikki, "The Promise of Liberalism and the Performance of Freedom," in *Foucault and the Political Reason*, eds Barry, A., Osborne, T. and Rose, N. (London: UCL Press, 1996), 81–97.

Benjamin, Walter, "Critique of Violence," in *Reflections: Essays, Aphorisms, Autobiographical Writings*, ed. Demetz, P., trans. Edmund Jephcott (New York: Harcourt Brace Jovanovich, 1978), 277–300.

Benjamin, Walter, *Reflections: Essays, Aphorisms, Autobiographical Writings*, ed. Demetz, P., trans. Edmund Jephcott (New York: Harcourt Brace Jovanovich, 1978).

Bergen, Bernard, *The Banality of Evil: Hannah Arendt and the Final Solution* (Oxford: Rowman & Littlefield, 1998).

Bertolino, Elisabetta, "Is There such a Thing as a Mediterranean Feminism? A Contribution from the Margins," in *Feminisms: Within and Without*, ed. Pelan, R. (Galway: National University of Ireland, 2005), 36–55.

Bertolino, Elisabetta, "Forgiveness, One's Voice and the Law," in *The Philosophy of Forgiveness. New Dimensions of Forgiveness*, ed. Lewis, C.D. II (Wilmington: Vernon Press, 2016), 187–214.

Bertolino, Elisabetta, "Pasolini, le Lucciole and the Law," in *Rileggendo Pasolini. Il Diritto dopo la Scomparsa delle Lucciole*. Vol. 2, eds Contu, E., Guerrieri, A. and Romano, G. (Ariccia: Aracne Editrice, 2016), 255–264.

Bettelheim, Bruno, *Symbolic Wounds: Puberty Rites and the Envious Male* (London: Thames and Hudson, 1995).

Birmingham, Peg, "On Action: The Appearance of Law," in *Action and Appearance: Ethics and the Politics of Writing in Hannah Arendt*, eds Yeatman, A. et al. (London: Continuum, 2011), 103–116.

Boddy, Janice, "Gender Crusade: The Female Circumcision Controversy in Cultural Perspective," in *Transcultural Bodies: Female Genital Cutting in Global Context*, eds Hernlund, Y. and Shell-Duncan, B. (London: Rutgers University Press, 2007), 44–66.

Bonaparte, Marie, *Notes on Excision* (New York: International University Press, 1950).

Bono, Paola and Kemp, Sandra, *Italian Feminist Thought: A Reader* (Oxford: Basil Blackwell, 1991).

Bowen-Moore, Patricia, *Hannah Arendt's Philosophy of Natality* (London: Macmillan Press, 1989).

Bravo, Anna and Cereja, Federico, *Intervista a Primo Levi, Ex Deportato* (Turin: Einaudi, 2011).

Bridgeman, Jo and Millns, Susan, *Feminist Perspectives on Law. Law's Engagement with the Female Body* (London: Sweet & Maxwell, 1998).

Brown, Vicki, *Listening to the Streets: A Study of Young People Involved in Prostitution.* (University of Manchester: Thesis, 2005).

Butler, Judith, *Subjects of Desire: Hegelian Reflections in Twentieth-Century France* (New York: Columbia University Press, 1987).

Butler, Judith, *Gender Trouble: Feminism and the Subversion of Identity* (New York: Routledge, 1990).

Butler, Judith, *Bodies that Matter. On the Discursive Limits of Sex* (New York: Routledge, 1993).

Butler, Judith, "How Can I Deny that These Hands and This Body are Mine?" in *Material Events: Paul De Man and the Afterlife of Theory*, eds Cohen, T., Cohen, B., Miller, J. and Warminski, A. (Minneapolis: University of Minnesota Press, 2001), 254–276.

Butler, Judith, *Giving an Account of Oneself* (New York: Fordham University Press, 2005).

Butler, Judith, "Critique, Coercion and Sacred Life in Benjamin's Critique of Violence," in *Political Theologies*, eds De Vries, H. and Sullivan, L.E. (New York: Fordham University Press, 2006), 201–219.

Butler, Judith, *Frames of War: When Is Life Grievable?* (London: Verso, 2010).

Butler, Judith, "Rethinking Vulnerability and Resistance," in *Vulnerability in Resistance*, eds Butler, J., Gambetti, Z. and Sabsay, L. (Durham: Duke University Press, 2016), 12–27.

Butler, Judith, Laclau, Ernesto and Žižek, Slavoj, *Contingency, Hegemony, Universality: Contemporary Dialogues on the Left* (London: Verso, 2000).

Cahill, Anne, *Overcoming Objectification: A Carnal Ethics* (New York: Routledge, 2011).

Calhoun, Craig and McGowan, John, *Hannah Arendt and the Meaning of Politics* (Minneapolis: Minnesota University Press, 1997).

Canetti, Elias, *The Conscience of Words* (New York: Seabury, 1979).

Canetti, Elias, *Crowds and Power* (New York: Farrar, Straus and Giroux, 1984).

Carlen, Pat, *Women's Imprisonment: A Study in Social Control* (London: Routledge and Kegan Paul, 1983).

Carline, Anna, "Criminalisation or Protection? Tensions in the Construction of Prevention Strategies Concerning Trafficking for the Purposes of Sexual Exploitation," in *Gender, Sexualities and Law*, eds Jones, J. and Grear, A. (Oxon: Routledge 2011), 175–187.

Carline, Anna, "Perspectives on Trafficking and the Policing and Crime Act 2009: Challenging Notions of Vulnerability Through a Butlerian Lens," in *Regulating the International Movement of Women. From Protection to Control*, eds Sharron, A. and FitzGerald, A. (Oxon: Routledge, 2011), 135–140.

Cavarero, Adriana, *In Spite of Plato: A Feminist Rewriting of Ancient Philosophy*, trans. Serena Anderlini-D'Onofrio and Aine O'Healy (Cambridge: Polity Press, 1995).

Cavarero, Adriana, "Demeter," in *In Spite of Plato: A Feminist Rewriting of Ancient Philosophy*, ed. Cavarero, A., trans. Serena Anderlini D'Onofrio (Cambridge: Polity Press, 1995), 57–90.

Cavarero, Adriana, *Relating Narratives. Storytelling and Selfhood*, trans. Paul Kottman (London: Routledge, 2000).

Cavarero, Adriana, *For More Than One Voice: Toward a Philosophy of Vocal Expression*, trans. Paul Kottman (Stanford: Stanford University Press, 2005).

Cavarero, Adriana, "Dedicated to Derrida," in *For More Than One Voice: Toward a Philosophy of Vocal Expression*, trans. Paul Kottman (Stanford: Stanford University Press, 2005), 213–241.

Cavarero, Adriana, *Horrorism: Naming Contemporary Violence*, trans. William McCuaig (New York: Columbia University Press, 2009).

Cavarero, Adriana, "Inclining the Subject: Ethics, Alterity and Natality," in *Theory After Theory*, eds Elliot, J. and Attridge, D. (New York: Routledge, 2011), 194–204.

Cavarero, Adriana, "Archeologia dell'Omicidio," in *I Comandamenti. Non Uccidere*, eds Cavarero, A. and Scola, A. (Bologna: Il Mulino, 2013), 68–139.

Cavarero, Adriana, *Inclinazioni: Critica della Rettitudine* (Milan: Raffaella Cortina Editore, 2013). This last book by Cavarero has also been translated into English: Cavarero, Adriana, *Inclinationations: A Critique of Rectitude*, trans. Adam Sitze and Amanda Minervini (Stanford: Stanford University Press, 2016).

Cavarero, Adriana, "Canetti: Dritto Davanti al Morto," in *Inclinazioni: Critica alla Rettitudine* (Milan: Raffaella Cortina Editore, 2013), 118–130.

Cavarero, Adriana and Restaino, Franco, *Le Filosofie Femministe* (Milan: Bruno Mondadori, 2002).

Caygill, Howard, *On Resistance: A Philosophy of Defiance* (London: Bloomsbury, 2013).

Clarkson, C.M.V. and Keating, S.R., *Criminal Law: Text and Material.* Seventh Edition (London: Sweet & Maxwell, 2010).

Constable, Marianne, *Our World is Our Bond. How Legal Speech Acts* (Stanford: Stanford University Press, 2014).

Cook, Rebecca G., ed., *Human Rights of Women. National and International Perspectives* (Philadelphia: University of Pennsylvania Press, 1995).

Couldry, Nick, *Why Voice Matters* (London: Sage, 2010).

Cowan, Jane, *Culture and Rights. Anthropological Perspectives* (Cambridge: Cambridge University Press, 2001).

Culbert, Jennifer, *Dead Certainty. The Death Penalty and the Problem of Judgment* (Stanford: Stanford University Press, 2008).

Culbert, Jennifer and Sarat, Austin, "Interpreting the Violent State," in *States of Violence. War, Capital Punishment and Letting Die*, eds Culbert, J. and Sarat, A. (Cambridge: Cambridge University Press, 2009), 1–24.

Day, Sophie, "What Counts as Rape? Physical Assault and Broken Contracts: Contrasting Views of Rape among London Sex Workers," in *Sex and Violence*, eds Harvey, P. and Gow, P. (London: Routledge, 1994), 172–189.

Deleuze, Gilles, "From Ressentiment to the Bad Conscience," in *Nietzsche and Philosophy*, ed. Deleuze, G., trans. Hugh Tomlinson (New York: Columbia University Press, 1983), 111–146.

Derrida, Jacques, *Speech and Phenomena: And Other Essays on Husserl's Theory of Signs*, trans. David B. Allison (Evanston: Northwestern University Press, 1973).

Derrida, Jacques, *Limited INC.*, trans. Samuel Weber (Evanston: Northwestern University Press, 1977).

Derrida, Jacques, *Of Grammatology*, trans. Gayatri Chakravorty Spivak (London: Johns Hopkins University Press, 1997).

Derrida, Jacques, *On Cosmopolitanism and Forgiveness*, trans. Michael Hughes (London: Routledge, 2001).

Dolar, Mladen, *A Voice and Nothing More* (Cambridge: The MIT Press, 2006).

Dorkenoo, Efua, *Cutting the Rose: The Practice and its Prevention* (London: Minority Rights, 1994).

Douzinas, Costas, *Philosophy and Resistance in the Crisis: Greece and the Future of Europe* (London: Wiley and Sons, 2013).

Douzinas, Costas and Gearey, Adam, *Critical Jurisprudence: The Political Philosophy of Justice* (Oxford: Hart Publishing, 2005).

Douzinas, Costas, Goodrich, Peter and Hachamovitch, Yifat, *Politics, Postmodernity and Critical Legal Studies: The Legality of the Contingent* (New York: Routledge, 1994).

Douzinas, Costas, Stone, Matthew and Wall, Illan, eds, *New Critical Legal Thinking. Law and the Political* (New York: Routledge, 2012).

Douzinas, Costas and Warrington, Ronnie with McVeigh, Shaun, *Postmodern Jurisprudence: The Law of Text in the Texts of Law* (London: Routledge, 1991).

Douzinas, Costas and Warrington, Ronnie, "Antigone's Law: A Genealogy of Jurisprudence," in *Politics, Postmodernity and Critical Legal Studies*, eds Douzinas, C., Goodrich, P. and Hachamovitch, Y. (London: Routledge, 1994), 187–225.

Drakopoulou, Maria, ed., *Feminist Encounters with Legal Philosophy*, (Oxon: Routledge, 2014).

Drakopoulou, Maria, "Introduction: Reading Law, Reading Woman," in *Feminist Encounters with Legal Philosophy*, ed. Drakopoulou, M. (Oxon: Routledge, 2014), 1–8).

Drakopoulou, Maria, "Samuel Pufendorf, Feminism and the Question of Women and Law," in *Feminist Encounters with Legal Philosophy*, ed. Drakopoulou, M. (Oxon: Routledge, 2014), 66–99.

Engle Merry, Sally, "Wife Battering and the Ambiguities of Rights," in *Identities, Politics, and Rights*, eds Sarat, A. and Kearns, T.R. (Ann Arbor: University of Michigan Press, 1995), 271–306.

Euripides, *Medea*, ed. Denys, L.P. (Oxford: Clarendon Press, 1971).

Felman, Shoshana, *The Scandal of the Speaking Body: Don Juan with J.L. Austin or the Seduction in Two Languages*, trans. Catherine Porter (Stanford: Stanford University Press, 2003).

Freeman, Michael, *Lloyd's Introduction to Jurisprudence*. Eighth Edition (London: Sweet & Maxwell, 2008).

Gilligan, Carol, *In a Different Voice* (Cambridge: Harvard University Press, 1982).
Goodrich, Peter, *Languages of Law: From Logics of Memory to Nomadic Masks* (London: Weidenfeld and Nicholson, 1990).
Goodrich, Peter, "Gender and Contracts," in *Feminist Perspectives on the Foundational Subjects of Law*, ed. Bottomley, A. (London: Cavendish, 1996), 17–46.
Goodrich, Peter, *The Law of Love. A Brief Historical and Practical Manual* (New York: Palgrave Macmillan, 2006).
Gregory, Katherine, *The Everyday Lives of Sex Workers in the Netherlands* (New York: Routledge, 2005).
Guenther, Lisa, *The Gift of the Other: Levinas and the Politics of Reproduction* (Albany: State University of New York Press, 2006).
Halion, Kevin J., *Speech Act Theory and Deconstruction* (McMaster University: Thesis, 1989).
Hamacher, Werner, "Afformative Strike," in *Benjamin's Philosophy: Destruction and Experience*, eds Benjamin, A. and Osborne, P. (London: Routledge, 1994), 113–163).
Hanafin, Patrick, "A Voice Beyond the Law: Reading Plato, Reading Cavarero," in *Feminist Encounters with Legal Philosophy*, ed. Drakopoulou, M. (Oxon: Routledge, 2014), 9–19.
Hoigard, Cecile and Finstad, Liv, *Prostitution, Money and Love* (Philadelphia: Pennsylvania University Press, 1986).
Jackson, Emily, *Medical Law: Text, Cases and Materials*. Third Edition (Oxford: Oxford University Press, 2013).
Kalyvas, Andreas, *Democracy and the Politics of the Extraordinary: Max Weber, Carl Schmitt and Hannah Arendt* (Cambridge: Cambridge University Press, 2008).
Kelman, Mark, *A Guide to Critical Legal Studies* (Cambridge: Harvard University Press, 1987).
Kennedy, Ian, *Treat Me Right* (Oxford: Clarendon Press, 1998).
Laite, Julia, *Common Prostitutes and Ordinary Citizens. Commercial Sex in London 1885–1960* (London: Palgrave Macmillan, 2012).
Lawrence, D.H., *Lady Chatterley's Lover* (London: Penguin Books, 2006).
Levi, Primo, *Survival in Auschwitz and the Reawakening*, trans. Stuart Woolf (New York: Summit, 1986).
Loizidou, Elena, *Judith Butler: Ethics, Law, Politics* (Oxon: Routledge, 2007).
Loizidou, Elena, "This Is What Democracy Looks Like," in *How Not to Be Governed: Readings and Interpretations from a Critical Anarchist Left*, eds Klausen, J.C. and Martel, J. (Lanham: Rowman & Littlefield, 2011), 167–187.
Loizidou, Elena, "Before the Law, Encounters at the Borderline," in *New Critical Legal Thinking. Law and the Political*, eds Douzinas, C., Stone, M. and Wall, I. (New York: Routledge, 2012), 181–197.
Loizidou, Elena, "Disobedience Subjectively Speaking," in *Disobedience: Concept and Practice*, ed. Loizidou, E. (Oxon: Routledge, 2013), 108–124.
Lombroso, Cesare and Ferrero, William, *The Female Offender* (London: Fisher, 1895).
Lovett, Frank, *Rawls's A Theory of Justice: A Reader's Guide* (London: Continuum, 2011).
Maraini, Dacia, *Chiara di Assisi: Elogio della Disubbidienza* (Milan: Rizzoli, 2013).
Martel, James, "The Ambivalent Anarchism of Hannah Arendt," in *How Not to Be Governed: Readings and Interpretations from a Critical Anarchist Left*, eds Klausen, J.C. and Martel, J. (Lanham: Rowman & Littlefield, 2011), 143–155.
Mauss, Marcel, *The Gift. Forms and Functions of Exchange in Archaic Societies* (Glencoe: The Free Press, 1954).

McLeod, Carolyn and Sherwin, Susan, "Relational Autonomy: Feminist Perspectives on Autonomy, Self-Trust, and Health Care for Patients who are Oppressed," in *Relational Autonomy: Feminist Perspectives on Autonomy, Agency and the Social Self*, eds Mackenzie, C. and Stoljar, N. (Oxford: Oxford University Press, 2000), 259–279.

Nancy, Jean Luc, *Being Singular Plural*, trans. Robert D. Richardson and Anne E. O'Byrne (Stanford: Stanford University Press, 2000).

Nancy, Jean Luc, *Listening*, trans. Charlotte Mandell (New York: Fordham University Press, 2007).

Nussbaum, Martha, *Sex and Social Justice* (Oxford: Oxford University Press, 1999).

Nussbaum, Martha, "Objectification," in *Sex and Social Justice*, ed. Nussbaum, M. (Oxford: Oxford University Press, 1999), 213–239.

Nussbaum, Martha, "'Whether from Reason or Prejudice': Taking Money for Bodily Services," in *Sex and Social Justice*, ed. Nussbaum, M. (Oxford: Oxford University Press, 1999), 276–298.

Nussbaum, Martha, *Women and Human Development: The Capability Approach* (Cambridge: Cambridge University Press, 2000).

Nussbaum, Martha, *Upheavals of Thought* (Cambridge: Cambridge University Press, 2001).

Nussbaum, Martha, *Hiding from Humanity: Disgust, Shame and the Law* (Princeton: Princeton University Press, 2004).

O' Neill, Maggie, *Prostitution and Feminism: Towards a Politics of Feeling* (Cambridge: Polity Press, 2001).

Orbach, Susan, *Bodies* (London: Profile Books, 2009).

Parati, Graziella and West, Rebecca J., eds, *Italian Feminist Theory and Practice. Equality and Sexual Difference* (London: Associated University Press, 2002).

Purdom, Judy, "Judging Women: Rethinking Shame Through Corporeality," in *Feminist Perspectives on Law and Theory*, eds Richardson, J. and Sandland, R. (London: Cavendish Publishing, 2000), 209–228.

Rawls, John, *A Theory of Justice* (Cambridge: Harvard University Press, 1971).

Rawls, John, "The Justification of Civil Disobedience," in *Revolution and the Rule of Law*, ed. Kent, E. (Princeton: Princeton University Press, 1971), 30–45.

Rawls, John, *Political Liberalism* (New York: Columbia University Press, 1996).

Ricoeur, Paul, *Memory, History, Forgetting* (Chicago: The University of Chicago Press, 2004).

Rogers, Juliet, "Flesh Made Law: The Economics of Female Genital Mutilation Legislation," in *International Law and Its Others*, ed. Orford, A. (Cambridge: Cambridge University Press, 2006), 197–220.

Roman-Lagerspetz, Sari, *Striving for the Impossible: The Hegelian Background of Judith Butler* (Department of Political Science, University of Helsinki: Academic Dissertation, 2009).

Salecl, Renata, "Cut in the Body: From Clitoridectomy to Body Art," in *(Per)versions of Love and Hate*, ed. Salecl, R. (London: Verso, 1998), 141–168.

Sanders, Teela, *Sex Work: A Risky Business* (London: Willan Publishing, 2005).

Self, Helen J., *Prostitution, Women and the Misuse of the Law: The Fallen Daughters of Eve* (London: Frank Cass, 2003).

Sharpe, Andrew, *Transgender Jurisprudence: Dysphoric Bodies of Law* (London: Cavendish, 2002).

Stauffer, Jill, *Ethical Loneliness. The Injustice of Not Being Heard* (New York: Columbia University Press, 2015).

Van der Walt, Johan, *Law and Sacrifice: Towards a Post-Apartheid Theory of Law* (London: Birkbeck Law Press, 2005).

Van der Walt, Johan, "Law and the Space of Appearance," in *Hannah Arendt and the Law*, eds Goldoni, M. and McCorkindale, C. (Oxford: Hart Publishing, 2012), 63–97.
Van Marle, Karin, "Introduction: Towards a Politics of Living," in *Sex, Gender, Becoming: Post-Apartheid Reflections*, ed. Van Marle, K. (Pretoria: Pretoria University Law Press, 2006), VII–1.
Vaneigem, Raoul, *The Revolution of Everyday Life* (London: Left Bank Book and Rebel Press, 1983).
Wall, Illan, *Human Rights and Constituent Power* (Oxon: Routledge, 2011).
Wilkinson, Michael, A., "Between Freedom and Law: Hannah Arendt on the Promise of Modern Revolution and the Burden of the Tradition," in *Hannah Arendt and the Law*, eds Goldoni, M. and McCorkindale, C. (Oxford: Hart Publishing, 2012), 35–61.
Young, Alison, *Imagining Crime* (London: Sage, 1996).
Zerilli, Linda M.G., *Feminism and the Abyss of Freedom* (Chicago: The University of Chicago Press, 2005).
Žižek, Slavoj, *Enjoy your Symptom!: Jacques Lacan in Hollywood and Out* (New York: Routledge, 1992).
Žižek, Slavoj, *Plague of Fantasies* (London: Verso, 1997).

Articles in periodicals

Abusharaf, Rogaia Mustafa, "Virtuous Cuts: Female Genital Circumcision in an African Ontology," *differences: A Journal of Feminist Cultural Studies*, 12(1) (2001): 112–140.
Bandes, Susan, "When Victims Seek Closure: Forgiveness, Vengeance and the Role of Government," *Fordham Urban Law Journal*, 27 (1999–2000): 1599–1606.
Baraitser, Lisa, "Mothers Who Make Things Public," *Feminist Review*, 93 (2009): 8–26.
Bertolino, Elisabetta, "The Politics of Subjectivity in the Women, Law and Development Discourse," *Australian Feminist Law Journal*, 25 (2006): 119–142.
Bertolino, Elisabetta, "Predictable Medea," *Studies in the Maternal*, 2(1) (2010): 1–10.
Bertolino, Elisabetta, "The Injustice of Justice. Feminist Ethical Reflections on Subjectivity," *WAGADU Special Issue on Epistemic Justice in Practice*, 15 (2016): 72–121.
Broussard, Patricia, "The Importation of Female Genital Mutilation to the West: The Cruellest Cut of All," *University of San Francisco Law Review*, 44 (2009–2010): 787–824.
Brown, Wendy, "Wounded Attachments," *Political Theory*, 21(3) (1993): 340–410.
Buss, Doris, "The Curious Visibility of Wartime Rape: Gender and Ethnicity in International Criminal Law," *Windsor Yearbook of Access to Justice*, 25 (2007): 3–22.
Carline, Anna, "Critical Perspectives on the Policing and Crime Act 2009. An Unethical Approach to the Regulation of Prostitution," *Contemporary Issues in Law*, 10 (2010): 77–100.
Carline, Anna, "Constructing the Subject of Prostitution: A Butlerian Reading of the Regulation of Sex Work," *International Journal of the Semiotic of Law*, 24(1) (2011): 61–78.
Cavarero, Adriana, "Birth, Love, Politics," *Radical Philosophy*, 86 (1997): 19–23.
Cavarero, Adriana, "Politicizing Theory," *Political Theory*, 30 (2002): 505–532.
Cavarero, Adriana, "L'Orecchio di Nancy," *Aut Aut*, 316–317 (2003): 68–76.
Cavarero, Adriana, "Recritude: Reflections on Postural Ontology," *Journal of Speculative Philosophy*, 27(3) (2013): 220–235.
Cavarero, Adriana with Bertolino, Elisabetta, "Beyond Ontology and Sexual Difference: An Interview with the Italian Feminist Philosopher Adriana Cavarero," *differences: A Journal of Feminist Cultural Studies*, 19(1) (2008): 128–167.

Cook, Rebecca G., "International Human Rights Law Concerning Women: Case Notes and Comments," *Vanderbilt Journal of Transnational Law*, 23 (1990–1991): 779–796.
Deuber-Mankowsky, Astrid, "Walter Benjamin's Theological-Political Fragment as a response to Ernst Bloch's Spirit of Utopia," *The Leo Baeck Institute Year Book*, 47 (1) (2002): 3–19.
Douzinas, Costas, "A Note from the Editor," *Law and Critique*, 20 (2009): 1–2.
Drakopoulou, Maria, "Feminism, Governmentality and the Politics of Legal Reforms," *Griffith Law Review*, 17 (2008): 330–356.
Dustin, Moira, "Female Genital Cutting in the UK: Challenging the Inconsistencies," *European Journal of Women's Studies*, 17 (2010): 7–23.
Exline, Julie Juola, et al., "Forgiveness and Justice: A Research Agenda for Social and Personality Psychology," *Personality and Social Psychology Review*, 7 (2003): 337–348.
Gabel, Peter and Harris, Paul, "Building Power and Breaking Images: Critical Legal Theory and the Practice of Law," *Review of Law and Social Change*, XI (1982/1983): 369–411.
Goodrich, Peter, "The Critic's Love of the Law: Intimate Observations on an Insular Jurisdiction," *Law and Critique*, 10 (1999): 343–360.
Guenther, Lisa, "Being from Others: Reading Heidegger after Cavarero," *Hypatia*, 23(1) (2008): 99–116.
Hanafin, Patrick, "An Ethics for Dead Voices: Law and the Politics of Sexual Difference in Dacia Maraini's Isolina," *Law and Humanities*, 4 (2010): 195–209.
Hayter, Kearns, "Female Circumcision. Is There a Legal Solution?," *Journal of Social Welfare Law*, 6 (1984): 323–333.
Hughes, Donna, "The Use of New Communications and Information Technologies for Sexual Exploitations of Women and Children," *Hastings Women's Law Journal*, 13 (2002): 127–146.
Huzar, Timothy J., "Horrorism in the Scene of Torture: Reading Scarry with Cavarero," *Journal of Interdisciplinary Voice Studies*, 2 (1) (2017): 25–43.
Jaldesa, Guyo, Askew, Ian, Njue, Caroline and Wanjiru, Monica, "Female Genital Cutting Among the Somali of Kenya and Management of its Complications," *USAID* (2005).
Jeffries, Stuart, "Orlan's Art of Sex and Surgery," *theguardian.com* (1 July 2009).
Kantola, Johanna and Squires, Judith, "Discourses Surrounding Prostitution Policies in the UK," *European Journal of Women's Studies*, 11 (2004): 77–101.
Kennedy, Ian, "Commentary to Re MB (Medical Treatment) Consent: Adult Refusal of Consent, Capacity," *Medical Law Review*, 5 (1997): 317–328.
Latham, Melanie, "The Shape of Things to Come: Feminism, Regulation and Cosmetic Surgery," *Medical Law Review*, 16 (2008): 437–457.
Lerman, David M., "Forgiveness in the Criminal Justice System: If it Belongs, then Why Is it so Hard to Find?" *Fordham Urban Law Journal*, 27 (1999–2000): 1663–1675.
Loizidou, Elena, "The Trouble with Rape: Gender Matters and Legal Transformation," *Feminist Legal Studies*, 7 (1999): 275–279.
Mackay, R.D., "Is Female Genital Circumcision Unlawful?" *Criminal Law Review* (November 1983): 717–722.
MacKinnon, Catharine, "Feminism, Marxism, Method, and the State: Toward a Feminist Jurisprudence," *Signs: Journal of Women in Culture and Society*, 8(4) (1983): 635–658.
Magnus, Kathy Dow, "The Unaccountable Subject: Judith Butler and the Social Conditions of Intersubjective Agency," *Hypatia*, 21(2) (2006): 81–103.
Marino, Patricia, "The Ethics of Sexual Objectification: Autonomy and Consent," *Inquiry*, 15(4) (2008): 345–364.
Mattar, Mohamed, "Trafficking in Persons, Especially Women and Children in Countries of the Middle East: The Scope of the Problem and the Appropriate Legislative Response," *Fordham International Law Journal*, 26 (2002–2003): 721–743.

Michalowski, Sabine, "Court-Authorised Caesarean Sections – The End of a Trend?" *Modern Law Review*, 62 (1999): 115–127.

Mills, Catherine, "Efficacy and Vulnerability: Judith Butler on Reiteration and Resistance," *Australian Feminist Studies*, 15(32) (2000): 265–279.

Munro, Vanessa, "A Tale of Two Servitudes: Defining and Implementing a Domestic Response to Trafficking of Men for Prostitution in the UK and Australia," *Social and Legal Studies*, 14 (2005): 91–114.

Murphy, Tim, "Brit Crits: Subversion and Submission, Past, Present and Future," *Law and Critique*, 10 (1999): 237–278.

Nussbaum, Martha, "The Professor of Parody," *New Republic* (22 February 1999): 37–45.

Pogge, Thomas, "Can the Capability Approach Be Justified?" *Philosophical Topics*, 30(2) (2002): 167–228.

Pyle, Jeffrey J., "Equality and the Rule of Law. Critical Race Theory's Attack on the Promises of Liberalism," *Boston College Law Review*, 40(3) (1999): 787–827.

Ramachandran, Banu, "Re-Reading Difference. Feminist Critiques of the Law School Classroom and the Problem with Speaking from Experience," *Columbia Law Review*, 98(7) (1998): 1757–1794.

Schneider, David M., "Book Review: Symbolic Wounds. Puberty and the Envious Male by Bruno Bettelheim," *American Anthropologist*, 57(2) (1955), 390–391.

Sheldon, Shelly and Wilkinson, Stephen, "Female Genital Mutilation and Cosmetic Surgery: Regulating Non-Therapeutic Body Modification," *Bioethics*, 12 (1998): 263–285.

Simmons, John, "Tacit Consent and Political Obligation," *Philosophy and Public Affairs*, 5 (1976): 247–291.

Steinman, Kathy, "Sex Tourism and the Child: Latin America's and the United States' Failure to Prosecute Sex Tourists," *Hastings Women's Law Journal*, 13 (2002): 53–76.

Sullivan, Barbara, "Rape, Prostitution and Consent," *Australian and New Zealand Journal of Criminology*, 40 (2007): 127–142.

Sunstein, Cass, "A Review of Nadine Strossen," *New Republic* (9 January 1995): 42–46.

Tincani, Persio, "I Beni Principali Come Capacitazioni," *Politeia*, 83 (2006): 21–44.

Van Marle, Karin, "The Capabilities Approach, the Imaginary Domain and the Asymmetrical Reciprocity: Feminist Perspectives on Equality and Justice," *Feminist Legal Studies*, 11 (2003): 255–278.

West, Robin, "Jurisprudence and Gender," *University of Chicago Law Review*, 55 (1988): 1–72.

Wicks, Elizabeth, "The Right to Refuse Medical Treatment under the European Convention on Human Rights," *Medical Law Review*, 9 (2001): 17–40.

Worthington, Everett, "Is There a Place for Forgiveness in the Justice System?" *Fordham Urban Law Journal*, 27 (1999–2000), 1721–1732.

Conference papers and talks

Butler, Judith, "Speaking of Rage and Grief," Talk at *10th Annual PEN: World Voices Festival of International Literature*, New York: 28 April–4 May 2014.

Main case law

Adesanya (1974) *The Times*, 16 and 17 July.

Airedale NHS v Bland (1993) AC 789 (House of Lords).

Attorney General's Reference (No. 6 of 1980).
R v Brown [1994] 1 AC 212 (House of Lords).
R v Gary Lee Cole and Stephen Kevin Barik (1993) 14 Cr. App. R.(S.) 764.
R v Linekar (1994) *The Times*, 26 October. Queen's Bench Division.
Re MB (Caesarean Section) [1997] 8 Med LR 217.
Norfolk and Norwich Healthcare NHS Trust v W [1996] 2 FLR 613.
Rochdale Healthcare (NHS) Trust v C [1997] 1 FCR 269.
St George's Healthcare NHS Trust v S (1998) 3 All ER 673.
Strunk v Strunk (1969).
Re T (Adult Refusal of Treatment) [1993].
Tameside and Glossop Acute Services Trust v CH [1996] 1 FLR 762.
Re Y [1996].

Index